From Plato to Wittgenstein

ST ANDREWS STUDIES
IN PHILOSOPHY AND PUBLIC AFFAIRS

Founding and General Editor:
John Haldane, University of St Andrews

Values, Education and the Human World
edited by John Haldane

Philosophy and its Public Role
edited by William Aiken and John Haldane

Relativism and the Foundations of Liberalism
by Graham Long

Human Life, Action and Ethics: Essays by G.E.M. Anscombe
edited by Mary Geach and Luke Gormally

The Institution of Intellectual Values:
Realism and Idealism in Higher Education
by Gordon Graham

Life, Liberty and the Pursuit of Utility
by Anthony Kenny and Charles Kenny

Distributing Healthcare: Principles, Practices and Politics
edited by Niall Maclean

Liberalism, Education and Schooling: Essays by T.M. Mclaughlin
edited by David Carr, Mark Halstead and Richard Pring

The Landscape of Humanity: Art, Culture & Society
by Anthony O'Hear

Faith in a Hard Ground:
Essays on Religion, Philosophy and Ethics by G.E.M. Anscombe
edited by Mary Geach and Luke Gormally

Subjectivity and Being Somebody
by Grant Gillett

Understanding Faith: Religious Belief and Its Place in Society
by Stephen R.L. Clark

Profit, Prudence and Virtue: Essays in Ethics, Business & Management
edited by Samuel Gregg and James Stoner

Practical Philosophy: Ethics, Society and Culture
by John Haldane

Sensibility and Sense: Aesthetic Transformation of the World
by Arnold Berleant

Understanding Teaching and Learning: Classic Texts on Education
edited by T. Brian Mooney and Mark Nowacki

Truth and Faith in Ethics
edited by Hayden Ramsay

From Plato to Wittgenstein: Essays by G.E.M. Anscombe
edited by Mary Geach and Luke Gormally

From Plato to Wittgenstein

Essays by G.E.M. Anscombe

Edited by
Mary Geach and Luke Gormally

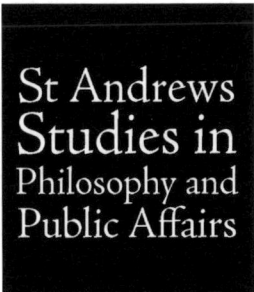

St Andrews
Studies in
Philosophy and
Public Affairs

ia
IMPRINT ACADEMIC

Published in the UK by Imprint Academic
PO Box 200, Exeter EX5 5YX, UK

Published in the USA by Imprint Academic
Philosophy Documentation Center
PO Box 7147, Charlottesville, VA 22906-7147, USA

ISBN 9781845402334 paperback
ISBN 9781845402327 cloth

A CIP catalogue record for this book is available from the
British Library and US Library of Congress

Cover Photograph:
St Salvator's Quadrangle, St Andrews by Peter Adamson
from the University of St Andrews collection

For

Dermot Fenlon C.O.

Faithful pastor, scholar,

and friend of Elizabeth Anscombe.

Contents

Preface

The present volume is the third in a series designed to collect in book form hitherto uncollected and unpublished papers by the late Professor Elizabeth Anscombe.[1] The title of the present collection of papers, *From Plato to Wittgenstein*, mimics the title of the first volume of her *Collected Philosophical Papers – From Parmenides to Wittgenstein*: both volumes collect papers in which Anscombe engages analytically and argumentatively with the thought of major philosophers of the past, including the thought of her teacher and friend Ludwig Wittgenstein. The *Collected Philosophical Papers* were published in 1981, twenty years before her death. In those intervening years she went on to publish over 50 papers and a small number of extended reviews of the work of other philosophers. It is interest in this body of published work which has partly inspired this new series of collected papers. But the inspiration for this enterprise also derives from research among Anscombe's unpublished papers and notebooks, a very large body of material which she was not assiduous in keeping in orderly fashion and which still remains to be adequately organised. An initial ordering of this material has, however, uncovered a number of papers, some typescripts (often with author's corrections), others handwritten manuscripts, which have claims to see the light of publication. There are eight papers in the present collection which have not been previously published in English, though versions of two have appeared in Spanish translation.

One question reviewers might reasonably ask is: Would Anscombe herself have published this material? In some cases it

---

[1] The two previously published volumes are: *Human Life, Action and Ethics. Essays by G E M Anscombe*, edited by Mary Geach and Luke Gormally (Exeter, UK & Charlottesville, VA, USA: Imprint Academic, 2005); *Faith in a Hard Ground. Essays on Religion, Philosophy and Ethics by G E M Anscombe*, edited by Mary Geach and Luke Gormally (Exeter, UK & Charlottesville, VA, USA: Imprint Adademic, 2008).

seems likely that she was not offered the occasion to do so. But in other cases it is evident that she would have considered the paper incomplete. The paper 'On Piety, or: Plato's *Euthyphro*' in the present volume is a case in point. But anyone with an interest in the debates about that Platonic dialogue will surely find Anscombe's incomplete paper on it engaging. And still other papers represent extended analyses and argumentative engagements from which Anscombe subsequently extracted brief and illuminating papers which she did publish. In the present volume the lengthy paper 'Hume on causality: introductory' is the matrix from which Anscombe extracted 'Hume and Julius Caesar' and '"Whatever has a beginning of existence must have a cause": Hume's Argument Exposed'.[2] It is published here as an example of the scrupulous and attentive study she devoted to major philosophers which is abundantly evident in her unpublished papers. There one finds in notebooks and papers extensive work on a number of Platonic dialogues (the *Meno*, the *Phaedo*, the *Theaetetus* and the *Sophist*), on Anselm's *Proslogion* argument and on his *De Veritate*, on Locke's *Essay concerning Human Understanding*, on Berkeley, on Hume on causality and on his *Dialogues concerning Natural Religion*, on Frege and Russell, and—voluminously—on themes from Wittgenstein. Interestingly, there is very little on Aristotle and Aquinas.

In view of cavils about editorial policy from a small number of reviewers, a brief explanation of the policy adopted in distributing papers between different volumes in this series seems called for. The principal focus of the first volume, *Human Life, Action and Ethics* was on ethics. As explained in the preface to that volume, it began with a number of papers on the nature and proper valuation of human life because Anscombe's reflections on those topics were fundamental to what she had to say about morality. So also was her understanding of human action and practical reason, the topics of the second part of that volume. The focus of the second volume, *Faith in a Hard Ground*, was on topics which engaged Anscombe's philosophical attention because of her Catholic faith. The volume contained papers whose subject matter materially coincided with the subject matter of papers in the first volume. But the treatment of those topics in the second volume was more evidently inspired by the challenge of Catholic teaching or influenced by its content. It is to be hoped that

---

[2]   Originally published in 1973 and 1974, and reprinted in G E M Anscombe, *From Parmenides to Wittgenstein. Collected Philosophical Papers, Volume I* (Oxford: Basil Blackwell, 1981), pp. 86–99.

the rationale for the selection of papers in the present volume is fairly perspicuous, and that reviewers will not find editorial policy a reason for failing to engage with Anscombe's thinking.

As in previous volumes, footnotes flagged in Arabic numerals are the author's, those flagged in symbols (∗, †, §, etc) have been supplied by me. In the initial footnote to each paper, where information is provided about the source and date of the paper, the distinction between 'manuscript' and 'typescript', as the names suggest, is between handwritten and typed documents. Insertions in square brackets in quotations from other authors were made by Anscombe; insertions in square brackets in her text have been made by me, usually to supply fairly obviously missing words.

I am indebted to the advice of two scholars in particular in deciding on the selection of papers for the present volume. Nicholas Denyer of Trinity College, Cambridge (and former graduate student of Anscombe), offered advice on the inclusion of the Plato papers. Anselm Müller, former Professor of Philosophy of the University of Trier (and also sometime graduate student of Anscombe) not only advised on the inclusion of a number of the Wittgenstein papers, but also helped in answering questions about the texts of some of those papers.

The whole project of publishing these volumes of Elizabeth Anscombe's papers could not have made the progress it has had John Haldane not welcomed the volumes into the series he edits. His sustained and sustaining interest in the project has been a constant encouragement to make progress with it for which I am very grateful.

Gratitude is again owing to the Earhart Foundation for the grants given to me in 2009 and 2011 to work on archiving Elizabeth Anscombe's papers and publishing a selection of her uncollected and unpublished papers. Much of my time has been spent on a preliminary organisation of a somewhat disorganised mass of papers. I hope to continue to make progress with this work and to produce a further volume of papers in due course.

My wife and I are at one in wishing to dedicate this volume to Fr Dermot Fenlon, a noble priest and fine scholar, who was a friend of Elizabeth Anscombe.

Luke Gormally
June, 2011

Introduction

Elizabeth Anscombe's interest in the great philosophers of the past was that of a participant in their debate. She learned to take part in their perennial conversation by having a teacher who was himself a great philosopher, Ludwig Wittgenstein. She recorded that before she knew him, the great philosophers of the past had appeared to her like beautiful statues: knowing him had brought them alive for her.

She said to me once that the contemporary philosophy teachers who called themselves philosophers were not philosophers: she would not call herself one. Who was, I asked, and she named Wittgenstein. She had learned, by walking and talking in the company of one of them, to move in the company of people who were, in this restricted sense, philosophers; not merely listening, but seriously entering into their concerns and criticizing their thoughts. This did not mean using a philosopher's work as a text about which to make erudite observations, nor did it mean taking him as a banner for her cause, nor employing his name as a label for a mindset which she might dislike: it meant interesting herself in the topics that the philosopher discusses, taking his thoughts apart, adopting some, finding deep problems through others, and rejecting what she found silly. For she was quite capable of finding a great philosopher silly. She used to say to me that we are all stupid in some ways. I suppose she thought this because she had found in talk with him that even Wittgenstein had his absurd attitudes. He had enthused to her about the phrase 'moves without moving' as used about God by Saint Augustine, and had been visibly annoyed when she explained that it meant 'moves other things without himself moving'.

I don't know if he saw the expression 'moves without moving' as being analogous to something mathematical or as a bit of great but obscure poetry. He would not have wished his own work to be looked at in this latter way. She told me how he had explained the popular success of a man whose work he despised by saying that he made people feel as though philosophy was a fairy cave. Anscombe does not do this. You will not find a fairy cave here, but a tough inquisition into the problems: such questions as whether all truths are eternal or timeless, a topic approached in their different ways by Anselm and Aquinas and Russell.

We should remember that time-denying McTaggart thought that Russell basically agreed with him about time, and that though people try to refute the former philosopher's argument for the unreality of time, the sense in which Russell believed in the timeless truth of all properly analysed propositions is one in which large numbers of philosophers do believe in it nowadays. Anscombe, by contrast, was ready to accept both the idea that a proposition might become true or cease to be so, and the idea that the proposition itself was not eternal. She ascribes to Anselm, and seems to sympathise with, the view that an expression might have truth from all eternity without ever existing.

Anscombe did not on the whole have the interests typical of an historian, but in respect of Anselm she did on one occasion do some research into primary sources, and that was when she wished to check whether there was any textual reason for placing a comma in the crucial sentence of the *Proslogion*, where occurs the argument called — in her view falsely — his 'ontological' argument. Her interpretation of the sentence depended on whether (in our modern punctuation) we should put in the usually-inserted comma before the phrase 'quod maius est'. She held that if one left out the comma the sentence was better Latin. She saw this as bearing out her interpretation, since Anselm wrote beautiful Latin. 'I don't know if it's better Latin' said an American professor who had been teaching about the ontological argument, and to whom I had reported the news of the new interpretation, 'but it's certainly better philosophy.'

Anscombe thought that to count existence itself as a perfection was absurd, and it is only fair to Anselm to consider her interpretation of him, which finds him not guilty of this absurdity. She was uncertain about the validity of Anselm's argument as construed by her, though if she had thought it invalid she would have said as much. When giving me an account of a debate of hers with a noted Christian apologist, she had told me that bad arguments for the truth should be refuted.

Anscombe would compare things which Wittgenstein had said with what the philosophers of the past had said on the same subjects. For example, Anselm in discussing truth comes up against the same question as Wittgenstein in the *Tractatus*, of whether a proposition might not be said to have two equally correct ways of signifying, a true way and a false one. She was not a philosophizer about philosophy, but showed, by her readiness to make such comparisons, that certain ways of setting the past at a distance were entirely alien to her. Thus she compared a passage in Frege with one in the *Phaedo*, saying 'When I read the introduction to Frege's *Grundlagen* my spirit bounded with the recognition of a brother to Socrates as so depicted by Plato.' She was a translator in a deep sense: she showed this in her book *Intention* by using the phrase 'under a description' in some contexts in which scholastics use sentences containing the word 'qua.'

Her essay 'Wittgenstein: whose philosopher?' seems an exception to the rule that she was not a philosophizer about philosophy, but really the paper seems to prove that she was incorrigibly a philosopher rather than such a philosophizer. She distinguishes two kinds of philosopher, tells a tale to illustrate the way in which certain problems do not seem like problems to people who are not philosophers, and then she is away, thinking about the problems themselves, caught up by them, not really making generalizations about philosophy any more. What she says about Plato and Wittgenstein is true of her: that though there was much in her work to interest people who were not philosophers, still she was also interested in the sort of problems which only strike philosophers as problematic.

Of Wittgenstein's two philosophies, Anscombe was clearly attached to the later: though she saw much solid material in the *Tractatus*, she thought that it disallowed too much human discourse: not just metaphysical and religious discourse, but plain historical narrative.

In analysing an historical proposition, say, of the form 'A assassinated B' one cannot suppose that the meaning of the proposition consists in those facts (atomic or otherwise) in which the fact of the assassination consists. To do this is to commit what Anscombe named 'the fallacy of being guided by the truth': for the assassination might not have occurred, might then not consist in any facts, atomic or otherwise. She sees both in Wittgenstein's *Tractatus* and in Anselm the point which explains this expression of hers: that a proposition must be capable of signifying what it does both when what it signifies actually is, and when it signifies what is not, and is false.

In her essay on Wittgenstein and Anselm she not only shows her belief in the translatability of the past, but also the reasonableness of seeing past philosophers as having something definite to say to pres-

ent day ones. It is to be remembered, however, that she did regard
some present-day concepts as untranslatable: the special moral
senses of duty, obligation, right and wrong, but this was because she
thought these concepts confused and deracinated.

Wittgenstein was no doubt the dying teacher who said to her that
he had loved truth, and it was this love of truth which caused him to
make the second great change which he did make in philosophy: he
was honest enough to see that his *Tractatus* theories did not describe
language adequately. Anscombe found a lot in the *Tractatus* —
indeed, she wrote a book about it.[1] For example, she sympathised
with its attack on the belief that there is such a thing as the causal
connection. Anscombe expressed to me the view that, correctly
translated, the sentence should be not 'Belief in the causal nexus is
superstition', but 'Superstition is belief in the causal nexus'. Thus
translated, the sentence gives us a definition of superstition. I suppose he did not think that superstition was to believe in the different
things we call causes (constructing, pushing, breaking, begetting,
suppressing, assisting, poisoning, informing) but to believe in the
causal nexus as a sort of all-purpose glue which attaches each cause
to its proper effect which, as Anscombe expresses it, 'drags' the
effect into existence. One sees the harmfulness of the idea of the
causal connection in the causal theories about memory, perception,
and so on that people have. To think you have explained remembering by saying that there is a causal connection between memory and
thing remembered is like thinking you have explained addition by
saying that there is an arithmetical connection between the addition
sum and its answer.

Causality is one of Anscombe's great topics, and in the paper here
she subjects Hume, who seems never to have expected that people
would examine his philosophy for internal consistency, to such an
examination, one which considers whether his assertions about
ideas and impressions are really consistent with either of Hume's
definitions of a cause. Out of this work, as is noted in the Preface, she
drew two of her previously-published papers: the one on Hume and
Julius Caesar is apt to make one read a philosopher with much more
care, lest one allow him such feats of prestidigitation as Hume
performs, slipping unnoticed between his talk of our experience in
reading about Caesar, and the experience of those who presumably
were eyewitnesses of the events.

---

[1]   G E M Anscombe, *An Introduction to Wittgenstein's Tractatus* (London:
Hutchinson, 1959; third edition 1971).

There is a relation between her treatment here of knowledge of the past and her treatment of proper names in her essay on Russell. Our knowledge that there is a chain of testimony through which we have our knowledge of past events derives from our believing the testimony we have seen or heard. One such chain is the chain of use of a proper name, e.g. Julius Caesar. On the supposition that Julius Caesar existed, we can take the name to be a proper name by her account of proper names. If Julius Caesar did not exist, his name does not exist.

Russell, seeing that all kinds of presuppositions went into treating ordinary proper names as names, thought that proper names were really definite descriptions, and that the only real proper names stood for experience contents, like 'red' or 'this'. Russell's use of the word guaranteed its reference, but Anscombe had been freed by Wittgenstein from the phenomenalist belief in the private sense of 'this', guaranteed to onself but inaccessible to others. She was not imprisoned by the requirement of personal infallibility which has bedevilled philosophy since Descartes. I remember her speaking of how the word 'this' latches onto things, giving the example of someone coming in with a box and saying 'This is what is left of poor old Jones', meaning the contents of the box. Obviously, the man who did this might be mistaken, there might be nothing in the box. 'This' as used in her example is not Russell's 'this', with its guaranteed reference. It is understandable that people who think of 'this', referring to an immediately perceived sense datum, as the only real proper name, should think that the atomic propositions of the *Tractatus* were about sense data, but Anscombe in her own book on that work confutes such a view, arguing against it from the text.

Anscombe was chiefly attached to Wittgenstein's later philosophy, though not to most of what he said about ethics and religion. She does not accept Kripke's interpretation of Wittgenstein as one who pushed scepticism further. I found that interpretation quite convincing, when I heard Saul Kripke set it forth in Cambridge, but she quotes chapter and verse to refute it, giving Kripke and not Wittgenstein the credit for the new sceptical difficulty. She also denied that there was a theory of language in Wittgenstein, and that his use of the concept of grammar was in any way peculiar. People's thinking it is peculiar has to do with the notion that to identify a fact about a language as a grammatical fact is to show that a certain way of speaking is grammatical, and a failure to talk in that way is ungrammatical. For example, a philologist to whom I said that the grammar of questions means that they have answers, responded by saying that it was not a grammatical mistake to fail to answer a question. But to know what a question is one has to know what it is to answer a question, and this sort of knowledge is knowledge of grammar.

But if Wittgenstein's obstinate questioning of the riddle about how we carry on applying concepts correctly is not the raising of a sceptical difficulty, what is it? Anscombe does not try an alternative account to Kripke's of what Wittgenstein is doing here. The problem of how we keep on doing things correctly — like adding two — is one which is found in the first book of the *Republic*, when Socrates points to the infinite regress involved in thinking that there is an art by which we check up on an art. Anscombe liked Lao Tzu, but I never heard her say anything about him except that she liked him. It seems to me that the same problem is addressed by him.

It is hard, if not impossible, to summarize Wittgenstein's later philosophy because in that philosophy he neither tries to set forth principles, nor to give an epistemological account of everything. He had said to her that this was the difference he had made to philosophy: philosophy books before him were either about epistemology, or had titles about the principles of something or other. The question then is: how can one be doing philosophy if one neither tries to set forth the most general principles nor to found everything on one's own infallible perceptions? Clearly, Anscombe is doing philosophy here, and can be seen to be doing so. She wrote once that philosophy was thinking about the most difficult and general questions, and she does do that.

Her paper on Plato's theory of forms shows that she thought that though the mind worked in a way which was general, immaterial and timeless, this did not mean that she believed in an intervening object, the form or idea, itself general, immaterial and timeless. In her paper on the immortality of the soul[2] she denies also that the immateriality of thought shows that the soul is an immaterial substance. In this sort of attitude she clearly shows the influence of Wittgenstein. She showed it also in her book on intention,[3] where she denied that the intention in an action was some internal event

---

[2]   'The Immortality of the Soul', in *Faith in a Hard Ground. Essays on Religion, Philosophy and Ethics by G E M Anscombe* edited by Mary Geach and Luke Gormally (Exeter, UK & Charlottesville, VA, USA: Imprint Academic, 2008), pp. 69–83.

[3]   G E M Anscombe, *Intention* (Oxford: Basil Blackwell, 1957; second edition 1963; reprinted, Harvard University Press, 2000).

taking place separately from the action. I do not know that one could formulate a *doctrine* of Wittgenstein's which is applied in all these instances. There is however a somehow characteristically Wittgensteinian way of countering the philosopher's tendency to explain a philosophically puzzling thing by inventing an entity or event which causes it, as physicists invent particles like the graviton.

Anscombe told me that it was through the thought of Aquinas, who held that the ideas were in the mind of God, that the word 'idea' came to have its modern meaning. It is interesting that only one of these papers is about Aquinas. Anscombe drew upon his thought to an unknowable extent: she said to me that it aroused prejudice in people to tell them that a thought came from him: to my sister she said that to ascribe a thought to him made people boringly ignore the philosophical interest of it, whether they were for Aquinas or against him. The way in which she and my father combined analytic and Thomistic thought was not the way of people deciding to construct a combined philosophy of analytical Thomism, but the way of people who were in pursuit of truth and good philosophy, and took it where they found it. She once called Aquinas a 'strikingly good philosopher', contrasting him with another saint and revered authority, Alphonsus Liguori, who, she said, was not. However, she seems from her remains not to have done much expounding of Aquinas.

My parents, though they were not in general at loggerheads about philosophy, were very different in their approaches, which is well illustrated by comparing their treatment of the *Euthyphro*. Geach is struck by what he called the Socratic fallacy, the fallacy of thinking that one does not understand a concept unless one can define it. He is also struck by the fact that Euthyphro is actually in the right, in that his father has committed murder. I have read a defence of euthanasia by a man who cited the ancient Greeks, with their practice of infanticide, to show that having a legal practice of killing innocents does not make people think that murder is all right in other cases. Against this, people should point out that when Euthyphro prosecuted his father for leaving a man tied up in a ditch until he died it was a gesture which no-one was going to take seriously except as a gesture. The man was a serf who had killed another serf in a drunken quarrel, and no-one thought that Euthyphro's case against his father had a chance in the court. So much for the ancient Greek attitude to murder.

By contrast with Geach, Anscombe observes that Plato wrote the *Euthyphro* and that the nobility of Euthyphro's position emerges from that dialogue. She thinks Plato must have seen how fine that position was. Also, she enters carefully and analytically into the dialogue's central question about piety, the question of whether actions are pious because god pleasing or god pleasing because pious.

Hasty reading of her essay *Modern Moral Philosophy* has caused some people to think that she made a crude identification of morality with divine law, and that she held that morality vanishes if one does not believe in God. She did not: it was only the modern concept of the moral that she thought senseless without the concept of a divine law. In this essay on the *Euthyphro*, she confronts the question (lately seen simply as something to use almost rhetorically as a self-evident refutation of the identification of morality and divine law) as that question arises, not in respect of 'morality', but in respect of the particular virtue which is under discussion in the dialogue. She remarks dryly that modern commentators are not particularly interested in piety, which prevents them from getting to the heart of the problem. She compares and contrasts piety with obedience in respect of the same central question asked *mutatis mutandis*.

I asked her when I was a girl whether she or my father was the better philosopher, and she said that he had the more powerful intellect, but that she had the greater ability to see about and around a problem. Their respective essays on the *Euthyphro* illustrate this well. No doubt Geach's identification of the Socratic fallacy has done a great deal of good, but the question about piety just is an interesting question, if asked not as people tend to ask it, as a rhetorical attack on a divine law account of morality, but seriously as a philosophical problem.

Mary Geach
July 2011

PART 1

ANCIENT, MEDIEVAL

& MODERN

The origin of Plato's theory of forms

S. V. Keeling was a learned man who attracted attention in France as well as in the UK. His major distinction from almost all other philosophers was that he was a follower of the Cambridge philosopher McTaggert. McTaggert himself had also the rare distinction of inventing an argument for a paradoxical conclusion, an argument that has been discussed ever since. Like Zeno, who argued that there was no such thing as motion, he has inspired many to refute him, but there is little agreement between the refuters. He was an atheist and his general view of things was that we—human persons—are all enjoying an eternal life of love and mutual knowledge without realizing this. In short, he thought that we were all gods, though he would not have put it like that. He wrote in a very good prose style.

Keeling was a teacher at University College, London, and when he died he left money to a former student of his who decided to found the Keeling Memorial Lecture. To him, therefore, I express gratitude, as also to those who chose to invite me to give the lecture this year.

Now for my title: 'The origin of Plato's theory of forms'. I am going to argue, not for any source in earlier philosophers' writings, but for a root in the doctrine that like-knows-like. If you mention this doctrine to a cultivated native German speaker, you are almost certain to be given a quotation from Goethe, the lines:

* The Stanley Victor Keeling Memorial Lecture delivered at University College, London, on 8 March 1990, and published in Robert W Sharples (ed) *Modern Thinkers and Ancient Thinkers. The Stanley Victor Keeling Memorial Lectures at University College, London, 1981–1991.* (London: UCL Press, 1993).

> Waer' nicht das Auge sonnenhaft
> Wie koennt' die Sonne es erblicken?
> Waer' nicht in uns des Gottes eigne Kraft
> Wie koennt' uns Goettliches entzuecken?†

To translate:

> If the eye were not sunny
> How could it glimpse the sun?
> If God's own power were not in us
> How could what is divine enchant us?

Goethe does not claim to be more than translating from someone he calls Johannes Secundus. So far as I have been able to find out, it is not known who this was. It sounds as if it might be a Pope, but I don't know of any other reason to think it was, or how Goethe stumbled upon it.

The doctrine that like-knows-like was a frequent one among the early Greek philosophers. It is reported by Theophrastus that Anaxagoras strongly rejected it, and maintained that, rather, *un*like-knows-like. He mentioned among other examples that sensation will show you that something is warm if your hand is cooler, and vice versa. 'Like things cannot be affected by like. An image is cast upon what is not the same colour, but a different one.' (This is about sight.) We do not apprehend sweet and sour by sweet and sour respectively but by contrasts.

When I first heard Anaxagoras' objection, I was much impressed by it: it seemed to be a successful dismissal of the 'like-knows-like' doctrine. Now I am not so sure. You know that something is cool by way of the warmth of your hand; but coolness and warmth are different degrees of the same thing. (They are not, as the Greeks thought, different mixtures of contraries.) Sweet and sour make us recognise each in the presence of the other by contrast, but again it is contrast within a range of the same kind of properties. It is by difference of colour that we see the pattern of the image presented to the eye. This may be a sufficient reply to Anaxagoras. If so, it would mean that we had to give a more sophisticated version of 'like-knows-like' than he was rebutting.

---

† Anscombe seems to have been (mis)quoting from memory. Goethe's text reads: Wär' nicht das Auge sonnenhaft/ Die Sonne könnt' es nie erblicken;/ Läg' nicht in uns des Gottes eigne Kraft/ Wie könnt' uns Göttliches entzücken?/

There is a statement in Plato's *Phaedo* which appears to be based upon some, perhaps restricted, form of the doctrine that like-knows-like. It is the statement that the soul (the human soul, he means) is akin to the forms. He says it there in the *Phaedo* without arguing for it. But why did he think it? The reason would seem to be that the soul must in its *nature* be something like the forms in order to know them. On the other hand, it is not suggested that the soul of a man *is* a Platonic form. That the human soul must have known the forms from forever we know partly from Plato's way of having Socrates argue in the *Meno* for the eternal pre-existence of the soul, and partly from the theses of the *Phaedrus* and the *Phaedo* about the process of acquiring knowledge of a form F. In the *Phaedrus* this is described as a process of contracting into *one* unitary object what is got from a multitude of perceptions — for example, the knowledge of 'the equal' by seeing equal sticks and stones. The descriptions seem equivalent and make one think of the British Empiricists. But the process is described as a process of being *reminded*, by the many things that are F, of the form or type F itself, which the mind has so to speak seen in a previous existence. Thus there is no commitment to a doctrine of sense impressions as a source of all our ideas.

From the argument in the *Meno* we can derive that Plato's Socrates thought — or ought to have thought — that no matter when one could *manifest* knowledge of mathematical facts, it would always turn out that the apparently new knowledge was really being reminded. Socrates indeed does not explicitly come to this conclusion, but produces a phoney argument which he then has the grace to say he 'wouldn't exactly insist on'. The argument is that, without having been taught it in this life, Meno's slave has turned out to know that the square which is double the size of the given square is the square on the diagonal of the given square. So he was *reminded* (by Socrates' questions) of something he already knew when he was not a man. But — and this is what Socrates is a bit shamefaced about — the time of his being a man and the time of his not being a man add up to the whole of time. So for the whole of time he has been a knower of the mathematical fact, and by the same methods Socrates will be able to prove the slave's previous knowledge of the whole of mathematics.

Without Socrates explicitly *saying* so, the example does prove that in a certain sense there is no such thing as being taught mathematics. At any rate it is not like being taught history, where you know all you know in the first place by being told. The restriction of the term 'knowledge' to necessary and invariable truth was inherited from the Greeks even as late as the thirteenth century. It is to be found then in scholastic philosophy. In consequence of it there has been a known philosophical problem 'whether one human being can teach another' which is not part of the familiar repertory of problems in modern Anglo-American and related philosophy.

It is possible to continue the discussion in the *Meno* from the point where Socrates is a bit shamefaced about his argument for the eternal pre-existence of the soul. One can enlarge the subject matter so that it comprises understanding proofs, which need not be mathematical proofs. Socrates can be made to point out that there is no such thing as understanding valid reasoning and not accepting it as valid. If that is so then the understanding of the validity of valid arguments cannot be taught as something one essentially learns from being told it, like so much that we learn. This enlarges the interest of the argument in the *Meno*, for it covers much more than mathematics.

However, the argument in the *Meno* does just concern the slave's knowledge of geometry, i.e. of mathematics, and we have to remember that Plato thought that mathematicians were trying to reach forms, the only really real things, but that they did not succeed, but only 'dreamed of reality'. In short, their thoughts and arguments concerned not forms, of which there is only one for any type of thing, but 'mathematicals'. In the understanding that is 'revived' in Meno's slave, there were *two* squares, and any square has *two* diagonals. I don't think Plato ever tells us how the geometrical knowledge (which is 'revived' in the slave's coming to know the theorem) is to be expressed in terms of the forms *the square, the diagonal* and *the triangle*. But in the *Phaedo* and the *Phaedrus* he is definitely concerned with the forms, although his example of 'the equal' in the *Phaedo* has to introduce a designation of a form which ought to be *necessarily* plural: *auta ta isa*, meaning *the equals*. If, following a suggestion of Wittgenstein, one compares the notion of a form to that of the standard yard at Greenwich, this leads to one's asking oneself: 'Wouldn't the standard *equals* have to be two equal lengths side by side, or something of that sort?' Furthermore, if someone were willing to accept that, together perhaps with some more 'standard sames', the question would arise how the standards were to be used as standards.

Once more, so far as I know, though Plato does make Socrates speak of 'the equals', *auta ta isa*, which are plural, he does not offer us any solution of the problem here presented. It is perhaps only a slight problem. Can't we say: 'there can be only *one* form of the equals, even though you have to conceive it as consisting of two things which as being the form in question are essentially equal?' It appears to me that we can, if we are at all justified in speaking of forms as Plato conceived them. We can just ascribe it to Plato's perception of awkwardness that his Socrates sometimes says *auto to ison* – singular, *the equal itself*, and sometimes *auta ta isa* – plural, *the equals themselves*.

So much by way of introduction to the topic of my title: the source of Plato's theory of forms. As I have said, I am interested not in a derivation from previous thinkers who influenced Socrates or Plato but rather in the philosophical thinking involved in believing in Platonic forms. This thinking is so connected with a doctrine that like-knows-like that I am inclined to look for a form of that doctrine that fits its use to postulate forms, which are not particular but universal, not variable but unchangeable, and each not multiple but single.

Before my account of this source of Platonic thinking, however, I will advert to remarks he makes about knowledge, ignorance and opinion in the *Republic*. He says that knowledge (*episteme*) is related to *to on* – i.e. to what is; non-knowing, or ignorance (*agnosia*) to *to me on* – i.e. to what is not; opinion (*doxa*) comes in between: it is brighter than non-knowing and darker than knowing. So there must be something in between what is and what is not, and that is what opinion is related to. (*Republic* V, 477–8.)

One cannot cite this as illustrating a belief that 'like-knows-like', as two of the states are not states of knowledge. But we may say: what a state (a state of the cognitive mind, to use later language) is related to is *like* the state; hence, as opinion is between knowing and ignorance, it must be related to something between what they are respectively related to. The word (*epi*) which I translate 'related to' is a preposition, but I cannot find an English preposition that will do the same job. Perhaps I could use an emphatic 'of': knowledge is *of* what is, ignorance *of* what is not, opinion *of* what is between. We may note that it is tempting to translate *agnosia* by 'error' rather than by 'ignorance' or 'non-knowing', but I think we must resist the temptation. Error would be an *example* of non-knowing, and the only example for which it is reasonable to say 'here the object is *what is not*'. Nevertheless it would be a mistranslation, and the correct translation emphasises for us that we have here an example of how weird Plato's thought sometimes is.

Leaving this, however, we can say that the basic thought displayed in this passage of the *Republic* is very much the same as that displayed by reasonings which would appeal to the principle 'like-knows-like'. For example, it might be argued 'there cannot be discursive thought concerning the deity, because discursive thought is essentially complex, and God is essentially simple'. Or again 'you cannot intellectually grasp there being two men; because the proposition does not distinguish the two men, in order to think that proposition you would have to double your idea of a man, but that is impossible because the idea "man" is single in anybody who conceives it'. Similarly, if you think of such a proposition as 'any boy will pick a fight with any boy' you have to think the idea 'any boy' twice over, and yet that idea is single in your mind. In all such cases there is reasoning from the essential features of some thought to what would have to be a feature of the object of thought.

Now I come to the exposition of my title subject: the source of Plato's theory of forms. A little history is relevant. The first Greek philosophers to enquire into the nature of things thought that there was nothing — no substance — in the world except bodies. Further, they observed that all bodies are movable, or capable of motion, whether this is being moved by others or is moving in the intransitive sense of the word. Indeed, it was thought that bodies were in continual flux, and in consequence some thought that we could not have any certainty about things: *certain truth* was not available to us. For what is in continual flux cannot be grasped with certainty, because it has slid on before the mind judges it. As Heraclitus said: 'You cannot step in the same river twice', and this was not just an observation about rivers with their obviously flowing water: everything is flowing, *panta rei*, and his utterance can be taken as symbolic of the whole non-*state* of things.

Upon this stage came Plato. In order to preserve the possibility of our having certain knowledge of truth through our intellects, he laid down that there was another genus of things besides those corporeal ones, a genus separated from matter and motion, which he called *kinds* or *ideas*, by 'participation' in which any of those particular and sensible things is called a man or a horse or anything else. In this way he declared that pieces of knowledge and definitions and whatever pertains to the action of the intellect do not relate to those sense-perceptible bodies, but rather to such immaterial and separate things. Thus the mind's thinking is not thought of those corporeal things, but is of the separated 'kinds' of such things.

Now there are obviously two falsehoods here. First, with these *kinds* being immaterial and unmoving, the understanding of matter and motion would be excluded from natural science — whose proper preserve they are. So too would proof by material causes and by any ordinary causes which move things. Secondly, it seems ridiculous to bring in other beings, when we are looking for an account of our knowledge of the very objects that *are* clearly in our view; other beings, that is, which cannot be the substance of the familiar objects, since they have a logically quite different sort of existence. That being so, having acquired knowledge of these separate substances, we would not be able thereby to make inferences to, or judge well about, the sensible objects. We may remember that in the first part of the *Parmenides*, in which Parmenides wipes the floor with Socrates, this objection is made by the great man to Socrates' theory of ideas and Socrates is not able to answer it, or indeed any other.

However, to return to our theme, it does appear that Plato has got misled precisely by an application of the like-knows-like principle. One can use this in either of two ways, take either of two directions with it. One may say: *this* is how what we are acquainted with *is*, therefore we have to describe our mode of acquaintance in such a way that *it* too has these features, or somehow accommodates these features even if it does not seem to have them. Or we may say: *this* is what our process or apparatus for knowing something is like, therefore what we know with it must be like that too. An example of a problem arising in the context of the first way is to be found in recent discoveries about colour vision: a ray of a certain green combined with a ray of a certain red yields sight of pure yellow. How is this to be explained? Well, why does one want it explained? Because it seems so odd that our power of sight should get such a result out of red and green. How can we accommodate that yellow in our account of colour vision? We'd not be puzzled like that about seeing green when something green was presented to our eyes.

So the most usual use of the like-knows-like principle would be to argue from the object to the kind of thing that being acquainted with it is. Now Plato seems to have moved in the opposite direction: to have thought that the way some known object is *in* the knowing mind shows us how the known object must be in itself. Now, we may say, he could tell in what way what is known is in the knowing mind when the knowing mind's knowledge is what is expressed by propositions. Propositions almost always have general terms in them. A general term is expressive of some general feature of the things it is rightly used to describe. So we can say that at least the substance known is a universal — i.e. common to all the members of a given class. (Here I will remark on the fact that Aristotle's term *ousia*, which we regularly translate 'substance', is a steal from Plato: an *ousia* is a *being*, and Plato thought the only *ousiai* were forms. Aristotle successfully impounded the word for *his* philosophical account of the most fundamental beings.)

A further property of the meaning of a general term is that it is not only general but it *cannot change*: if it changed, it would be a different term. This thought is to be found in William James's *Principles of Psychology*:

> Conceptions form the one class of entities that cannot under any circumstances change. They can cease to be altogether; or they can stay as what they severally are; but there is for them no middle way. They form an essentially discontinuous system and translate the process of our perceptual experience, which is naturally a flux, into a set of stagnant and petrified terms. The very conception of flux itself is an absolutely changeless meaning in the mind: it signifies just that one thing, flux, immovably.‡

Coming back to the existence of such-and-such a meaning in the mind, it is also immaterial. Making then the transition from the properties of an object of thought *as it exists in the mind* to what the mind is thinking of in using the term, there is a temptation, to which it seems Plato succumbed, to ascribe to the object of thought as it exists outside the mind the very properties which characterise it as a mental object: being a universal, being immaterial, being unchangeable. The form of the object of thought is in the intellect in these ways, with these characteristics: so much is obvious if you simply consider meanings of a vast number of words — words that stand for objects in the widest sense of 'object'. And so Plato thought that the things which *were* objects of thought must have all these properties *as they existed apart from being thought about*: they must be general, immaterial and unchangeable. This of course puts the understanding at a great distance from material things.

There is however no need for this to be the case. It is true that the understanding gets hold of the material and moveable kinds of objects in an immaterial, and in a sense changeless, kind of way, according thus with its own way of getting hold of anything. Thus it can and ought to be said that the mind can and does know corporeal

‡ William James, *Principles of Psychology*. Authorised edition in two unabridged volumes bound as one (Dover Publications, 1950), Volume 1, pp. 467–8.

objects with a knowledge-of that is immaterial, 'universal' (i.e. by way of *general* concepts) and in a way unchangeable, without introducing intervening objects with those properties, and without supposing that the corporeal objects themselves have those properties.

2

On Piety, or:
Plato's Euthyphro

I

Modern commentators are not particularly interested in piety. Lacking this interest, it seems to me they do not get to the heart of the questions discussed in the *Euthyphro*.

We can make a parallel between piety and obedience:

> What actions are obedient? — Actions ordered by people. — Do people order them because they are obedient, or are they obedient because of being ordered?

> To this double question the answer is: (a) there is no general reason why anyone orders an action, but a possible reason is the obedience of the action, i.e. that if the recipient of the order does what is ordered he will have done something obedient. And (b) actions are obedient because or at least partly because they are ordered. That is, to be obedient an action has to be ordered, even if that is not all that is necessary.

There is, we see, no incompatibility between saying that a superior, say, orders you to do something because it will be an act of obedience if you do it, and saying that it is an obedient act because you do what the superior ordered.

If we hear of an act's being ordered for the sake of obedience, that tells us nothing of what it is an order to do. This may even be a matter of indifference to the one giving the order. He must just order something or other — the most obedient person in the world, who leaps to

---

* From an unpublished, undated typescript of which there are two variously corrected copies among Anscombe's papers. Each copy extends to only three parts, though the text clearly envisages a further part. Despite its uncompleted state the text is sufficiently interesting to warrant publication.

attention at the words 'Do just what I tell you', will do nothing obedient if the order-giver does not go on to say e.g. 'Jump off that cliff' or 'Move that object from there to there'.

Still, the one may give such an order for no other reason than that it will be obedience for the other to carry it out. And it, the act itself, will be obedient because it was ordered and was done because it was ordered. It will be as it were a vehicle of the desired obedience.

Let us try these considerations for fit, as it were, with *piety*:

> What actions are pious? — Ones which are god-pleasing. — Do they please the gods because they are pious, or are they pious because they are god-pleasing?

> To this double question the answer is: (a) there is no general reason why a god is pleased by an action, but a possible reason is the piety of the action, i.e. if [   ] does it he will have done something pious. And (b) actions are pious because, or at least partly because, they are god-pleasing. That is, in order to be pious, an action has to be pleasing to a god, even if that is not all that is necessary.

The space between square brackets is blank because it is not off-hand clear what would occupy this space comformably to the model passage. Should we put 'anyone'? But that might include another god, perhaps equal. 'A man'? Perhaps, but that makes large assumptions. 'A devotee'? That would introduce confusion: people may be impious as well as pious. 'One whose god it is', though familiar, is mysterious. — Socrates gives the lightest of hints that there is a question here. Caring for horses is the concern of horse-experts, caring for dogs of dog-trainers, but care for gods?[1] But on the whole the dialogue assumes that it is men as such who will be pious or impious, men as such who are related thus, in some problematical fashion, to 'the gods'. So we will settle for 'a man' to fill the gap, while noting that, in idea, we are making some assumptions.

The next thing to notice is that what was obvious about giving orders — that there is no general reason — is not evidently true about what pleases gods. Euthyphro and Socrates seem to agree that there is a general reason for an action to please a deity, namely that it is pious.

Socrates argues from this that 'pious' cannot mean 'god-pleasing'. We may indeed note a circle:

---

[1]   *Euthyphro* 13a 5ff

actions are pious if god-pleasing, god-pleasing if a god is pleased with them, and a god is pleased with them if they are pious,

but a circle is harmless, only non-explanatory until we can break into it. Socrates' argument does not rest on this circularity; he leads Euthyphro into a contradiction.

Still, it is not clear that we should accept that there is a general reason — its piety — why a deity is pleased with an action. At least Euthyphro held that the gross injustice of murder was hateful to the gods. If, then, he derives 'impious' from 'god-hated', still he seems not in this case to explain 'god-hated' as 'hated by the gods for its impiety' but rather 'hated by the gods for its injustice'. Why not then, in parallel fashion, derive 'pious' from 'god-pleasing' and explain 'god-pleasing' as 'pleasing to the gods for being just'? — Well, it does not really sound right: as Socrates later remarks, an act is not pious merely because it is just. But this leaves us with a problem: why is it impious if it is unjust, at least if it is unjust killing?

Euthyphro denies that a pious act is pious because the gods like it, thus delivering himself into Socrates' hand. In view of his definition 'the pious is what the gods like', this denial is disastrous for him. Socrates secures it by asking whether the gods like what is pious because it is pious, or it is pious because they like it — as if both could not be true, as may hold for what is ordered and what is obedient.

We may display the contradiction clearly as follows with the parallel situation for obedience. First, we define a pious act as a god-pleasing one, and an obedient act as an act done according to orders. Then we give Euthyphro's admissions, followed by what would be the parallel ones for obedience:

1. Acts are god-pleasing because they please the gods.

2. Not: Acts please the gods because they are god-pleasing.

3. Acts please the gods because they are pious.

4. Not: Acts are pious because they please the gods.

1. Acts are done according to orders because they are ordered.

2. Not: Acts are ordered because they are done according to orders.

3. Acts are ordered because they are obedient.

4. Not: Acts are obedient because they are ordered.

If we replace 'pious' and 'obedient' in (3) and (4) by their definitions we get (3) contradicting (2) and (4) contradicting (1). So the definitions, assertions and denials are inconsistent. Socrates assumes we retain the assertions and denials and so faults the definition of 'pious'.

But Euthyphro ought never to have accepted the negations. He ought to have rejected (4) and distinguished two senses in (2).

That definition of obedience will be found faulty but not on account of such an argument. Of course (3) 'Actions are ordered because obedient' is generally false; Socrates would no doubt happily delete the 'not' in (4) for obedience, and grant that 'Actions are obedient because ordered' is true, as it must be if (1) is true and the definition right. But though (3) is generally false about orders, we have noticed that it may be true. If Socrates' argument is sound the truth of (3) *at all* will be incompatible with (2), if we replace 'obedient' with its definition.

Socrates' Either/Or was merely forcing a card on Euthyphro. The right solution, for both piety and obedience, is to delete the 'nots' in (4), and to retain them in (2) only if we can understand (2) as stating 'logical priority' of 'the act pleases the gods' and 'the act was ordered' over 'the act is god-pleasing'[2] and 'the act is according to orders'. In this, very obscure, sense, in which alone (2) is true, there is no conflict with the truth, general or occasional, of (3).

The definition of obedience was defective, however. It should have run 'an obedient act is an act done *intentionally* according to orders'. If someone had 'Open Sesame' powers in respect of any order he gave, he might give orders purely for the sake of happenings' being in accordance with his orders, but that would not be the same as giving orders for the sake of obedience. Now how is it with piety? We have a definition of the pious as the god-pleasing and the statement that the gods are pleased with the pious act precisely for being pious. It sounds like 'My favourite colour is the colour I like best; and I like it best for being my favourite colour'. If it is, then it is absurd and either the definition or the statement must be dropped. But there is another possibility: that 'god-pleasing act' is not a description that applies to an act independent of the intention of pleasing the deity. (Compare 'act of honouring'.) If we do so understand 'god-pleasing' the definition of piety is not defective like that

[2]   I have used the tenuous contrast between the actives 'to please' and 'to be pleasing' in place of the equally tenuous contrast between passives which we find in Plato. There is no way of making Plato's passives go over into English.

of obedience, and its conjunction with the statement is not absurd. The description 'intentionally god-pleasing' will be pleonastic; 'unintentionally god-pleasing' absurd.

What we have here is a substantive doctrine that gods are not pleased with any acts that are not done with the intention of pleasing them. This is obviously a theological doctrine of enormous importance, to accept or reject.

We should like a description which parallels 'what was ordered' in being a description of what was done independent of whether it was pious or not, so that we can define the pious by means of that description with the intention added.

Our explanation will then run: 'Pious acts are such acts as please the gods when done with the intention of pleasing them, when done with the intention of pleasing them'.

And now we can ask what are examples of such acts, i.e. are acts which may or may not be done with the intention of pleasing the gods, and which do please them if so done. But how can we hope to learn what these acts are? We cannot observe divine pleasure, so there is no path from the definition of the pious like the path from the definition of the obedient. Even when an act is ordered for no reason but its obedience, the one who wishes to be obedient knows what to do as soon as he grasps a performable order.

Observation is of course not the only conceivable way of knowing what will please. If it could be argued out that acts of such-and-such a character must please the gods if done with the intention of pleasing them, that would do. But there is a difficulty about this, in our information that what pleases them about the acts is the piety and only the piety. If we argue for example (by any process of internal reasoning) that deeds of signal virtue must please the gods if done with the intention of pleasing them, are we not *eo ipso* suggesting that the virtuousness pleases them, at least on condition of the extra intention? Then they will be pleased with actions, not just for their piety, but for their virtue together with their piety.

It is rather as if we thought we could argue what sort of performable acts *must* be ordered by one who orders things to be done only for the sake of obedience. It seems clear that other than performability there can be no restriction placed on what such an order-giver may order, no restriction implying any other point for him in the act besides it obedience.

We must stress that the thesis being considered is not that the pious is whatever is done with the intention of pleasing the deity.

Indeed such an idea hardly makes sense for the pious agent. For the agent must have some idea that what he does will please. Geach[3] remarks that parents may be pleased with something done with the intention to please; but the child at least must think that the thing he actually does will please. I cannot say: *anything* I do with the intention to please will please, so I will just choose something to do, and do it with the intention to please. That is a point about intention: if I do *a* with the intention of bringing about *b*, I must believe that doing it will effect *b*; it may be that — and that I recognise that — it will bring about *b* only if I do it with the intention of bringing *b* about, but at any rate I must think that *a* is an appropriate thing to do with this intention.

There will then be the question: what makes it an appropriate thing? Now the pious agent need not have any answer to this; he will have no internal grounds, but merely believe on external grounds, on information perhaps from someone like Euthyphro, that certain things are appropriate. Euthyphro said he knew a lot about piety; no doubt he could give expert information here. Another source of belief about what are materially pious things to do would be custom. And so long as the pious agent believed that such-and-such were pious things to do, he could do them with the intention of pleasing the gods, without racking his brains about why they were pleasing to the gods beyond the fact of being done to please them.

But Socrates will quiz the expert. The pious agent can perhaps do pious things without answering the question; but still the question remains: what does make these actions and not those appropriate vehicles of piety? Whatever it is, won't the gods be interested in it and not just in the piety? But Euthyphro defined the pious as the god-pleasing, and said that what the gods were pleased with the pious for *was* the piety.

That is to say: the suggestion was that piety is always what obedience is sometimes. Obedience is sometimes what the order-giver is after. But piety is always what the god is pleased with. Then just as, when obedience is what the order-giver is after, it may not matter what the particular content of the order is, so the pious act may always be in itself indifferent. In order for there to be a pious act at all, there will have to be something or other specified to be the vehicle of the piety, something for the gods to be pleased at one's doing. But it will be substantively pointless.

[3]   'Plato's *Euthyphro*. An Analysis and Commentary', reprinted in P T Geach, *Logic Matters* (Oxford: Basil Blackwell, 1972), pp. 31–44, at p. 44.

Now there are many pious acts — acts conceived to be pious — of which this is strikingly true. For example, pouring a libation. And the argument may be aided by another: Euthyphro speaks of the 'cultivation' (cult) or service of the gods, but is quick to agree that gods cannot need anything from men, cannot possibly be benefitted by anything men do. Then if there is a type of act called 'pious', if there are material classes of action which are supposed to be acts of piety, given just as 'god-pleasing', and with no significance except that they are 'for' a god — they must be acts with no substantive purpose.

At least we have come to see point in the characteristic pointlessness of acts of formal piety. And there would be a logically faultless answer to the question 'Why *these* acts?', if it could be given: namely, that they had been ordered by the gods. (The expert Euthyphro would no doubt claim to give information about this too.) We have so far adduced orders and obedience as an object of logical comparison to help clarify the questions arising from piety; but if this is right, obedience is even materially relevant to our topic. If the gods ordained certain things for men to do in order to please them, they were like the order-giver who was out for obedience; and the particular things ordained would be in themselves as arbitrary and indifferent as in his case. This saves the explanation that the gods are pleased with the pious just for its piety. It makes piety into a form of obedience, and it equates the gods with the order-giver whose aim is obedience. But it raises the question: Why should they want obedience? (On the other hand, if the answer to the question 'Why *these* acts?' were that men choose them as expressive, that explanation is not saved — a god will be pleased with the pious because of what is expressed by it.)

And there is that other matter outstanding, of the impiety of murder. What we have said might throw some light on piety narrowly conceived, on the specific acts of religious piety, though it leaves us perplexed about the nature of gods. But their hatred of murder, of unjust killing, makes it seem that they have some interest in actions other than those of formal piety; an interest in justice and injustice. How does this fit in with the claim that what pleases the gods is piety; and, more specifically, that only pious acts please them? We may distinguish between the formally pious, i.e. the acts with no point but piety, and other acts, which may have a point of their own but which will be acts of piety if done in order to please the gods. But the question will arise, why they are supposed to be god-pleasing.

Will it be because of the 'point of their own' or because they are done to please? If Euthyphro's definition and explanation of what pleases the gods are right, then the latter will be true. Such actions could still be arbitrarily specified as pious, merely because something has to be. But if some things that an order-giver ordered for the sake of obedience were also, say, systematically useful or systematically harmful to the order-receiver, one would be puzzled at the suggestion that they were matters of indifference to the order-giver. It would certainly seem that he was not giving orders for the sake of obedience to them, or not for that alone. And similarly it would seem that a deity was not pleased with—or at least did not want—the pious actions only for their piety.

II

As the *Euthyphro* obliquely reminds us, piety is not necessarily piety towards gods. Euthyphro was going to prosecute his father for murder. Some called this an impious act on the part of a son: an act of *filial impiety*.

Let us consider filial piety. We shall find that it has some of the obscure and paradoxical character which Socrates has uncovered in religious piety:

> What actions are filially pious? Actions which give honour to a parent. Do they give him honour because they are filially pious or are they filially pious because they give him honour?

The same pattern-of-a-problem occurs here as before. But we know now that the double question does not—as Euthyphro was made to think—hold the gun of an Either/Or to our heads. We know that we can say yes to both arms of the question. We do say yes to the second because of the definition, which is not going to be faulted. What about the first? 'A parent is honoured by filially pious acts because they are filially pious.' Is that always or merely sometimes true?

It will be useful to speak of the *honouring aspect* of something that gives honour to a person. A parent (at least given certain conditions) may be said to get honour from any known creditable actions on the part of his child. Then the honouring aspect is the creditability. 'He got honour from his child's discovery, because it was a great achievement.' Now when we ask whether a parent is honoured by such and such acts because they are filially pious, we are asking whether the piety is the, or at least an, honouring aspect of what was done. It is plain that not all actions which are honouring to parents are acts of filial piety. To be so, they have also to be done in order to honour the parents. But the question before us is whether in all acts which *are* acts of filial piety, the piety is necessarily the — or an — honouring aspect. And it appears that the answer is: no. For the piety may not be known. Suppose that the great discovery was what brought honour to the parents; and suppose that the child worked to achieve something worthwhile, precisely in order for this to be an honour to the parents. The child succeeds; and the work was for the child an act of filial piety. But this motive has been a secret one. Here we have a case in which a parent gets honour from a filially pious act, but *not* because it is filially pious. The achievement, not the piety which inspired the achievement, is the honouring aspect. By contrast, suppose the child showed the motive, dedicated the work to the parent, made acknowledgment of the parent in connection with it, even, as it were, performed the work as an explicit present to the parent, then the parent would not merely get honour from acts which were filially pious, but would get honour from them because they were filially pious. (As well as because they were substantively creditable.)

An order's being given only for the sake of the obedience of the act, though possible, is relatively rare, and it might have seemed that there was an absolute contrast between obedience and filial piety in this respect. That the obedience is a merely possible reason, while the piety is an integral aspect of parental honour, when this is effected by a pious act. But we have now seen that this is not so: that, just as we can think of cases where the ordering was because of the obedience, so we can construct a case where the honour is not (in the relevant sense of 'because') *because* of the piety.

However, it is important that our cases are relatively rare. That the natural and typical picture of an order and its relation to obedience is that it is for the sake of some substantive purpose of the act done in obedience to it, and that the natural and typical picture of parents being honoured by an act of filial piety is that the honouring aspect is precisely the piety. This contrast may do something to explain why we have the feeling: Wouldn't there be something really pointless and disgusting about an act's being required for the sake of obedience if the *sole* ground was the obedience, there not being even any further utility in the fact of obedience? But not the feeling that there is something really pointless about acts, gestures, performances, whose sole point is filial piety.

We stressed that when the order-giver only wants obedience and has no further purpose, it doesn't matter what he orders, he just has to order something or other that the other can do. Now this feature is reproduced, at least to some extent, in the case of filial piety: if the sole honouring aspect is the piety, it might be said, it doesn't matter what the act is, just so long as it is done for the sake of honouring the parent. But here a new logical difference appears. The substantive content of the order given for the sake of obedience can be anything; or rather, the only restriction on it is that it is performable by the recipient. The connection between the act and the order, which makes it possible for this act to be an act of obedience to (intentional execution of) the order, is the identity of description between the act and what the order orders. Nothing like that is to be found which may connect the act done to honour the parent with the intention to honour. We said that the act's being creditable meant (given the right circumstances) that it did honour the parent, and we may say that a requirement of creditability puts a restriction on what can be an act of filial piety, comparable to the restriction in ordering to the act's being performable by the recipient of the order. But beyond that — what makes the connection? Simply that the act is done with the intention of honour? And what sort of intention is that? Is having such an intention a special, recognisable experience, such that if you have it, then what you decide to do (so long as it is creditable) is an act of honouring? And how is *it* creditable, if there isn't a separate substantive creditability, but the whole honouring aspect is only the piety? Must we not say: *anything* will do and be creditable — so long as it is not discreditable? Just as we would say in the obedience case: anything will do — so long as it is performable. But then we are left with the motive of honouring as an inexplicable, indefinable phenomenon, apparently just a special mental experience. It seems obvious that we are making a mistake about this. How would one explain what feeling was meant, what 'honouring' meant, if *that* is what it is? How know if we all mean the same? One doesn't *at all* want to say: 'You just have to be acquainted with it' — as one is rather inclined to say 'You just have to be acquainted with blue'.

But it is not true that anything will do. I mean that when actions have no substantive point except that they are honouring, then they may vary from one society to another but are fixed for the society. In Mexico, for example, they used to burn incense in honour of a guest; this, then, would be a *guest-honouring action* there. It is thus a matter of civilisation which actions are tokens of honour, varying perhaps according to the object of honour — a guest, an uncle, a parent, a god — and when we speak of a 'pious' act, narrowly, but in a very general kind of way, we may mean precisely an act without a substantive point, but one which is intelligible in the society as an act of honour to those of some class to whom honour is paid.

'Narrowly', because I am now speaking of the 'act of piety' in a sense in which it is restricted to what I call 'substantively pointless' acts. In this narrow sense, sending an aged parent the means of making a journey in comfort is not an act of filial piety; but, since it might be done partly with the motive of showing him respect and consideration such as are his due, it would be an act of piety in the broader sense when done with that motive.

A different example: feeding an aged needy parent. This is different, because one does not fail in respect and consideration by not sending the means of special comfort on a journey; just what is done in the way of showing respect and consideration is highly optional; whereas if you let your parent starve, you are unjust to him, and *to be unjust to* is to treat with dishonour. Feeding him is an act of justice; it can hardly be an act of piety in the sense of being done to honour him; but it may be an act of piety in the sense that the injustice of letting starve, when done to a parent, is gross filial impiety, and you want not to be guilty of that.

In the wide sense, then, the filially pious will be anything (creditable) done with the motive of honouring, or at least with the motive of not dishonouring, while in the narrow sense filially pious acts will be acts, substantively pointless, which get their point from being acts of honour. In any society there will be many such types of act. (Given that honouring exists, the purely individual and only personally significant act or gesture of honour becomes possible.) And now the pious in the narrow sense is regarded as creditable because of being pious.

III

Socrates and Euthyphro come to a new definition of piety as *that part of justice which concerns the cultivation or service of gods.*

Piety may be argued to be a part of justice as rendering a god his due. Socrates does not argue this. He merely starts with the assertion, which Euthyphro naturally accepts, that the pious is just; he does not go into why it is just. One would like to know whether it is just only because it is not unjust, like the act of any other virtue such as friendship, mercy, hospitality, courage. The connection looks to be closer than that: piety is a subdivision of justice; is justice towards deity. I suppose that Plato does not make Socrates explore this aspect because it would perforce make the enquiry touch on the general nature of justice; whereas this dialogue focussed simply on piety. But that is not to say that we are not meant to consider why piety is just.

What exercises Socrates is: what can serving the gods amount to? The serving doesn't do them any good: they need nothing. It is suggested that it is the service of a servant who cooperates in a work. But what work?

Euthyphro replies that it is a laborious business to understand these matters accurately. 'However, I simply say this to you: if someone knows how to say and do what is acceptable to the gods, praying and sacrificing, those are the pious things, and such things preserve both private houses and commonwealths. The opposite of the acceptable is impious, and that overturns and destroys everything.' The 'work', then, is the good state of men, private and civil.

Socrates does not challenge this, but wants to elucidate prayer and sacrifice as asking and giving; this strikes him as a sort of commercial transaction. He does not remark that Euthyphro counted the prayers (i.e. the asking) as part of what is 'acceptable to the gods'; hence he is able to say: 'Piety would then be a sort of commercial art, the art of commercial transactions between gods and men.' It will be the art of *giving* something acceptable, and *asking* for what you can hope to get in return. Euthyphro shows signs of weariness ('Call it commercial if you like!') and does not notice the shift that Socrates made. Asked what the gifts are, he dismisses with scorn the suggestion that *he* thinks gods can be benefitted by men anymore than Socrates does: the gifts are honour, respect and thanks.

Socrates now says: 'So the pious is the acceptable, but is neither profitable to the gods nor dear to them'. Euthyphro insists that it *is* dear to them. Socrates: 'But this is where we were before! We agreed that the pious and what is dear to the gods are not the same thing. Either we were wrong then, or we are wrong now.' So the dialogue ends with the usual aporia.

Commentators remark that Plato fails to distinguish between *the pious* and *the dear-to-the-gods* being the same in meaning and their applying to the same acts — only the identity of meaning was (supposedly) refuted before, and all that Euthyphro is saying now is that the gifts of honour, respect and thanks *are* dear to the gods. The point is not well taken. The acceptability, the welcomeness, of what is done by the man who knows what to do was offered by Euthyphro as an explanation of that just service of the gods which is piety, and when Socrates says 'Welcome, but neither profitable nor liked' he is seizing on what would be an absurdity. How could something be welcome but in being either profitable or pleasing?

We ought to accept as genuine the aporia, and take seriously Socrates' remark 'Either we were wrong then, or we are wrong now, and the whole thing needs going into from the beginning.'

A Platonic dialogue of this type is not the impertinent publication of failed work, but a display of skill in starting a hundred hares and in exposing the problematic character of its topic. A dialogue may very well do this if, like the *Theaetetus*, it produces nothing but failed definitions. But the *Euthyphro* is not even in that sense a failure: it has given us two very good definitions of piety and has pointed to problems about them. Plato *may* have thought the definitions failures; like many of his readers he may have been convinced by the argument against the first one, to which the second also looks back. But we cannot tell: all we know is that Socrates says 'The whole thing needs reinvestigation'.

Beginning that reinvestigation, we have seen that Socrates did not after all succeed in refuting Euthyphro's original definition, but his argument helps us to grasp various interesting things about piety (and similar properties). We have several problems outstanding.

Before going back to them, I should like to consider the character so skilfully portrayed to us as Euthyphro, 'Right-mind'. People usually seem to think of him as a cardboard character, a conventional religious type, who is thoughtlessly stuck in his attitudes. Socrates is good, Euthyphro is bad and a fool. Now dialectically Euthyphro has the role of the man who is got into difficulties by Socrates; like all who have this role in the dialogues, he is set up to be tied in knots and as usual some answers which he need not have given are put in his mouth so that he shall be tied in knots. This is no more than the well-known Platonic technique for reaching the points he wants to concentrate on. Euthyphro also has the particular character of one who, like the very different Protagoras, thinks he knows, thinks, that is, that he has full knowledge of the *theory* of the thing: his insistence that he is an expert on piety puts him into the class of Socratic interlocutors who are, as it were, fair game. There is something ludicrous about his manner of making his claims. All the same, he is not at all on the make, and not at all a conventional character. He is at odds with his world, and to his own hurt; precisely because of his seriousness. He is willing to go against everything conventional, to incur the rage of his family and the derision and contempt of the citizens, because he cannot brush aside the fact that his father has callously killed a poor helpless man out of mere negligence. No one cares, because the victim was a nobody and a worthless person — except Euthyphro. I do not believe that Plato was unconscious of the power of Euthyphro's complaint where he makes him say that his father 'made little of the man, and did not care whether he died of cold or hunger and his chains, which indeed happened' and also says that it doesn't matter who the victim is — serf or his own social equal. I find it astonishing that readers do not notice the justice with which Plato makes Euthyphro speak at this point and the way in which the conceitedness drops out of his style, but mostly seem set on taking him as a contemptible figure. Geach takes the opposite view: he is all on Euthyphro's side and is furious with Plato for the poisonous attitude expressed by Socrates. But we ought to remember that Plato wrote all those words! This is so, whether or not Euthyphro was a fictitious character. I do not find it credible that Plato wrote the best words he put into Euthyphro's mouth, all unconscious of their quality.

Euthyphro is portrayed as a man who has thought rather intently, and come to very definite conclusions about what are cases of unjust killing, about piety and impiety, about not letting oneself be compromised by 'respect of persons'. That is indicated at several places. Socrates does not allow him to expound these thoughts, and he is quite unprepared for Socrates' kind of question. He does regard the idea of serving the gods and its purpose as one with a lot of difficulty about it, but he has no nose for logical and linguistic points; he grasps them with difficulty (and indeed some of them look like mere will o' the wisps) and is obviously not much impressed by them. Above all, he has no nose for the more narrowly philosophical problems. That belongs to Socrates and the author.

3

Plato, soul and 'the unity of apperception'

Plato introduced the topic called 'the unity of apperception' in his *Theaetetus*.† There Socrates asks Theaetetus whether we see *with* our eyes, or rather through them, i.e. by means of them; whether we hear *with* our ears or through them. Theaetetus answers 'through', and Socrates commends him for his decision, saying how odd it would be 'if there were a number of senses sitting inside us, as if we were wooden horses, and there were not some single form (soul or whatever one ought to call it) in which all of them converge, something *with* which, *through* the senses as instruments, we perceive all that is perceptible'.

Plato did not treat this as a problem or puzzle, a matter arousing perplexity about the senses. Nor am I sure that Kant did, in giving it the name 'the unity of apperception'. In this century, however, it is more likely to be seen as a puzzle. You hear a bang and see a flash. You hear and see the bang and the flash *simultaneously*. That is not yet enough to raise a problem: as Kneale has remarked, John might hear the bang at the same moment as Tom sees the flash and that observation is unproblematic, and it would remain so even if just one — John, say — hears the bang and sees the flash at the same time. A problem arises only for one person's *being conscious of* both hearing a bang and seeing a flash at the same time. The perception of the simultaneity can't be by sight or by hearing. How then can there be such a *perception*? By what sensory faculty does one perceive this?

---

* From an undated, unpublished manuscript. Title supplied.

† See *Theaetetus* 184c and following for the part of the dialogue discussed in this paper.

Plato doesn't have this example or indeed show a feel for this problem in the *Theaetetus*. He is after other game. There must be some one form of thing in which all the senses converge. This thing is a part of the perceiver. Can it be a part of his body, as the special sense organs are? What is perceived by means of one of them can't be perceived by means of another of them. So if there is a *thought* about both, this can't mean that there is a *perception* of both at once *through* either *one* of the special senses *or* the other. *Through* what then are you thinking of both? Suppose it were possible for you to try and find out whether sound and colour were both *brackish*, you'd find this out by the faculty that uses the tongue. Well, then, *through* what faculty do you get 'exists', 'doesn't exist', 'are alike', 'are unalike', 'the same', 'different', and unity and numbers and their properties like odd and even? Theaetetus both grasps and helps to elaborate the question, and delights Socrates by saying 'there isn't any special organ for all these things — the soul itself is its own instrument for contemplating these common terms which apply to everything.'

Does Socrates, like Berkeley, insist that *no* sensory power *can* take in both objects of sight and objects of another sense? Not exactly. He does seem to suggest this when he says 'suppose it *were* possible to try and find out whether sound and colour were both brackish'. That is, he refers implicitly to the impossibility. But the *point* here is not that impossibility: he wants to suppose (*per impossibile* indeed) that you *could* try and find this out but his purpose is only to elicit the realisation that it would be by the exercise of a faculty *other than* sight or hearing — the faculty that uses the tongue. His aim is to elucidate the question he wants to ask. Through what instrument do you tell that the objects of sight and hearing are, say, existent, unlike, different, and numerous? If you *could* find out they were brackish it would be by means of the tongue. Well, you actually *can* say those other things about them. What's the faculty, what's the instrument? Is it part of the body as the special sense organs are?

We do indeed have Plato making Socrates assert that what is perceived by one of the special senses can't be perceived by another of them. Object and sense-faculty are correlative: more precisely, they are related by a many-one relation. If O is object of special sense faculty F, it is not an object of any other special sense faculty. So *red*, for example, is an object of sight and cannot be object of any other special sense. But the relation is not one-one; for the fact that red is an object of sight does not imply that nothing else is — blue is, for example. Thus it is only many-one and not one-one.

The only sensory powers and objects that Plato *mentions* in this discussion are the special ones, the ones that Aristotle later called 'proper' or 'peculiar'. It's probably most natural for us to call them 'particular' senses. And Plato certainly seems to hold that no *such* sensory power can take in any *such* object of another *such* sensory power. The point is hardly controversial. But Berkeley's thesis is a much stronger one — there cannot be *a sensory power* that takes in objects which another sensory power also takes in. What has Plato to offer about this in the *Theaetetus* discussion? Nothing! He does not mention any properties that strike one as 'common sensibles'. He does not mention shape and size, for example. Concerning these, Berkeley said that truly *visual* shape and size are hardly ever mentioned or considered. But he is quite sure they exist and are not the same properties as the size and shape perceived by touch. Thus he denies the existence and indeed the possibility of common sensibles. Plato does not here consider this, except in the way of considering whether there is some faculty using a corporeal sense through which the soul perceives *existence, resemblance, same* and *different, unity* and *number, odd* and *even*. Of these only unity and number counted among Aristotle's 'common sensibles'. But Plato's interest is evidently not in the topic of common sensibles, let alone a common sense by which they are taken in, but rather in the question whether that list — existence, same, different, etc, — is a list of things apprehended, as the objects of the particular senses are, by a faculty *using a part of the body as an organ*. And his answer is evidently: no.

His interest is in that list and the power being exercised in the formation of judgments using members of it. For example, that sound and colour are not the same. The question is whether 'same' and 'not the same' can be referred to some special faculty as colour can be referred to sight.

Let us now consider Socrates' commendation of Theaetetus for his 'thought'. We *can* see what Plato means by 'with' as opposed to 'through'. At first sight it sounds as if the senses are supposed to be windows *through* which the soul sees and hears, sitting within. But the reference to instruments shows that that is not what is intended: the soul uses the sensory powers as instruments in perceiving their objects. Therefore, as this is the explanation of 'through' in contrast with 'with', he doesn't intend the rejected proposition 'He sees *with* his eyes' to be understood instrumentally (he is not denying that eyes are instruments of sight); nor, when he accepts talk of the soul as something *with* which, *through* the senses, *we* perceive all that is perceptible, does he intend to suggest that the soul (or mind) is itself an *instrument* we use, with which we perceive, think and so on.

I take it that we are to understand the Greek dative or our 'with' in such a way that, if you do something *with* something, e.g. you walk *with* your legs, the first something is *actually done by* the second something; your legs walk, you walk *with* your legs. This walking of your legs is, we may note, an exercise by you of the power of walking. If there is 'a single form, call it the soul, *with* which through the senses, we perceive', then it is the soul that perceives, not the sense organs, and our soul's perceivings are *our* exercisings of our powers of perceiving. That's the meaning of 'one perceives with one's soul'. It itself is what has the objects as objects of perception or thought. When those objects are objects of the special senses there is *also* the instrument, the sense organ through or by means of which the soul perceives.

To sum up: if I am right in my understanding of the matter, the difference between the legs and the sense organs is that the legs *do* walk, and are not instruments by means of which the soul walks; the eyes, on the other hand, do *not* see, but are instruments by means of which the soul sees. There is nothing *with* which the soul perceives or thinks as the animal walks *with* its legs, except indeed itself.

But, we may ask, *should* we not say that the eye sees, the ear hears, the skin is sensitive, the olfactory apparatus smells, the tongue and palate taste? The answer to this must be found in the comparison with men sitting in the Trojan horse. Each of these men judges things himself. If the eye sees and we see *with* our eyes in the way I have explained, then the eye itself would be a judging subject. But as the eyes and the sense of sight cannot take in sounds, *each* of us would be or contain a whole set of distinct judging subjects. But there *are* judgments which concern the special objects of the particular senses, and whose expressions include terms like 'same', 'exists', etc., which are *not* names of objects of sense perception. Therefore there must be some single thing which takes in the special objects of the particular senses and frames judgments containing terms for them as well as those other terms which do *not* stand for special objects of particular senses.

All this quite by-passes the topic of common sensibles. All we have in Plato are: objects of the particular senses, and here there is always a sense organ which is a particular bodily part; and terms standing for what according to Socrates and Theaetetus are not objects of sense at all, for *there is no organ*. But what perceives the objects of sense and *also* has as its objects *existence, like* and *unlike, same* and *different, one* and *many*, is the soul. 'Soul' is introduced only as a possible term for that necessary single thing in which all the senses converge. *That* they do so converge and so that there must be 'some one thing' is proved by the fact that one can think such things as 'sound and colour are different'.

The argument seems to me to be a good one and for the moment the thing that bothers me is the total bypassing of the topic of common sensibles. I have mentioned that Berkeley rejected these: at least he rejected shape and size as common to sight and touch. I see no reason why Plato should have rejected them. *The* objects of sight are colours, light and darkness. To say that is not to say that there cannot be any other objects of seeing or that such other objects can't be also objects of tactile feelings. Objects so apprehended by more than one sense don't thereby have to have a 'special' sensorium, what Aristotle calls a κοινον ἀισθητηριον, a common sensorium of their own. To call them common sensibles is to say they are common to more than one sense, *not* to say they are the objects of a *new* particular sense, oddly called 'common'. And indeed Aristotle seems a bit ambiguous, on occasion denying the possibility of any such κοινον ἀισθητηριον, I think for the reason I've just given.

On the other hand, there is the following question: Is there not such a thing as a *perceptual judgment*? Say: 'This object (whatever it is) is blue', or 'This is a chord, two or three notes combined'. We need enter into no dispute here about whether perception *is* judgment. We need not quarrel with Plato about the soul being what sees and hears. He, just because he thought that, would have no difficulty, I should think, about the idea of a perceptual judgment. Judgment being an act of mind, that there are judgments *on* the 'recepta' of sense whose very reception is itself an act of mind, or soul, would be unproblematic for Plato. As for other people who perhaps don't go along with Plato, we can simply point to examples of perceptual judgment.

Now 'Sound is not the same as colour' is not a perceptual judgment: for I lay it down that a perceptual judgment is particular, always involving something one could point to, a particular occurrence, some object of sense. Here I am Humpty Dumpty and claim to tell the phrase 'perceptual judgment' what it is to mean. Under these orders, a perceptual judgment restricts itself to being a judgment about something that is or was being perceived, and any such thing, if the being perceived comes essentially into the judgment, makes the judgment a perceptual one, so long as it is simple. By 'simple' I mean neither conditional nor general. Let this suffice as an explanation. Now aren't 'This pattern of colours is gayer than that tune' or our old friend 'The bang was simultaneous with the flash' perceptual judgments? If we allow ourselves to call 'This is blue' a deliverance of sense, should we not also call those judgments deliverances of sense? How might Plato express this? Just by saying that in these cases the soul perceives and judges something about what it perceives. What is involved is a sensory power, surely; but the simultaneity of the bang and flash, or greater gaiety of the colours than the tune are *not* objects of either sight or hearing, although sight and hearing are also involved.

Berkeley would not have granted that there were sensory judgments. Here apparently he has a recourse available. He could make use of his thesis that there are no *ideas* of relations; for a relation involves a comparing mind and nothing involving a comparing mind can be given in sense. I protest against this: many relations between objects of sense are just as perceptible as non-relational sensible properties. 'This blue', I say with my eye on a pair of blue ribbons, 'this blue is darker than that one'. After all, Berkeley thinks that perceiving too is an act of mind, hence that perceiving is not an idea, perceiving is not perceived. That didn't mean that there were no ideas which were perceived: in fact ideas are the very thing whose being is to be perceived. In giving expression to a perception, then, you aren't *using* the concept of perception. No more are you *using the concept* of a comparison when you compare or of a comparing mind when you judge one colour sample to be lighter than another. So he has no right to that thesis that there are no *ideas of relations* and hence that 'The bang and the flash are simultaneous' isn't a perceptual judgment.

If then there are perceptual judgments straddling different sense modalities, haven't we got a problem which is *not* solved by saying: the unitary item in which the senses converge is the soul? If there is an argument that the senses mustn't be thought of as like a lot of men sitting in a Trojan Horse, but they must converge in some one thing, call it the soul; won't there equally be an argument that they must converge in some one *sensory* power, call it the common sense, whose deliverances are still *sensory*?

I see no reason to think that Plato would have been disturbed by this. The 'one thing, call it the soul' does not have to be something unitary in the sense of having no departments—indeed we know that he believed in a tripartite division of the soul. Must there be a unitary, i.e. uniform, simple, constant character in the soul's judging? Well, he doesn't think so, as he distinguishes between what the soul uses instruments (sense organs) for and what it doesn't. Might he say: where is the organ? With what bodily part is associated the sensory power through which the soul perceives simultaneity and greater or less multiplicity *across* different sense modalities?

This implies you can't call something sensory unless there is an organ for that sensory power which it instances. This conception would mean that the fact there isn't an organ would be a sufficient reason for saying this is a purely mental thing.

That the special senses have organs is true. It is not true that every different type of special sense object has a different organ. Aristotle remarks that taste would be counted part of touch *if* we tasted all over our bodies. And it is natural to regard hot and cold, rough and smooth, hard and soft, as different types; or again tingling, which hasn't got a contrary; all are perceived through touch. Touch is, then, divided into many kinds of sensation. The skin isn't the special organ of a special sense. But for simultaneity there seems to be no organ at all. And as it is a relation *between* the things called simultaneous you couldn't handle it as we handled size and shape — saying *it* can be perceived by more than one sense.

Should I give up the idea that these judgments are perceptual judgments? Or should I say: they *are* so in as much as the perception of the bang and the perception of the flash are essentially involved in them; but 'simultaneous' is not a sensible characteristic — i.e. is never a sensible characteristic. Resemblance is not one either, though it can come into perceptual judgments. We would quarrel with Hume's attempt to explain abstract ideas as different resemblances. If we form the idea of black and white and a cube and a globe because of the different resemblances to be found in a pair of cubes and a pair of globes, each pair containing one black and one white member, the question must arise how we derive ideas of *resemblance* since the resemblances are so different. Why are they all *resemblances*? Is *that* fact something sensory? It might be better to follow Plato and hold that resemblance like identity and difference are terms of intellect and not of sense. And so perhaps it is with simultaneity.

The thing that is striking about the terms that Plato chooses in order to give examples of thoughts about objects of sense, and ask 'through what organ do you have these thoughts?', is indeed that the terms are extremely abstract and general. Like and unlike, existent,

same and different, number and unity, odd and even. They are as
Frege might say: reason's ownest own; they are properties (or whatever we choose to call them) grasped by intellect. What is here common to objects of sense is *not* grasped by the particular senses. So
there seem to be two ways in which he reaches the 'single form, call it
the soul'. One is that it won't do to picture the senses like the war-
riors sitting in the Trojan Horse, and the other is that the perceiver of
objects of sense judges things about them (and thus has these too as
his objects of thought) which specially belong to intellect, not to
sense.

The bringing together in judgments that no particular sense could
make – in case you think of the particular senses as making judgments – applies to a host of terms which appear to be sensory or perceptual in the sense I gave those words. If it is absurd to think of a
faculty of 'common' sense, then these terms appear to be manufac-
tured by the intelligence in a very complicated relationship to the
special senses. It is here of great importance that the special senses
are not confined to their own proper objects. One can see the expression of a man's face, for example. Here we don't invoke any sense
other than sight; but the object of this seeing is not a member of the
class: colours, light and darkness.

'I do sensibly perceive the simultaneity of the bang and the flash.'

If this is a sense perception what is the organ of it?

'There are *two* organs, eyes and ears.'

But neither of them is the instrument of *this* perception.

'Both are jointly. The soul whose instrument they are, perceives
the bang and flash through them and, being equipped with the concept of simultaneity, uses it in the judgment that it forms. The judgment is a perceptual one.'

But how does the soul *perceive* the simultaneity?

'By simultaneously perceiving the bang and the flash and considering them under the aspect of the concept of *simultaneity*.'

But then it wasn't a perception *of* simultaneity!

You are entangled in a prejudice about what to call a perception of
something. You want to model it on the way the proper objects of the
particular senses are perceived. It cannot be so modelled. That is
what throws you into perplexity. The soul which is the life of the
individual, is his vegetative and sensitive as well as his intellectual
life and is able to acquire concepts in a great variety of ways. The
sunflower turning to the sun is a bit of vegetative life. If the sunflower were an animal, its vegetative life would be greatly modified

by that fact; but so would its animal life be modified by its vegetative processes. And if it were also intellectual and had a language this would affect its vegetative and animal life and be affected by it. So simultaneity of reaction in one form of life may become reaction *to* simultaneity in another and this become part of thought in the third.

You teach the concept of simultaneity by teaching a reaction to simultaneous events.

Hume may not have been so wrong as appears in explaining the idea of succession in terms of having a succession of impressions. Only he would have to grant that here the idea was not a copy of any impression, and in that way not derived from any impressions.

4

Why Anselm's proof in the Proslogion is not an ontological argument

I

An argument for something's existence should be called 'ontological' only if it depends on taking existence to be a perfection. Descartes' second argument for God got called 'ontological' because it is
like that. Anselm's *Proslogion* proof is called 'ontological' by assimilation to Descartes'. People are sometimes unscholarly and report as
Anselm's the argument later formulated by Descartes.

Those who are more careful read Anselm and can at least observe
differences:

1. Descartes defines God as supremely perfect being. Anselm, as:
that than which nothing greater can be conceived.

2. Descartes' proof is extracted from the definition — together with
existence's being a perfection. He uses no premise that the idea of a

* Published in *The Thoreau Quarterly* 17 (1985): 32–40. The text of a lecture given at
the XIX Reuniones Filosóficas, University of Navarre, on the 9th of March 1982.
The Spanish version, 'Por que la prueba de Anselmo en el *Proslogion* no es un
argumento ontológico', appeared in *Annuario Filosófico* 25 (1982): 9-18. Anscombe
gave a more concise treatment of the same topic in a lecture at the XXXth Confer-
ence of the History of Logic, Cracow, October 19-21, 1984: 'Descartes and
Anselm', in Jerzy Perzanowski (ed) *Essays on Philosophy and Logic* (Cracow:
Jagiellonian University Press, 1987), pp.15–18.

deity is in his mind, any more than it is a premise for him that the idea of a triangle is in his mind. Rather: when the idea 'triangle' or 'deity' is in his mind, it is not a figment of his, but something that, *whether or not there is any such thing in the real world*, has a determinate nature which is eternal and immutable. And this is shown by the fact that various properties can be demonstrated of it. Existence is not a property that can be proved of a triangle; but it can be proved of a deity:

> God = Def. supremely perfect being.
>
> Existence is a perfection.
>
> Therefore God has existence.

3. Anselm's argument, on the traditional reading of the text, goes:

i.   God = Def. that than which nothing greater can be conceived.

ii. That than which nothing greater can be conceived at any rate exists in the mind of the fool who says there is no such thing.

iii. If that than which nothing greater can be conceived is only in a mind, it can be thought to exist in reality too, which is greater.

iv. Therefore if that than which nothing greater can be conceived is only in a mind, it is not that than which nothing greater can be conceived.

v.   But it is a contradiction to say that something than which nothing greater can be conceived is something than which a greater can be conceived.

vi. Therefore that than which nothing greater can be conceived exists in reality as well as in the mind.

These arguments are so different that they do not deserve to be handled together.

Anselm's has an existential premise, Descartes' has none.

Anselm claims to derive a contradiction from this existential premise and the supposition that *that than which nothing greater can be conceived is only in the mind.*

Descartes claims that 'everlasting existence' can be as clearly and distinctly perceived to be a property of God as it can be perceived that a triangle's angles add up to two right angles.

There is an objection to Descartes' argument. The question, 'Does any G exist?' or 'Is there such a thing as a G?' is equivalent to the question whether the concept-term we put in place of G is *empty*. Or we might say it is equivalent to the question 'Is anything a G?' or 'Is it true that (∃x)Gx?'. So only if one can say that it is a perfection of something *that there is such a thing as it*, can we say that existence *in this sense* is a perfection. But in that case existence will be a perfection when blindness exists, and all sorts of evils and privations.

Descartes has confused the sense of 'existence' in which a statement of existence says 'There is such a thing as G', or, better 'For some x, Gx', and the sense of 'existence' in which it is like 'life'. In this latter sense we can speak of everlasting existence, of the fact that something used to exist, or still will exist at some future date, of a long or short span of existence, of coming into and passing out of existence.

Now Descartes speaks of the determinate nature of a triangle, calling it immutable and eternal. He is not thereby saying it has such existence as I have just been speaking of. He is speaking of an essence, the various properties in whose make-up do not include living or existing, either always or for a long or short time.

His argument about God is that in this case the essence or nature does include everlasting existence, and he takes this to be a proof that God exists.

Now 'God exists' in the sense in which he wants to prove it, means that the concept of a deity is not empty — that something is a deity. But this does not follow from the premises. One may grant, indeed, that everlasting existence is part of the notion of a deity, and still ask: But *is* there such a thing?

Nevertheless this does not quite cover the matter. Descartes thinks he has a proof that God exists and does not distinguish the senses of 'existence'. But could he not have accepted the distinction, and argued that, since God is necessarily an everlasting being, God must be *extant* now — and always.

A parallel. He could have argued as well or ill that the nature which he can conceive includes everlasting life, and taken this as a proof that God *is alive now* — and always.

This whole matter, then, needs a bit more attention.

We ought to contrast 'being a living being' and 'being alive'. (I understand that in Spanish one actually uses different verbs 'to be' in the two cases.) That it belongs to the concept of something to be a living being does not prove that it is alive. What is a Dodo? A living thing of an extinct species. So *being a living thing* and *being alive* are not the same.

Similarly *existing everlastingly* or *being the kind of thing to have an everlasting existence* is not the same as *being extant* — or as *always being extant*. 'Being extant' is logically a term like 'being alive', and 'being an everlasting existent' like 'being an endlessly living thing'.

It can belong to the concept of something to have everlasting life, endless existence — but that does not prove that such a thing is actually alive, or is extant, and hence that the concept is not empty.

Descartes in effect thought that it did. Interestingly, he does consider the objection: 'Perhaps I cannot think of God except as existing, just as I cannot think of a hill without a valley. But from my thinking of a hill with a valley, it does not follow that there *is* any hill in the world; similarly, it appears not to follow, from my thinking of God as existent, that God does exist. For my thought imposes no necessity on things …'.

But he says there is a lurking fallacy here. It is things that impose necessity on his thought: '… from my inability to think of God as non-existent, it follows that existence is inseparable from God, and thus that he really exists.'§

Thus Descartes plainly takes that endless existence which belongs to the concept of deity to be the same as that existence which is *there being such a thing as* …

From the endless existence's being part of the concept it follows, indeed, that *if* the concept is not empty, then God not only is an endlessly existent being, but is actually extant, alive, at all times. That God is an endlessly existing being is a truth like red's being a colour. And this truth entails that, *if* the concept God is not empty, a deity is not only actual and alive, but that this actuality and life are perpetual and from forever.

This, however, all hangs on the *if*. I said 'if the concept is not empty …' And our considerations don't show that it is not. And so we must reject the ontological argument of Descartes.

II

We have seen that Anselm's argument is not the same. Nevertheless it is still an ontological argument, given the standard reading of the text. This standard reading yields step (iii) of the argument as I set it forth:

   iii.   If that than which nothing greater can be conceived is only in a mind, it can be thought to exist in reality too, *which is greater*.

---

§ See Descartes, *Meditations on First Philosophy*, Meditation V.

As I said, there is an existential premise. The argument runs:

> So, something greater can be conceived than something than which nothing greater can be conceived, *if* this exists only in the mind. Hence, either it does not exist in any mind, or it exists in reality as well. But it does exist in someone's mind. Therefore it exists in reality as well.

I make no doubt that this last paragraph gives the argument. Except that the 'So' of the first sentence refers us to (iii). What that sentence says,

> Something greater can be conceived than that than which nothing greater can be conceived, *if* this exists only in the mind

is supposed to follow from my (iii), in which I give the standard reading of the text at this point.

But now — what this (iii) says is that existing in reality as well as in someone's mind is greater than existing only in a mind.

But this does not mean that what exists in reality as well *is a greater thing!* And if that were put in as a step in the argument, one would want to know how it was reached.

Therefore one can fault the argument in either of two ways. (1) The missing step would lead on to the next proposition, which is about *something greater*, but would not seem to be justified by (iii). Or (2): how would anything that followed from existence in reality being greater lead to the next proposition.

At the very best there is a gap. We might put the following in as an extra premise:

> What exists in the mind and in reality is greater that what exists only in the mind.

Then the argument would seem complete.

But why should we accept this premise? And if we do insert it, what then is the role of the phrase 'which is greater' in (iii)? It looks as if we ought to drop this phrase, and have:

iii.   If that than which nothing greater can be conceived is only in a mind, still it can be thought to exist in reality as well.

iiia.   What exists in reality as well as in a mind is greater than what exists only in a mind.

This would give us a coherent argument. But, once again, why should we accept (iiia)? Perhaps at this point we invoke Descartes' assumption: existence is a perfection. A hundred dollars in the pocket is more than a hundred dollars in the imagination — a whole hundred dollars more.

This then is the reason for calling Anselm's argument ontological. Existence in reality is better and greater than existence only in the mind. What has it is better and greater than the same thing not having it. So the supremely perfect being, or being than which nothing greater can be conceived, must have this perfection too.

It is traditional at least since Leibniz to assimilate Anselm to Descartes. Leibniz thought Anselm's a fine argument, sadly rejected by the Scholastics, and revived by Descartes. He knew indeed that it was part of the argument in Anselm that the idea was in someone's mind, but that did not make him distinguish it. He thought the fact of something being in the mind was an 'indice trompeur', because impossible things can be in the mind. So the argument was incomplete. Both in Anselm and in Descartes it needed supplementing by an argument to show that the idea was an idea of something *possible*.

It may be that Leibniz is the man responsible for the modern assimilation to Descartes. He is, however, not responsible for the interpretation which involves saying that what is in reality also is greater than what is in the mind alone. That goes back at least to Aquinas. For I take it that an argument essentially using the description 'that than which nothing greater can be conceived' must derive from Anselm's, even if it was misinterpreted.[1]

I will now show that the whole thing *is* a misinterpretation.

In modern times the standard interpretation is forced on us by the punctuation of the Latin. The crucial sentence is:

> Si enim vel in solo intellectu est, potest cogitari esse et in re quod maius est.

All modern editions that I have seen have a comma between 're' and 'quod', thus forcing the translation:

> For if it is only in the intellect, it can be thought to be in reality as well, which is greater.

If, however, you leave out that comma, you get better Latin and the rendering is:

> For if it is only in the intellect, what is greater can be thought to be in reality as well.

Anselm wrote beautiful Latin. And commas are pure editorial opinion. What the MSS of his text have are dots; sometimes these look a

---

[1]　St Thomas Aquinas, *Summa theologiae* 1a, q.2, a.1 ad 2.

bit random. When not random and not functioning like our period, they are supposed to be a help to the man who is reading the text out loud; or sometimes they have something to do with abbreviations; say of a proper name.

I have looked at many MSS of this passage and have not seen even one of such dots in this place.[2] Not that it would signify if there were one; it is the comma of modern editions that forces a particular Latin construe, and so a translation, upon us.

With a proper reading the argument runs:

i. God = Def. that than which nothing greater can be conceived.

ii. That than which nothing greater can be conceived exists at any rate in the intellect of the fool who says no such thing exists.

iii. If this does exist only in an intellect, what is greater than it can be thought to exist in reality as well.

iv. Therefore if something than which nothing greater can be conceived is only in the intellect, it is not something than which nothing greater can be conceived.

v. But this involves a contradiction.

vi. Therefore that than which nothing greater can be conceived exists in reality as well.

This argument is not an ontological argument, except — indirectly — on the interpretation given to it by Aquinas. His comment does not suggest that he has construed the crucial sentence differently from the way I do in the new (iii). But if you say 'What is greater can be thought to exist in reality' the questions must arise 'What, that is greater? And what is greater about it?' Anselm gives no clue in *Proslogion II* to show us how he would answer these questions. And one possible answer might be: 'What is in reality as well as in the mind just *is* thereby greater than what is only in the mind.' And this St Thomas puts down as part of the argument.

If that is a correct explanation of 'what is greater', then even with a correct construe of the Latin we still have an ontological argument — for one of Anselm's premises.

But it is not a necessary explanation. Indeed, it is not even a possible one. For he denies the general proposition 'What is in reality is greater than what is only in the mind'. We find this denial in the reply to Gaunilo.

[2] Since writing this I have seen a dot in this place in one MS.

We might charitably expound the proposition by inserting 'the same': 'What is in reality is greater than the same thing existing only in the mind.' But we shall see that this won't do either: they turn out not to be the same.

Why, someone may ask, did Anselm not give an explanation in presenting the argument?

The answer to this, I think, is the following: we know he wanted to give a very short single argument. And this he did. On the assumption that that than which nothing greater can be conceived is only in the mind, something greater can be conceived. For something greater can be thought to exist in reality as well. The assumption is therefore contradictory. Either there is no such thing even in the intellect, or it exists only in reality. But it does exist in the mind of the fool. Therefore …

That is the strong short argument that flashed upon Anselm in choir. There are two ways to challenge it: you may call the premises in question, or you may fault it as invalid.

You may feel inclined to say: there *must* have been more to it than that. He must have had reason to say 'Something greater can be thought to exist in reality'.

Well, certainly he did. But *here* he was putting down the barest bones of the argument. He gives premises — which he undoubtedly believes — from which the conclusion is to follow. From one point of view the interesting thing is: *Does* the conclusion follow? It doesn't matter at all why he holds that particular premise. If the premises are true, is the conclusion proved?

Let me give a version of the argument, which is not quite St Anselm's but is very close to it:

A. Suppose there is a thought (in some mind) of: something such that nothing greater can be thought of, and suppose that what it's a thought of is only in the mind.

B. Then something greater can be thought actually to exist.

C. In that case the thought of something such that none greater can be thought of is a thought of something such that a greater than it can be thought of.

The question is: is (C) a contradiction? If so, then we could draw the conclusion that either the original thought described is an impossible thought, or it cannot be of something that is only in the mind.

I do not wish to say that the question about the premise is of no interest — I mean the premise that: If that is only in the mind, then what is greater can be thought to exist in reality. On the contrary, it is extremely interesting. If we examine Anselm's reply to Gaunilo, we find a crop of arguments, all interesting and powerful, and some giving the answer to the question about that premise.

On the assumption that that than which nothing greater can be conceived is nothing outside the mind, we can certainly say that it is something that can not-exist, can be non-existent. But it is possible to think that that than which nothing greater can be conceived *does* exist. If it is thought of as existing, it must not be thought of as possibly not-existing. For it could be thought of as not possibly not-existing, and the thought of it as not possibly not-existing is obviously a thought of it as greater than if it is thought of as possibly not-existing. Thus the thought of it as existing *leads* to a thought of it as greater than what was thought of as not-existing. But there is here no suggestion that it is the *existing* that is the greater thing about what is thought to exist.

This is only one of several arguments in the reply to Gaunilo, all subtle and powerful. We know that Anselm directed that Gaunilo's criticism be included in MSS copies of the *Proslogion*, and that he also thought Gaunilo had failed to understand his argument. Gaunilo for example keeps taking Anselm's description as 'what is greater than all things', and Anselm protests that he never based any argument on *that* description. Suppose, he says further, you were able to show me something that was greater than anything else, I might say to you 'But I can think of something greater still.'

As the reply to Gaunilo is an important source for the answer to our questions 'What greater thing?' and 'What is greater about it?' we can infer that Anselm saw the need to make that clear, and this will have been *one* of his reasons for including Gaunilo in the MS copies; for of course he also included his reply.

Before ending, let me notice one principal aspect of Anselm's argument and defence of it. He gets consequences, given the supposition of existence — consequences regarding the further description of the thing in question, which are different from parallel consequences given the supposition of non-existence.

This is clean contrary to a dominant tradition in modern philosophy.

5

Russelm or Anselm?

It is pleasing to have notice taken of my article 'Why Anselm's Proof in the *Proslogion* is not an Ontological Argument'. I thank Professor Williams.[1] In reply, I have to make some objections.

1. I did not argue that Anselm's argument could be 'saved by deletion of a comma', only that it could so be saved from the stupidity of an Ontological Argument. Note that commas in editing Anselm are merely editorial judgments, there being no commas in the mediaeval MSS.

2. I wanted to show what Anselm's was. I did not claim that it was a valid proof. I could not determine whether it was a valid argument.

3. I showed that if it was a valid argument of the 'Ontological' class, it has a missing, i.e., unstated, premise: 'What exists in reality is greater than if it exists only in the mind'. (This missing premise is supplied by Aquinas, *Summa Theologiae*, Part I, Q.2, art.1, ad 2, who discusses an argument, obviously current in his time and deriving from Anselm's, though he does not attribute it to Anselm. All the same, he thinks it wrong.)

4. Williams does not notice the need of this extra premise, saying directly (or perhaps taking me as saying) that the premise, which (with the editorial comma put into the text before '*quod maius est*') says that existing in reality is greater than existing only in a mind, 'seems to involve the fallacy of treating *being* as a real predicate.' It does not: the extra premise is requisite.

5. Williams does not notice that *Proslogion* 3 is an argument assuming the *conclusion* reached in *Proslogion* 2. The latter has supposedly proved the existence of that '*quo maius cogitari nequit*' ('than which

* Reprinted from *The Philosophical Quarterly* 43 (1993): 500-504, with the permission of the publishers, Wiley-Blackwell.

[1]   C J F Williams, 'Russelm', *The Philosophical Quarterly* 43 (1993): 496–499.

nothing greater can be thought of'). Henceforth I shall abbreviate this as *qmcn*, and '*quo maius cogitari potest*', 'than which a greater can be thought of', as *qmcp*.

Given that *qmcn* does exist *in re* (in reality), Anselm argues further that it *cannot* not exist. This impossibility must be an impossibility of its ceasing to exist. Hence Williams' accusation that I equate 'It can be the case that that than which nothing greater can be conceived is non-existent' with 'That than which nothing greater can be conceived can be non-existent' is wrong. Given that *id qmcn* has been proved to exist, it can further be shown that it cannot be non-existent, i.e. cannot become non-existent, i.e., cease to exist. The argument from non-conceivability applies: namely, that *qmcn*, if existent, cannot be thought of as ceasing to exist. For one can conceive something — call it *id qmcn* — to be capable of ceasing to exist. But then it is not *qmcn*, for one would be thinking of something greater if one thought of something *qmcn* which was incapable of ceasing to exist.

It is a mistake to treat *Proslogion* 3 as a new and independent argument for there being such a thing as something *qmcn*, i.e., for '*id qmcn*' as being a non-empty concept. This shows that Williams' arguments against *Proslogion* 3 are misconceived. He says that Anselm attempts a *reductio ad absurdum* proof of the proposition 'That than which nothing greater can be conceived cannot be conceived not to exist'. But, to repeat, Anselm's reasoning in *Proslogion* 3 assumes that *that qmcn* (that than which nothing greater can be conceived) has already been proved to exist, and he is arguing something further. Here he does rely on what Williams calls a premise for a *further proof* of the existence of *id qmcn*, namely that if you conceive of something as existing and capable of not existing, your conception is a conception of something inferior to what you conceive if you conceive of it as incapable of not existing.

6. It is a mistake to say that 'That than which nothing greater can be conceived' is a 'definite description' in the sense that Russell gave to that term. Anselm's first and repeated expression in *Proslogion* 2 is '*aliquid qmcn*', i.e., 'something *qmcn*'. In the same — short — chapter he later speaks of *id qmcn*, which we can render 'that than which …'. There is no reason to think he has switched to a Russellian definite description, which would have in strictness to be rendered 'that which *alone* is *qmcn*'.

It is worth observing that Russell in 'On Denoting' has a footnote: 'The argument [namely 'the most perfect Being has all perfections;

existence is a perfection; therefore the most perfect Being exists'] can be made to prove validly that all members of the class of most perfect Beings exist ...'. I do not complete this interesting footnote, but quote its beginning to show that Williams' assumption that '*id qmcn*' is a definite description *à la* Russell wants grounds. Reading Anselm's argument, I might say (to Anselm): 'You've proved the existence of some *qmcn*, but so far as that goes it leaves open the question "How many things fall under that description?"' In *Proslogion* 2 Anselm speaks of 'such a nature' ('*talis natura*'). It may be that there is only one 'such nature', but more than one thing that has it.

7. Here I will give briefly what ought to be the received version of Anselm's argument in *Proslogion* 2, accepting the editorial comma before '*quod maius est*'. (I put in square brackets the extra premise which that version needs, and which is not in Anselm.)

If *qmcn* exists only in the mind, still it can be conceived to exist in reality as well. Now, for any object, to exist in reality as well as in the mind is greater than for it to exist only in the mind. [And therefore it too is greater than if it exists only in the mind.] Hence conceiving it to exist in reality as well as in the mind is conceiving it as greater than one is conceiving it as if one thinks it exists only in a mind. Therefore one cannot conceive *qmcn* to exist *only* in a mind. For if *qmcn* is only in a mind, this *qmcn* is also *qmcp* — but that is a contradiction. But it certainly does exist in a mind — namely in that of the fool, who says there is no such thing in reality. Therefore *qmcn* exists in reality as well as in the mind.

This argument can be blamed like the Ontological Argument, since it derives a *thing's* being greater from its *existence in reality's* being greater than existence only in the mind.

8. Williams, like many others, writes as if 'greater than' in Anselm's argument is simply a binary relation between two things. Such a relation involves comparing, e.g., that both exist in reality. Some have indeed noticed that Anselm is not invoking such a binary relation, and it is sometimes suggested that one cannot compare what is 'in reality' with what is 'only in the mind'. This is a mistake: we often make such comparisons, e.g., 'The explosion was not as loud as I expected it to be'. Does this mean that the explosion in my imagination (expectation) was a louder explosion than 'the' explosion when it happened in reality? The suggestion makes clear that we cannot be operating as if we were comparing two explosions, one existing in the mind and the other actually happening. Williams' notation does not provide us with a tool for handling such matters. It

is clear that in Anselm's argument the comparatives are what is called 'intentional'. *Id qmcn* cannot exist only in the mind, for if it does, what is greater can be thought to exist in reality as well. Here I am disregarding that editorial comma and taking '*quod maius est*' to be the subject of 'can be thought to exist in reality as well' (*potest cogitari esse et in re quod maius est*). Anselm makes a very quick step in his argument here—his aim is to reach a contradiction between *id qmcn* existing in the mind of the fool who says there is no such thing in reality, and a greater thing, which can be thought to exist in reality as well. The fact that it *is* something that can be thought to exist in reality and not only 'in the mind' is essential to the contradiction, precisely because the fool's *thought* is of that than which nothing greater can be thought of—but here *is* something greater than what the fool's thought is of, if that exists only in the mind. Not: the existence in reality is the greater-making thing; but: the possible thought is of something that *is* greater. And so something greater *can* be thought of than what in the fool's mind was *that than which nothing greater can be thought of.* That produces a contradiction: the thought which Anselm describes is *a thought of* something greater than what, in the fool's mind, is: something than which nothing greater can be thought of.

A sort of parallel: I can think of a pain more intense than can be survived. That is just what my thought is, and that is all there is to it: it is 'only in my mind'. But now someone says that he had witnessed a pain more intense than could be survived: for the sufferer died of it. So he, the witness, has a thought which is of an actual pain, more intense than could be survived. Was not the pain that *he* can now think of (and believe to be possible) more intense than the pain that is 'only in the mind' of the man who conjures up the thought of 'a pain more intense than can be survived'? One might say: the former's description is real, the latter's is just imaginary.

This, as I said, is only a parallel. It does not quite hit the mark hit by Anselm's argument. For one brings in the pain that the witness witnessed, which did kill the sufferer. But in the Anselmian argument there is not an appeal to the object that *is* such that nothing greater can be conceived. We remain in the realm of thought: if the fool's object is 'only in the mind', then something greater can be thought to exist in reality as well. When Anselm says this, the questions immediately present themselves: 'What, that is greater? And what is greater about it? *Is* it "that it exists in reality as well"?' If so, then

Anselm is indeed guilty in a way of the fallacy alleged of the Onto-logical Argument.

But that is not the answer. To find the answer, we have to read Anselm's reply to Gaunilo, though we may get some help soon from the rest of the *Proslogion*. It is a greater thing that we are thinking of, if we are thinking, not merely that it exists in reality as well as in the mind, but that it can have neither a beginning nor an end of exis-tence. Or rather, we may have as the content of our thoughts not only something *qmcn*, and that it exists in reality, or can be thought to, but also that if there was something else, comparable to it, existing in reality also, but capable of ceasing to exist and having had a begin-ning, our thought of this latter thing *would* be a thought of a less great thing than was the thought of something *qmcn*, existing in reality and by inference having had no beginning and having no capability of ceasing to exist.

These and other arguments in the *Reply to Gaunilo* give body to the phrase 'what is greater' ('*quod maius est*') in *Proslogion* 2. *Proslogion* 3, which relies on the conclusion of *Proslogion* 2, and infers that non-existence — i.e., ceasing to exist — is not a possibility for *id qmcn*, might be said to give some body to the phrase '*quod maius est*' ('what is greater'); but the existence *in re* of *id qmcn* is given once one accepts the essential argument of *Proslogion* 2. Namely, that if *id qmcn* is 'only in the mind', something greater can be thought (believed) to exist in reality as well.

A final parallel: *the largest prime number* exists in the mind of the mathematics student, even one who knows — perhaps can prove — that there is no such thing. But suppose one who is at a more elemen-tary stage, though being something of a thinker, and he says 'I've got the idea of the biggest prime number in my head, but I bet there's really no such thing. However big a prime number you might show me, I'd feel it wasn't big enough to be the biggest — there'd have to be a bigger one.' (Cf. Anselm's reply to Gaunilo's taking him to be argu-ing about what is greater (and better) than anything else: 'You could show me something that was greater than everything else, but I could say: "But I can *think of* something greater still".') Perhaps our elementary mathematics student could formulate an explanation of why 'there'd have to be a bigger one'. He might even invent the famous proof, and learn quite a bit in doing so. At his stage of mere disbelief, we might compare him to Anselm thinking: 'If *that* were only in the mind, it would still be possible to think of something greater that would be there in reality.'

That is the impression one might form from that short crucial sentence in *Proslogion* 2. All that we are given is that it would be possible to think that something greater existed in reality as well as in the mind. However, that impression, which I have imagined, may be wrong, because that powerful mind produced that sentence and, we are told, very much wanted to produce a *short* knock-down argument. In thinking about it, we are led into the intricacies of thought about thought and of intentional comparatives. But the fact that Anselm directed that publication of his *Proslogion* should thereafter always include Gaunilo's attack and his reply (of which I have only mentioned a tiny bit, a single argument among several) – this fact suggests that he realised he should have been more explanatory of his *Proslogion* 2 sentence: 'For if it is only in the mind, what is greater can be thought to exist in reality as well'.

To end, I should bow to Professor Williams' consciously ironical title 'Russelm'. We know he is addicted to Russell on existence, but is there not in that title a hint of acknowledgement that he thinks he *may* be wrong about Anselm?

6

Truth:
Anselm or Thomas?

Anselm, called *doctor doctorum* by those who came after him, died in 1109, 116 years before Thomas Aquinas was born. So the sort of distance in time between them was something like that of Byron, or Napoleon, or even Kant, from us. In the writings of Thomas his name seems only less weighty than that of Augustine. It was not Thomas' way to express disagreement much with revered authorities; so he does this little or not at all with Anselm. Indeed, it looks as if he had found him very valuable and some things he certainly took from him.

Let me first give a brief sketch of the most significant early parts of Anselm's dialogue *On Truth*. He proposes to his pupil that they look through the various things that are said to have truth in them. They will begin with propositions, where, he also tells us, most people stop too; in any case, we rather often call propositions true or false. It is clear that he does not mean 'abstract propositions', but vocal utterances; and he remarks that the nature of truth in these can be equally considered in any signs that come about to signify something's being the case or not being the case, e.g. writings or speech with the fingers. The striking things about his discussion are two. First, the identification of truth with rightness of assertion. What is assertion for – i.e. what has it been created for? Answer: to signify as being the case what is the case. Since this answer contained in itself the only

---

* The text of the 1984 Aquinas Lecture delivered at Blackfriars, Oxford, on 16 February 1984, and published in *New Blackfriars* 66 (1985): 82–98. There are some occasional differences in the present text from the previously published version, introduced in the light of the original typescript and of annotations to the printed version by the author.

account the pupil had to give of a proposition's being true (namely, that it signified like that), the truth of a proposition, the truth or rightness of an assertion, and the truth or rightness of a signifying, are all identified with one another. The key is the teleology of assertion. We should note, however, that rightness of signifying is here being discussed only in the context of an assertion: it is assertion that is said to be right, as doing what it was created for, when it signifies as being the case what is the case. So we have the dialogue running:

T.   What does truth seem to you to be, in a proposition?

P.   I don't know, except that it is true when it signifies that to be the case, which *is* the case.

T.   What was assertion created for?

P.   To signify that to be the case which is the case.

T.   So that's what it ought to do?

P.   Certainly.

T.   So when it signifies, as being the case, what is the case, it signifies what it ought?

P.   Obviously.

T.   And when it signifies what it ought, it signifies rightly?

P.   Yes.

T.   But when it signifies rightly, the signifying is right?

P.   No doubt of it.†

And this rightness, they agree, is truth. I have quoted this discussion so that a reader can see how in it the *it* of 'it ought to do', 'it signifies rightly', 'it signifies what it ought', is always an assertion. Unasserted propositions or clauses within a longer proposition are not investigated. They are perhaps covered by the opening question and answer in my quotation.

The second striking thing follows immediately upon the identification of truth with rightness of assertion, i.e. with assertion's doing what it was created for. The pupil, who has already shown himself no stooge, asks:

> Tell me what I'm to answer, if someone should say that even when an expression signifies as being the case what isn't so, it is signifying what it ought. For it's been given it to signify a

† *De Veritate*, c.2. T = Teacher; P = Pupil.

thing's being so, equally when it is so and when it isn't so. For if it hadn't got it in it to signify the thing's being the case even when it isn't, it wouldn't signify that. Hence even when it signifies that what is not the case is the case, it signifies what it ought. But if it's right and true by signifying what it ought, an expression is true even when it signifies as being the case what is not the case.§

You might expect Anselm to reject this. But not at all. He ratifies it! We do not ordinarily call an utterance true when it signifies that to be the case which is not, but all the same it has got rightness and truth in it. But when it signifies that that is the case, which *is* so, it does what it ought in two ways, since it signifies both what it has had given it to signify, *and* what it was created to signify. We customarily call a proposition right and true according as it has this latter rightness, not the former. For it ought more — *plus debet* — to do what it was made for than what it was *not* made for. It could not get to signify a thing's being when it is not, or not being when it is, except because it could not be given it to signify something's being so *only* when it is so. So there are two kinds of rightness and truth: one, to do with what utterances are *for*, the other to do with their signifying what they do signify. The latter is constant, permanent and natural. The former is variable, inconstant, accidental and according to use.

This conception is no mere trick or *tour de force*. It is the second key thought of the *De Veritate* of St Anselm; the first being the identification of truth and rightness. 'Rightness', by the way, is not to be construed ambiguously, as being sometimes synonymous with truth, i.e. as meaning a correctness which in its turn would have to be explained as truth; some translators translate *rectitudo* so at the beginning of the book, where we are discussing propositions and opinions, and then go over to 'uprightness' when it comes to actions. No; it should always be translated 'rightness' and the idea of a 'non-moral' or a 'moral' sense of the word should not be allowed entry; it can only impede understanding. I suppose it might help to explain 'being done rightly' as 'being done properly', as you may speak of driving a screw or digesting your food or performing a deduction properly.

The second key thought, that of the two things, natural and non-natural rightness, leads to the treatment of justice — which has the longest chapter to itself, it is five whole pages long! — as a species

§ *Loc.cit.*

of truth; as also to the distinction between natural and non-natural truth in action. The action of a fire in heating is an example of natural truth, because the source of its doing that is the source of its existence; i.e. as we would say, it is its nature to; and it acts according to its true nature if it exists at all. Similarly, the utterance 'It's day', signifying that it is day whether it is or not, is doing what it has been naturally given it to do. That is to say: doing that is its nature. The pupil sighs with relief and says 'Now at last I see what's true about a false statement!'.

Considering all the things that may be called 'true' and 'right', Anselm puts aside the sort of rightness that is perceptible to the senses: that is not the sort he means in his search for the nature of truth — e.g. a right line (that is, a straight one) or a right angle. These are seen with the eyes as well as understood. So now he gives his definition of truth: truth is rightness that *only* the mind can perceive.

So far I have reported the groundwork in Anselm. Before going further, I will report that Thomas embraces all or most of what I have so far retailed. As to the teleology of assertion, I do not know. He would surely not reject it; still, I do not think it plays such a key role for him. But the idea of two kinds of truth, such that in one way even a false proposition is true because it does do the work, which defines it as a proposition, of signifying what it signifies, though in the *other* way it is not true — this certainly Thomas adopted. Discussing whether truth is immutable, which he does not think holds of *created* truth, he mentions Anselm's saying that truth is a certain rightness inasmuch as something fulfils — i.e. (here) *is* — what it is in the divine mind. That is to say, Anselm thinks that there is truth in objects, and that includes propositions. This offers an argument that truth is immutable: 'The proposition *Socrates is sitting* has it from the divine mind that it signifies that Socrates is sitting, which it does even when he is not sitting. So the truth of a proposition does not change in any way'.[1] Thomas answers the argument:

> A proposition does not only have truth as other things are said to do … but is said to do so in a certain special way in so far as it signifies truth of understanding. This consists in the conformity of understanding and thing. Take away the conformity, and the truth of the opinion is altered, and consequently that of the proposition. Thus, then, the proposition 'Socrates is sitting' is true while he is sitting, *both* with the truth of a thing, inasmuch as it is a *particular significant* utterance, *and* with the truth of signification,

[1]　*Summa theologiae* 1a, q.16, a.8, obj.3.

inasmuch as it signifies a true opinion. When Socrates stands up,
the first truth remains, but the second changes.[2]

The two kinds of truth are obviously taken directly from Anselm,
and Thomas' way of speaking of them also corresponds to the distinction between natural and non-natural truth.

He also embraces the definition 'rightness perceptible only to the
mind', though not exclusively; for he sees point in other definitions
of truth offered by Augustine (several), Hilary and (as he thinks) the
Rabbi Isaac. This was the famous 'measuring up to one another of
mind and object': 'adaequatio intellectus et rei' — a phrase which I
guess must be a source-stimulus for Locke's talk of 'adequate' and
'inadequate' ideas. The learned tell us that Isaac Israeli did *not* in fact
contrive that definition of truth but Avicenna inspired it.

I come now to try and explore the rather deep differences between
Anselm and Thomas. These primarily concern two great matters:
one is whether the proper seat of truth is the intellect — the
understanding — or whether there is truth in things. The second
is whether there is such a thing as created truth and — a sort of
appendage — whether truth is one thing, the same in all things that
have truth.

It may be a mistake to characterise the two philosophers as diver-
gent on any but the last point. For the others, Thomas can always say:
Anselm is speaking of things as they are in the divine mind, he does
not think the (non-natural) truth of a proposition is something that is
not created. And even about the third point, where I would say there
is a most definite disagreement, Thomas does not acknowledge it —
he insists that Anselm's single truth which is the same in all things is
the single eternal truth of the divine mind. Not that he is *professing*
exegesis — but *that* is the sense in which he can accept what Anselm
says as correct.

Nevertheless, I perceive a difference of feeling between the two,
which at the very least is a difference of slant. Thomas is sure that the
proper seat of truth is the intellect; and this is tied up with his examination of knowledge (*cognitio*) and desire (*appetitus*). There is knowledge according as the thing known is in the knowing mind
according to the manner of the mind; there is desire according as the
desire reaches out towards the desired thing itself. 'Good' names
what desire tends towards; 'true' what the understanding tends
towards. In consequence of these considerations, we must say that

[2]   *Ibid.* ad 3.

desire itself is called good so far as it is *of* what is good; the adjective 'good', primarily applicable to the desirable object, has a secondary, derived, use in which it applies to the desire. The primary logical seat of goodness is in the things (or states of affairs) which are the objects of desire. By contrast, because truth is in the intellect according as it conforms to the thing it is thinking of, the adjective 'true' has a secondary, derived, use in which *it* applies to the thing that is being thought of. Hence the thing thought of is called 'true' according as it has a certain relation to the intellect; the relation is called an 'order' (*ordo*).

However, we have to notice that a thing which is thought of may have this relation to an intellect either *per se* or *per accidens*. Let me try to explain these terms by others which may be clearer to some, darker to others. A thing may have a relation to a mind either in such a way that the relation is an internal one in the thing, or an external one. For example, a poem has an internal relation to the mind of the poet, an external relation to the mind of someone who is not the poet, but who reads it. And so generally for artefacts.

Any object can be called 'true' absolutely according to its relation to the intellect on which it depends: a house, for example, is true in this way if it is true to the plan of the architect. And a sentence is true in so far as it is a sign of a true understanding of its sense. And primarily, in signifying what has been given to it to signify.

'Every object is true according as it has the form proper to its nature.' Here Thomas and Anselm seem to come together again, the previous material having seemed to separate them. The natural objects in the world have the forms that they have, 'forms proper to their nature' says Thomas; 'they are and cannot but be *what* they are in the supreme truth' says Anselm; and Thomas will not disagree. But *his* analysis of the relations between 'true', 'good' and 'existent' fills a space that does not seem to be there in the work of Anselm: Anselm has moved fast from the peculiarity of the relations between truth, falsehood and signification of propositions to concepts of natural and non-natural truth. He gets truth into things without any consideration of 'true' as a term derived in this application from its native bearer, the intellect. Or: the derivation is purely the derivation from the *summa veritas*, which is God.

One definite large contrast between them is to be seen in the following. Thomas says: If no intellect were eternal, no truth would be eternal. But because only the divine intellect is eternal, in it alone does truth have eternity.

Now Anselm liked — at any rate he used — the Augustinian argument: 'If truth had a beginning or will have an end, then: before it began it was true that truth did not exist; and after it will end it will *be true* that truth will not exist. But there can't be anything true without truth. So there was truth before there was truth and there will be truth after truth will be ended, which is utterly absurd.'

It has been observed that if this argument is valid, it looks as if you could derive a parallel argument about falsehood to show that it can have had no beginning and can have no end. This is true up to a point, but up to that point it could not perturb Anselm. He does indeed say that in respect of the *summa veritas* truth and falsehood are in quite different positions: there, there is *no* falsehood. But in *this* argument what is in question is the truth of propositions; and the correlative falsehood of the contradictory propositions should offer no difficulty to someone who has seen that a proposition that can say what is the case can say the same thing when it is not the case. It may be that that only applies to things that are sometimes the case and at other times not. But if the 'utter absurdity' entails falsehood, as the Augustinian argument seems to imply, then we already have a perpetual falsehood introduced by the Augustinian argument itself: the falsehood that there was a time when nothing was true. If that entailment does not hold, then it is not so sure that we can parallel the Augustinian argument. Can we say 'There can't be anything false without falsehood'? The sense in which we certainly can is harmless; and the corresponding premise in the Augustinian argument, if similarly harmless, will be (similarly) redundant. The two arguments can be given without those premises:

> Suppose truth began.
>
> Then before truth began there was not truth, i.e. it was true that there was not truth. This is absurd.
>
> Suppose falsehood began.
>
> Then before falsehood began there was not falsehood, i.e. it was false that there was falsehood. This is absurd.

In the first argument we could replace 'it was true that there was not truth' by 'it was false that there was truth', and in the second 'it was false that there was falsehood' by 'it was true that there was not falsehood'. For the replacements are equivalent to what they replace. Yet 'this is absurd' does not seem to be an apt comment. 'What's absurd about it?' one might ask. But if the replacements are equivalent to what they replace, the absurdity should survive the replacements.

It follows that 'There cannot be anything true without truth' is not the harmless redundant premise we have been treating it as; and therefore we cannot allow a parallel construction with 'There can't be anything false without falsehood' as a harmless redundant premise. But there is no such thing as falsehood except in the sense of non-truth, which justifies the equivalences that I have mentioned. There is a primacy of truth over falsehood which excludes falsehood as a positive thing that confers its character on false propositions. The premise 'There can't be anything true without truth', on the other hand, may yet have a sense in which it is not harmless and redundant. Indeed, it must be so if the Augustinian argument is not to be thrown on the rubbish heap because of the considerations about those equivalences which I have offered.

For it is certainly not supposed to work *equally well* for falsehood.

Should the whole lot be thrown on the rubbish heap? That is to say, should we (a) disallow any but the harmless redundant sense of the propositions 'There can't be anything true/false without truth/falsehood' and (b) disallow the two parallel arguments because the absurdity in their conclusions does not remain after substitution of equivalents?

Someone might say: ' "It was true that there was not truth" only sounds absurd, but is not so. This is shown by the fact that "It was false that there was truth" is not absurd'. And someone else: ' "It was false that there was truth" doesn't sound absurd, but is, as is shown by the absurdity of its equivalent "It was true that there was not truth".'

If we say 'yes' to (a) and 'no' to (b), we shall either have to accept both of the parallel arguments or find some reason for preferring one to the other. As truth's/falsehood's having no beginning or end seems to entail falsehood's/truth's also having neither, and we are only concerned with propositions, it seems we must take the first course. We shall also surely think the two 'eternities' are one and the same and are trivial.

I am inclined to take this line about (b), but to say 'no' to (a). This leaves me holding that there is a sense in which an 'eternity' of truth is provable, trivial and the same as the 'eternity' of falsehood; but also, that the triviality shows that the nature of truth is hardly touched on in this discussion. If 'Nothing can be true without truth' is a non-redundant premise, the Augustinian argument may prove something non-trivial, as it purports to do.

Thomas considers the argument, e.g. in the *Summa Theologiae* (at 1a, q.16, a.7 obj.4 and answer). It poses a fairly serious problem for him. However, we must note, first, that the question he is discussing here is: 'Is *created* truth eternal?'; second, that his answer is 'No', so he considers the argument as an objection; and, third, that he explicitly treats it as an argument that there always was and always will be truth *of propositions*, which is a kind of created truth. His reply to the argument begins:

> Because our intellect is not eternal, the truth of the propositions we frame is not eternal either, but it began at some time. And before this kind of truth existed, it was not true to say that such truth did not exist, unless from the divine intellect in which alone truth is eternal. But it is true now to say that that truth did not exist then.

The middle sentence of this passage is puzzling because of the phrase 'unless from the divine intellect'. The Latin '*nisi ab intellectu divino*' is equally puzzling. The whole Latin sentence runs thus:

> *Et antequam huiusmodi veritas esset, non erat verum dicere veritatem talem non esse, nisi ab intellectu divino, in quo solum veritas est aeterna.*

In general — though not always — if it is true now to say something in the past tense, it will have been true at the appropriate time in the past to say it in the present tense. Thomas is claiming that its being true now to say that the truth of a proposition did not exist before a certain time does not imply that it was true then to say it did not exist then. For he claims that both the former is true to say now, and the latter was not true to say then.

This last is qualified by the mystifying 'unless from the divine intellect' — '*nisi ab intellectu divino*'. There is however a passage in the *Quaestiones Disputatae de Veritate* containing a use of the preposition '*a*' which not merely seems to be the same, but also explains itself:

> ... *veritatem primam, a qua sicut a*
> *mensura extrinseca enuntiatio vera dicitur.*

> ... the first truth, from which as by an
> extrinsic measure a proposition is called true.

In the same article (Q.1, a.5) he explains intrinsic and extrinsic measures by examples. The three dimensions (he actually says 'line, surface and depth') are intrinsic measures of a body. I conjecture that an intrinsic measure by which a proposition is called true might be an existence or happening which it describes, or something involved therein. However, truths about the non-existence of something, or about past events or what is not yet the case cannot be dealt with in the same way. 'There are no mermaids' is not a proposition whose truth is caused or measured by what does not exist. In the *Summa*, Thomas calls Socrates' sitting a cause of the truth of 'Socrates is sitting', and (if my conjecture is right) he would earlier have called it an 'intrinsic measure' by which that proposition is true. Now 'Socrates will be sitting' and 'Socrates sat', said respectively before and after that sitting, may have their truths caused by that same sitting; nevertheless it is certainly differently related to them, and the manner in which their truths are caused by it is marked by a different manner of signifying it. There is just one truth on the part of the event, but these differences characterise the senses of the propositions, and thereby constitute their truths as different.[3]

Earlier in the *Quaestiones Disputatae de Veritate* (Q.1, a.5 ad 2) he wrote about considering a non-existent outside the mind:

> It neither has anything by which it would answer to the divine intellect, nor by which it would produce knowledge of itself in ours. Hence, that it should answer to any intellect does not come from the nonentity, but from the intellect itself, which has received the concept of a non-existent.

If we may combine these passages, then Thomas held that there are features of the truth of some propositions which are caused by actually non-existent things, and other features which are contributions from our intellect. If my conjecture is right, the causes of all these features may be 'intrinsic measures' of truth. But — and this is no conjecture — there is also something comparable to anything's relation to an extrinsic measure in a proposition's relation to the 'first truth', i.e. to the divine intellect. He has given its place, time and an ell as examples of extrinsic measures of an object that is in a place, of motion, and of cloth. (We should remember that a pint pot is the place of the beer in it, and a day, e.g. from sunset to sunset, the time of a walk that goes on so long.)

The treatment of the Augustinian argument in this article of the *Quaestiones Disputatae* is partly wild and I would not cite these bits of the article but for its seeming that Thomas did not give them up in the *Summa Theologiae*, though his treatment of the argument is different there.

---

[3]   *Summa Theologiae* 1a, q.16, a.8 ad 4.

That he did not give all these points up comes out if we consider the rest of his reply to the argument. (I have quoted only the first half.) We are now confronted with the question: how can it be true now to say that the truth of a proposition did not exist then, though it was not true to say then that it did not exist? Thomas does not answer by saying: well, there were no human beings or anybody else to be formulating propositions, and so there was no possibility of *saying* that or anything else. This is shown by the mysterious restriction: 'unless from the divine intellect'. Whatever that means, it implies that the absence of sayers and the non-existence of propositions is not the reason it was not true then to say that that sort of truth did not exist then. At any rate, it is not the reason in a way that simply closes the topic. Let us consider the rest of the passage:

> But it is true now to say '*that* truth did not exist then'. This is not true except by a truth that is now in our intellect, but not through any truth on the part of the thing, because this is truth about a non-existent. A non-existent does not have it from itself that it should be true, but only from an intellect which grasps it. Hence it is true to say that a truth did not exist, inasmuch as we grasp its non-existence as preceding its existence.

It may be noticed that the idea of the truth of a thing or matter, or of a thing's having truth, occurs both in what I have just quoted ('truth on the part of the thing' — '*veritatem ex parte rei*') and in my own exposition in the matter of Socrates' sitting. The 'thing', or matter, in the just quoted passage, does not exist; but if a relevant thing existed, it would be a fact or state of affairs, as, for example, it takes a state of affairs to cause the truth of a proposition: 'The knife is longer than the fork'.

As Thomas' solution of the problem posed by the Augustinian argument is to say, in effect, 'this truth (about there then having been no truth of this sort) is an intellectual construct by a mind which grasps the concept of non-existence' it might be objected: 'You mean, it's all in the mind. But aren't you the one to say that *all* truth is in the mind?'

Here, presumably, the reply would be that there is such a thing as 'truth on the part of the thing' wherever we have positive entities and events and qualities and relations. But, it may be riposted, truth belonging to things is truth in a secondary, derived, use of the term; the primary seat of truth is supposed to be in the mind. That is a correct representation of Thomas. But we must remember that he also thinks that truth is in our intellect according as it conforms to the thing it is thinking of. So when it is thinking of a real positive thing the truth in the intellect is itself achieved by the intellect's measuring up to the thing. The fact that the adjective 'true' applies to the thing in a derived and secondary use does not mean that the truth in the intellect is not measured by the thing. In the case in hand, however, there is no thing to be the measure of the truth in the intellect: *this* truth is, we might say, a total do-it-yourself job on the part of the intellect working with and on resources it has within itself. It works with the present and past tenses and negation, and on the concepts *truth of a proposition, existence, before,* and *true to say.*

There is a further point we need to notice. Of course what Anselm calls 'natural' truth could not exist in a proposition that did not itself exist. But what he calls the 'non-natural' truth of a proposition (which is what we ordinarily mean by its truth) is attributed to it not in itself but as healthiness is attributed to urine; urine that is healthy is so called because it is a *sign* of health in an animal, which is the *proper* subject of health. So a proposition is called 'true' as the sign of truth in the intelligence. (Compare Wittgenstein's last sentence: 'Suppose someone in a dream says "I'm dreaming", even speaking audibly, he is no more right than if he says "It's raining" in a dream while it is raining in fact. Even if his dream is actually connected with the sound of the rain.')[4]

In writing about the truth of propositions, Thomas here means their non-natural truth, to the existence of which the actual occurrence of the propositions is not necessary. He does think that the existence of intelligences, of truth in which the propositions would be a sign, is necessary for the existence of this sort of truth, the non-natural truth of propositions. Why, is not clear to me yet. But I will attempt a rough sketch. He certainly thinks that an intelligence, or understanding, or intellect — I use these words interchangeably — is logically the seat of truth; so without intelligence there cannot be any truth. But a further reason is needed: namely that the truth existing in a created intelligence is of a different sort from the truth which is in, and is identical with, an uncreated intelligence. This might be shown by an analysis of the way truth exists in the created intelligences we are acquainted with, namely our own. And such is indeed Thomas' method, a method which also distinguishes between the ways in which knowledge occurs in different sorts of created intelligence — ours and the intelligences of angels. For knowledge to occur, it is a necessary condition that truth be *in* the

[4]   Ludwig Wittgenstein, *On Certainty*, §676.

mind that has knowledge. So it appears that there will be not merely created truth, different in kind from uncreated; but different *kinds* of created truth. The existence of each kind will depend on the existence of the kind of intelligence.

One further point about the truth of propositions: we count as truths the ratio of the circumference to the diameter of a circle, or two and three being five. Here we have truths expressed in propositions which we frame. Are not such truths eternal? Thomas' answer to this is that 'the ratio of a circle, and two and three being five have eternity in the divine mind'. The interest of the objection and answer is that they make clear that not everything which we would call a truth expressed in propositions is counted by him a created truth. This puts a restriction on what is meant by 'the truth of propositions framed by us' for which he insists that there was a beginning. I do not mean that we need to restrict that thesis to the truth of particular types of proposition. The mode and structure of a proposition whose truth is caused and measured by something eternal will surely affect its manner of signifying that cause of its truth, and that will produce a created aspect of its truth. We had an example of a difference of relation to the cause producing different truths when we considered the relation of Socrates' sitting to the past, present and future tensed propositions made true by it.

It remains now to explain the puzzling phrase 'unless from the divine intellect'. As the preposition is *'ab'* not *'in'*, the reference cannot be to such eternal truths as we have just been considering; anyway, as eternal truths they are not created. The explanation must be that the divine knowledge comprised everything, including the not yet existent propositions and truth in human minds. The divine knowledge is the same thing as the first truth, 'from which', Thomas had said in the *Quaestiones Disputatae*, 'as by an extrinsic measure, a proposition is called true'. Therefore *it* was in the first truth: that the later-to-be-framed proposition 'At one time the truth of propositions did not exist' was going to be true, and this would imply knowledge of the non-existence at the time when it did not exist. The comparison to an extrinsic measure I have already explained.

So much for the Augustinian argument, taken as an argument about the truth of propositions. Anselm himself was author of a subtler argument, which may at first sight seem to be of the same kind. On consideration, this turns out to be a false impression. The argument runs:

> Let anyone who can, think when this began or was not true:
> namely that there will be something; or when this will cease
> and will not be true: to wit, that there will have been some-
> thing.

The reason why this argument is not of the same type as the Augustinian is that we know e.g. 'the world is full of a number of things', so
it was always going to be that there would be something — and similarly for the future perfect.

This however is not the whole argument; it goes on:

> But if neither of these is conceivable, and neither can be true
> without truth, then it is impossible even to think of truth as
> having a beginning or end.

This part brings in the premise 'It cannot be true without truth',
whose character we have already debated in discussing the Augustinian argument.

I have separated the two parts because Thomas uses the first part
in the *Quaestiones Disputatae de Veritate* to help construct an objection
to his own views (Q.1, a.5, obj.6). He puts this objection next before
another one, an argument running:

> What is future always was future and what is past always will be
> past. But something is future and something is past. So the truth
> of a proposition about the future always existed and the truth of a
> proposition about the past always will exist; and so it is not only
> the primary truth that is eternal but many others. (Q.1, a.5, obj.7)

He deals with both arguments together at one blow: neither future
nor past as such exist, and so a truth about them has to be treated on
the same lines as truth about the non-existent, from which the eternity of any but the primary truth cannot be inferred.

In the *Summa Theologiae*, however, he deals with a similar but
slightly different argument. This is against the thesis that created
truth is not eternal:

> Present-tense truths were always going to be true. But just as
> the truth of a present-tense proposition is a created truth, so is
> the truth of a future-tense one. So there are many created
> truths which are eternal.

His reply is this:

> What is now the case was going to be the case because it lay in
> its cause that it would come about. Hence, with removal of
> the cause, the thing would not be going to happen. But only

the first cause is eternal. So it does not follow for current things that it will always have been true that they were going to be, except in so far as it lay in an eternal cause that they would be; and only God is such a cause.

All the combated arguments claim to prove an eternity for certain created truths without reference to the existence of the primary truth. Thus the bit of the *Monologion* which figures in the objection in the *Quaestiones Disputatae* leaves out the last sentence, where we noted the clause 'if neither can be true without truth', and the objection supplements the part it quotes with something further. Thomas answers these arguments without much difficulty.

In the *De Veritate*, chapter X, Anselm corrects a possible misinterpretation of his argument:

> When I said 'when was it not true that there was going to be something', I did not mean that that expression, saying that there would be something, had never had a beginning, or that its truth was God, but rather that it cannot be understood when, if that sentence were to exist, it would have failed to be true. So that, through not understanding when this truth could not have existed (given the existence of a sentence in which it could) we understand that that truth which is the first cause of this one had no beginning. For the truth of a sentence would not be always a possibility, if the cause of its truth was not always there; while a sentence saying there will be something is not true unless there really will be something, and nothing will come to be unless it exists in the supreme truth.

Thomas comments on this exposition of the *Monologion* argument (*Quaestiones Disputatae de Veritate* Q.1, a.5 ad 1). He attributes to Anselm a belief that at least certain true propositions had no beginning of being true, and he does not object so long as this is understood simply to refer to the permanence of the possibility of their truth: if they themselves existed, they would be true. But he takes the passage as showing that Anselm did not think that either a sentence, or a truth inhering in created things, was without any beginning or end: that holds only of the primary truth 'from which, as by an extrinsic measure, the proposition is called true'.

His comment is accurate so long as we take it strictly: Anselm did indeed not think that a truth inhering in created things was without beginning or end; but that does not imply that he thought that any truth inhering in created things did have a beginning or end. Unlike Thomas, he did not believe there was such a thing as truth inhering in created things. His exposition of the *Monologion* argument in the *De Veritate* does indeed suggest a dependence of the truth of a sentence on its existence: 'we cannot understand how this sentence, if it were to exist, would fail to be true'. But that does not actually imply that the sentence has to exist in order to be true. Acceptance of his argument does not depend on one's holding this. Nor is it excluded by one's doing so.

This brings us to the last chapter of Anselm's *De Veritate*. Here they discuss whether truth is the same in all things that have truth, and it is here that we get the clearest disagreement between Anselm and Thomas.

Anselm observes that the belief that there are different truths is based on the different kinds of thing that are true. So far as I have noticed, that is quite correct. He infers from this that if you believe there are different truths, you believe that truths and rightnesses depend for their existence on the things that have them. His pupil enthusiastically supports this. It is like colour in a coloured body, he says. Destroy the object, and the colour cannot remain.

Anselm says: 'The relation of colour to a body and of rightness to a signification are not the same'.

Asked to show this, he in turn asks if there would be any significations through signs if no one wanted to do any signifying. The pupil says: No. But does that mean that the rightness of signifying what should be signified would be stopped? – No. In that case, he concludes, the rightness – which is what truth is – is not something that began because signifying began. The rightness is in the signifying because the signifying happens (when it happens) according to a rightness that always exists. Nor is it absent because it dies when there is no signifying, or when signifying is not as it ought to be – but because signifying then falls short. It fails of a rightness which itself never fails.

Thomas' reply to this is not to refute it but simply to say that the truth which remains when things are destroyed is the truth of the divine intellect. This indeed is just one truth, but the truth which is in things or in the soul does vary according to the variety of things. There seems to be an impasse, an unsorted-out disagreement, not clearly announced as such.

In trying to clarify this, the first thing to note is that Thomas, like Anselm, thinks that a proposition does not have to exist in order to be true. But in view of his special way of setting truth essentially in intellects, we can at least speak for him and say he thinks – for he must so think — that created intellects have to exist in order for there to be created truth. Here Anselm might parallel his argument that the rightness of signifying remains even though no signifying is going on, and ask Thomas whether the rightness of thoughts and opinions would remain while nobody wanted to do any thinking. This argument would so far not be strong: people are said to have opinions regardless of whether they are asleep or not. So we would have to imagine an extinction of all human minds capable of thinking anything, in order to ask the parallel question we want. Would such extinction mean the extinction of such truth as there is in human minds? I take it that Anselm would say 'No', and Thomas 'Yes'. Now Anselm could ask 'Would it still be right for such-and-such things to be thought?' i.e. *are* they right things for someone to think if there *is* anyone to think them?' How could Thomas answer?

In view of his thinking that propositions do not have to exist in order to be true, he surely does not want to rebut Anselm's argument about signifying. He reports it thus:

> When the sign is destroyed, there remains the rightness of the signifying, because it is right that that should be signified which that sign did signify.[5]

But he surely does want to rebut the argument as continued in his account: 'and by the same reasoning, when anything that is true and right is destroyed, its truth and rightness remain.' The account is fair to Anselm's argument, and extends it. The extension is fair, since Anselm himself extends it to actions generally, and so presumably ought to insist on its extension to anything that can have truth and rightness. This, then, is a true account of his ground for believing that truths do not vary through the variations of true things.

But more needs to be said to show how it is his ground. For 'the variation of true things' covers the variety of kinds of thing that are true as well as the variability of propositions and opinions in respect of truth, as when a true proposition becomes false. On the first matter Anselm argues: if there are several truths according as there are several true things, then there is also a variety of truths according to the *variety* of true things. This conducts him to the second matter, for it implies that the rightnesses of things that have rightness exist according as the *things* do: e.g. the rightness of significations is other than the rightness of will because it is of signification, and the other is of will. The truths or rightnesses will then depend for their

[5] *Quaestiones Disputatae de Veritate* Q.1, a.4 obj.3.

existences on the existences of what have them. But they do not so depend.

Thomas says (*Quaestiones Disputatae de Veritate* Q.1, a.4 ad 3) that the truth which is in things or in the mind *does* vary according to the variation of things. This is supposed to answer the Anselmian argument which I have just given but it does not successfully do so. For the argument hangs on the unrebutted thesis that the truth and rightness of something – a sign, for example – *remain* when *it* is destroyed. Thomas says in this same reply that the truth which remains when the things are destroyed is the truth of the divine intellect. This hardly serves as a negation of what Anselm thinks. For that is just the difference between them: Anselm thinks there is only one truth, and it is indeed that unfailing and unchanging truth which is the divine intellect, the supreme truth.

Thomas has an analogy or metaphor: the truth in human intellects is like a reflection in a mirror: it is a reflection of the truth that he calls 'primary' and Anselm 'supreme'. The peculiarities of truth in the human mind – that it involves predication, for example, together with others, among them ones we have mentioned, involving tenses and non-existence – would, I suppose, be peculiarities of the mirror. Such an analogy suggests that there may after all be a way for Thomas to answer the question which I imagined: 'Suppose a total extinction of human intelligences; or suppose there never had been any. Are there right things for a human mind to think?' *He* could say 'No'. For if you destroy all the mirrors, all reflecting surfaces, you destroy all reflections.

Even on this supposition, human minds and their ways of thinking true things – and hence the sort of created truth that would exist if they did – would all exist in the divine mind as possibilities. That is, they would not exist *in re*, but the possibility of them would exist in the divine intelligence. Thomas would not disagree.

It is the actuality that matters, however, if we are speaking of things that are sometimes so and sometimes not; or which may be so, or not. Anselm's exposition of his *Monologion* argument in Chapter X of the *De Veritate* ended:

> … a sentence saying that there will be something is not true unless there really will be something, nor is anything going to be *unless it is in the supreme truth.*

He means actuality, not possibility, for the supreme truth is the cause of the truth of the propositions he is considering. But in the last chapter he shows that he thinks the truth of the true propositions is something eternal. We may conclude that he does think that truth is in the truth which is the supreme truth, and that there is no other truth in the proposition, except that we *call* it true, meaning that it does not fall short of the truth.

I will go no further. It is evident that as far as I have correctly described the doctrines of both philosophers, they involve many explorable problems. On the side of Thomas we have his own extensive explorations. On the side of Anselm, it would be necessary to comb through his beautifully brief writings with an eye alert for answers to the questions that arise: there is no obvious place to look for them.

7

Truth: Anselm and Wittgenstein

There is truth in many things. Looking at my title ['Truth'] I am somewhat awed by it, for what leaps out of the page at me is one of the names of God. 'I have loved the truth' a dying teacher once said to me, after speaking of the difficulty he felt about the idea of loving God. But: 'I have loved the truth'. And then, fearing lest I misconstrue his statement: 'I do not mean, when I say that, that I *have* the truth'.

To have the truth, to stand in the truth — what are these? And what did Our Lord mean by calling *himself* the truth? 'There is no such thing as truth, there are only truths', my father-in-law said to the first Mrs Bertrand Russell. Russell was his teacher; the influence is easily seen.

But what are the things that have truth in them?

Does the creation? Do actions? What did Aristotle mean when he said the good of practical reason was 'truth in agreement with right desire'? Do things made by men have truth in them? What, again, did Aristotle mean when he said that art or skill was a productive disposition with a true logos? Further: what is the force of counting truth among the 'transcendentals', the things that 'run through' all the categories and all the special forms of things; and don't belong each in one category, like the colour: yellow; or the area: an acre; or the animal: a horse.

* From the manuscript of the text of a lecture on 'Truth' given at the University of Navarre in October 1983, subsequently published in Spanish: 'Verdad', in J M Torralba and J Nubiola (eds) *La filosofía analítica y la espiritualidad del hombre.* (Pamplona: Eunsa, 2005), pp.47–54. The subtitle 'Anselm and Wittgenstein' is an editorial addition to the present printing of the text.

People ask now what is the primary bearer of truth, and they concentrate on a narrow range of possible answers: judgments, beliefs, premises, conclusions, reports, testimony, statements or assertions, propositions. Indeed, now as in the eleventh century, a great many would stop at statements or propositions and consider only those.

In the theory of meaning, these classes are obviously the ones most naturally thought of as containing the bearers of the predicate 'true'. And so I may say with St Anselm: 'Let us first look for what truth is in a proposition, since we rather often call that true or false'.† Reading the chapter that follows, we find he is above all *épris* with the question: what is the *primacy* of truth over falsehood?

This question makes its appearance as a result of the enquiry: what *is* the truth of a proposition or a statement? Is it the fact, the corresponding reality, the thing the true proposition tells, i.e. the *res enunciata*?

You might want to use the *res enunciata* — what is told by the true proposition — to explain its meaning. 'Now I am standing up' you say, having suited your posture to the words; and 'Now I am sitting down', having sat down. So these facts were the meanings of the sentence? What then was their being true? Having these facts as their meanings? If so, then when each ceases to be true it has lost its meaning, for the fact which was its meaning is no more. And if disappearance of the fact is the disappearance of the meaning and the truth, won't the fact *be the same thing* as both the meaning and the truth? But no, the fact is what makes it true: what the true propositions tells, the *res enunciata*, is the cause of its truth and not its truth: 'non eius veritas, sed causa veritatis eius dicenda est'.‡ And the proposition does *not* lose its meaning when the fact is no more. So its meaning (*significatio*) is not its truth; if it were, 'semper esset vera' — it would always be true. But its meaning, and everything belonging to its definition, 'manent … *et* cum est quod enunciat, *et* cum non est' [remain the same both when what is stated is the case and when it is not] — i.e. whether it is true or false. Thus we have it noted that 'the proposition has a sense which is independent of the facts', as Wittgenstein warns us not to forget in the *Tractatus*.§

Wittgenstein says that if we don't remember this, it is easy to think of true and false as 'equally justified relations between sign and

---

† St Anselm, *De Veritate*, c.2
‡ *Loc.cit.*
§ At 4.061.

thing signified'. Then we might say, e.g. that '*p*' signifies in the true way what '~*p*' signifies in the false way.

What is wrong with saying that? What is the inequality between truth and falsehood, where you have the sort of proposition which can be true *or* false, and which is now one, now the other? For the false proposition does not lack all relationship to the fact. 'I am sitting down' and 'I am not sitting down' are one true, the other false; the true one states the fact, the false one is connected with the fact too; the only difference is that it is the negation of the other. It isn't meaningless, it *contains* the description of the fact which makes the other one true. So why *not* say: it relates by the falsehood-relation to just the same fact as the other one does by the truth-relation. They could exchange roles. St Joan of Arc had a code for communicating with her subordinate generals, in letters written to them, with propositions they were to take in the contrary sense. She marked such letters with a cross. The code is a possible one. As Wittgenstein says, the fact that '*p*' and '~*p*' *can* say the same (i.e. that they can exchange roles) is important; for it shows that 'not' doesn't stand for anything in the reality. Further: '*p*' and '~*p*' are opposite in sense, but to them corresponds just one reality. What reality? Well, the fact, the *res enunciata* by the true one. This comes so close to saying that truth and falsehood are a sort of equal relations between sign and thing signified, and that one proposition — whichever of the two it is — signifies in the true way what the other signifies in the false way, that we wonder: what then *is* unequal about them? What *is* the primacy of truth? Wittgenstein is also *épris* with this, and he and Anselm are intellectual brothers on the subject.

Let us return to St Anselm and see how he also grasps and treats of this question. He actually formulates it *after* he has answered it. He has answered it by asking the pupil *what assertion is for*. The answer is given: for signifying that to be the case which is the case — 'ad significandum esse quod est'. And this was also the only account of *truth* that the pupil had been able to give: truth, he saw, was not the *res enuntiata* by a true proposition, nor was it the signification, nor anything belonging in the definition, but 'Nihil aliud scio nisi quia cum significat esse quod est, tunc est in ea veritas et est vera'. ['I only know that when it signfies something's being so and it is so, truth is in it and it is true']** From the next bit of the dialogue, after getting out of the pupil what assertion if *for*, we get him admitting that then,

** *Loc.cit.*

when assertion is doing what it is for, the signifying (*significatio*) is being done *rightly*. And that is what its truth is.

It is after this that the pupil explodes a bomb of a question. He says he *sees* that truth is this rightness. But

> tell me what I am to reply if someone says that even when an utterance signifies that something is the case which is *not* the case, it is signifying what it ought. For its being given to it equally to signify as being the case both what is the case and what isn't. For if it hadn't been given it to signify as being the case even what isn't so, it wouldn't signify *it*. So even when it signifies being the case of what is not the case, it is signifying what it ought. But if it is right and true by signifying what it ought, as you've shown, then an utterance is true even when it tells as being the case what is not the case.

This is a very clear assertion of the 'equally justified relations' between sign and what is signified. The two relations are spoken of as equal: '*pariter* accepit significare esse, et quod est, et quod non est'. And this parity is essential: if the proposition did *not* signify what it signifies equally when what it signifies is so and when it isn't so, it wouldn't signify that at all. And is this not evidently so according to Wittgenstein too? '*p*' and '*~p*' can signify the same, that is, '*p*' and '*~p*' could exchange roles; one and the same reality — whichever of the two possibilities *is* the reality — corresponds to both. He only seems to object to saying 'one signifies in the true way what the other signifies in the false way'. But to say that is *very close* to saying 'one and the same reality corresponds to both'. What is the difference?

Well, there is none, so long as you are clear that whichever is the reality that corresponds to both 'I am sitting' and 'I am not sitting', it *is no part of the sense* of either proposition. And equally, that 'signifying in the true way' and 'signifying in the false way' are not descriptions of the *senses* of the true and the false propositions. That is, if you did choose to speak of a proposition's 'signifying in the true way' you could perfectly well understand its *sense* without knowing whether it 'signified in the true way'.

What, though, of the 'not equally justified relations'? I have been arguing that there *is* an equality, a parity, and that what Wittgenstein says *supports* this; that is, what he says about a proposition and its negation, and about one and the same reality corresponding to both. And this parity is essential to the meaning, the sense or *significatio*, of the sort of proposition that can be true *or* false; and this parity is now announced by Anselm's pupil — at least, he imagines someone maintaining it, and asks 'What am I to reply?' The objection seems to undercut Anselm's account of signifying *rightly*. And with Wittgenstein, too, we are left wondering: What *was* wrong with the idea of 'equally justified relations' between sign and thing signified?

Is there an answer in Wittgenstein's passage:

> Couldn't we make ourselves understood using false proposi-
> tions as hitherto with true ones — so long as we know they are
> meant falsely? No! For a proposition is true if things are as we are
> using it to say they are, and if we use 'p' to say that $\sim p$ and the case
> is as we mean to say it is, then 'p' is true in our new way of taking
> it, not false.††

To give our instance of Joan of Arc: she was not lying with her code. And, *if* she was not in error about the facts, her sentences were true, not false.

That is quite correct. But what that answer comes to is: you can't be described as communicating with false propositions, understood as meant to be false. For, by the rule adopted, they would have become true ones, if they were indeed false before. Similarly for Michael Dummett's suggestion of an inner act of denial accompanying prop-ositions instead of the inner act of assertion he thought Frege's asser-tion sign was supposed to signify.

Thus true and false are supposed *not* to be 'equally justified rela-tions' because the false could not take over the role of the true in assertion and thought. This we can accept. But lies are possible. With a lie one means to assert as being the case what is not the case. Also error is possible. When one's assertions are mistaken, what one means to assert as being the case is again not the case. The general impossibility of exchanging the roles of true and false does not exclude either lies or error. Does the general impossibility then con-tain the whole substance of the 'not equally justified relations'? It may give a primacy to truth over falsehood in theory of meaning; but why should that be called a more *justified* relation because of that? (Translators tend to bungle this phrase; but there is no doubt the German means 'equally justified relations'.)

St Anselm's account does give an appropriate sense to 'not equally *justified* relations'. But before we consider that any further we should note that he does not rebut the pupil's suggested objection. He does

†† *Tractatus*, 4.062.

not say: No, that's quite wrong, the false utterance is in no way right and true. What he says is: we don't *call* it true, but there *is* a way in which it *is* true. 'Veritatem et rectitudinem habet, quia facit quod debet.' This doing what it ought lies precisely in signifying what it does, i.e. in signifying what it's ben given it to signify. But it's customarily called right and true only when it signifies the being so of what is so, not when it signifies that something is so when it isn't. For it ought more to do what it's been given signification for than what it wasn't given it for.

With this he retains the explanation starting from the question 'What is affirmation *for*?'

So, he tells us, the proposition that signifies that to be the case which *is* the case, does what it ought in *two* ways. In one of these, it signifies just what's been given it to signify — whether it's the case or not. In the other, it signifies what it was given that signification for — namely, to affirm as the case what *is* the case.

The observation: 'It wasn't given it to signify something's being so which is not so, [or not being so when it is so], *except* because it could not be given it to signify something's being so *only* when it is so, or its not being so *only* when it is not so'‡‡ comes near to Wittgenstein's account of the primacy of truth, if that is in his thought about communicating with false propositions as hitherto with true ones. No, he says, that is not possible. And Anselm says: the false is only possible because the true (in this sort of proposition) cannot be the sole possibility. Both indicate a sort of primacy of truth in the matter of meaning, though the reasons are different. The primacy of truth in Wittgenstein's account does not seem to explain his rejection of true and false as 'equally justified relations'.

Anselm's account of truth as rightness in signifying does not depend on using 'right' as a synonym for 'true'. It will lead, via considerations of truth in thought, will, action, and the being of things, to his definition of truth as 'rightness perceptible to the intellect alone'.

Of interest to students and lovers of St Thomas: he adopted that definition from St Anselm and also took from him the distinction between the two kinds of truth in a proposition.

---

‡‡ *Op.cit.* c.2.

8

Anselm and the unity of truth

There are properties of things which the things do not need to exist in order to have. That is to say, they do not have to exist at the time at which they have the properties. They may, for example, have ceased to exist. My great-grandfathers all became great-grandfathers of me after they had died and so ceased to exist. If some people would want to deny that because of the immortality of the human soul, take some other animal of which a corresponding thing is true. Another example is the property of being famous. Protagoras' monograph on truth is famous but not extant. Perhaps it does not exist at all in any copy anywhere in the world. It is nonetheless famous. So a thing does not have to exist in order to be famous.

I must here emphasise that when I speak of things that do not exist as having properties I am not including fictitious characters. Some people discuss the existence of characters in fiction. I do not want to get into this sort of topic at all. The things that have real properties when they do not exist are not fictitious things. The examples that I just gave are both of things that did exist (as I am speaking of existence here) and have properties (perhaps *acquired* those properties) after ceasing to exist. Your ceasing to exist does not make your name empty. It does not imply that you are no longer a possible verifying object for a proposition of the form 'For some x, Fx'. 'F' we might indeed suppose to be a past tense predicate. Thus 'For some x, x was

* From the manuscript of the text of a lecture on 'The Unity of Truth' given on 14 October 1983 at the University of Navarre. The manuscript on which the present text is based contains a number of alterations by the author to the original manuscript of the lecture on which a Spanish translation is based: 'La unidad de la verdad', in J M Torralba and J Nubiola (eds) *La filosofía analítica y la espiritualidad del hombre* (Pamplona: Eunsa, 2005), pp. 55–62.

a great French revolutionary general who made himself an Emperor'. Napoleon was such, and his name has not lost its meaning because he is dead. Nor has that of Alexander's horse Bucephalus. Also, both Napoleon and Bucephalus *are* famous.

Thus when I say there are properties which things can have when they do not exist I do not mean anything that would be exemplified by Cervantes' character Sancho Panza.

Here it is perhaps natural to say: we can accept this so long as the things in question *have* existed. There are those who would say, not that, but 'so long as the things in question either *have* existed or *will* exist'. I am disinclined to accept this suggestion about future existence being sufficient to give its meaning (as a proper name of an individual) to what is grammatically such. I will give you my reason for this. Suppose a prediction by someone: 'There will be two very young ravens, call them A and B, in this room at this time on this date, in ten years. A will have a white stripe on one wing, B will not.' Ten years go by, and we all crowd into this room to see if what was predicted comes about. There are just two ravens here, obviously very young. The predictor is there and he says: 'Oh! I was wrong. It is B that has the stripe; A is the one that doesn't'. Well, if what I told you was all there had been to the naming of the birds 'A' and 'B', then

> If to think it out you try
> You'll find it doesn't signify.

The same would be true of a pair of arbitrary names *similarly* imposed here and now on a pair of past things; but if you use names previously and severally given to the individuals in question, *then* being wrong about which was which becomes possible. For that, however, the individual has to *have* existed at the time of the statement.

I have mentioned this point because my thesis — things can have properties when they don't exist — may seem one that *can* be accepted with the proviso that such things must at least *have* existed; or — by people who think past and future are perfectly symmetrical — such things must *have* existed or *be going to exist*. I am not a 'symmetrist' about past and future; so I would be more sympathetic to people who restrict the thesis to things that *have* existed.

But I have an example which upsets this restriction. In Wittgenstein's *Philosophical Investigations* he considers an idea expressed like this:

What the names in language signify must be indestructible; for it must be possible to describe the state of affairs in which everything destructible is destroyed. And this description will contain words; and what corresponds to these cannot then be destroyed, for otherwise the words would have no meaning.†

He comments on this: 'One might of course object at once that this description would have to except *itself* from the destruction.' This objection seems to me false.

Suppose someone says: Let us suppose a time when nothing destructible existed. Would it be reasonable to say 'You will have to except this description, or its present-tense form 'Nothing destructible exists' from this generalisation about what will not have existed at such a time?' "Everything destructible is without existence". That sentence is thoroughly destructible. So would it have to except itself, in order to exist, compatibly with the truth of what it says?

No; a description, a proposition, a sentence—these are sets of signs intended in a certain meaning. Why should such things not have a property when they do not exist, e.g. the property of truth? If I am right, truth is a property the bearer (subject) of which does not have to exist at the time when that property holds of it.

If so, then the non-existent bearer need not *have* existed either; and it may also never be going to exist. For no one may ever formulate the proposition.

In the *Monologion* St Anselm offered two arguments for the eternity of the *summa veritas*, which the pupil quotes at the opening of the *De Veritate*. I am concerned just with part of the first one.

Think if you can, when this began, or was not true: namely, that there was going to be something... If that can't be thought it is impossible to think of truth as having a beginning.‡

In Chapter 10 of the *De Veritate* Anselm gives us an interesting gloss on this. I render it :

When I said 'when was it not true that there was going to be something?' I was not saying that that *expression*, saying that there would be something, existed without any beginning, or that its truth was God, but rather that it cannot be understood *when*, if that expression were to exist, it would have failed to be true. So the unintelligibility of when there could have been no

---

† *Philosophical Investigations*, I, §55.
‡ *De Veritate*, c.1.

such thing as this truth—given the existence of the expression that could *mention* there having been going to be something—yields *understanding* that the truth which is the first cause of this truth did not have any beginning. For the truth of the sentence would not always be a possibility if the cause of that truth did not always exist. For a sentence saying that there will be something is not true, if in reality there won't be anything, and there won't be anything if it is not in the supreme truth.

The *permanent possibility* of the truth of that sentence (whether the sentence exists or not) proves the *permanent actuality* of the cause, i.e. the ultimate cause, of that truth, which certainly exists if the sentence does come into existence. The sentence, when it exists, will not be true unless there will indeed be something; and there will not be anything unless *it* (i.e. what there will be) is already in the *summa veritas*.

In this exposition it may seem to be indicated that the truth of a proposition doesn't exist *unless* the proposition itself exists. This, however, does not follow from what is said in that argument. Rather, the argument relies on the existence of the truth of a certain sentence *if* the sentence itself exists. Nothing is said about whether that truth will exist if the sentence itself does not.

In the last chapter of the *De Veritate* Anselm returns to this topic. In the previous chapter he has discussed justice. This he explains as a species of that rectitude 'sola mente perceptibilis' which he has found to be truth. His question in the last chapter is whether this rectitude, this truth, is one in all things, is everywhere the same thing, or if it varies according to what is the subject of which rightness is predicated. The question is put: is rightness of signifying different from rightness of will? It may seem it is, because of the difference between signifying and willing or wanting. If these two rightnesses are different, then the rightness special to signifying *exists* because of the signifying, and will change with it accordingly. That is to say, when the signifying ceases to be of what is so, and comes to be of what is not so, the rightness which it had at first will cease to *exist*.

Anselm's pupil embraces this with enthusiasm. The rightness of a signification exists through it, just as the colour of a body exists through the body. If the body ceases to exist, the colour does not remain. For as long as the body exists, so long does its colour.

The analogy is in any case not quite exact, as the body can change in colour. What in signifying would correspond to colour in a body would be what we call 'truth-value'. This point could be taken care of without disturbing the argument, however. The two truth-values would be compared to two different colours a body may have at different times.

Anselm does not pause to make this point. He says: the relation of rightness to signifying is *not* the same as that of colour to a body. 'Show me the difference' says the pupil. The answer is a question:

> Suppose no one whatever wants to signify what there is to be signified by some sign or other: will there be any signifying then by way of signs? — [P] No, there won't. — Does that mean that it won't be right for what ought to be signified to be signified? — [P] No. — Then, even in the absence of the signifying the rightness does not perish. This is the rightness by which that — namely the signifying of what ought to be signified — *is* right; or the rightness which requires that what is to be signified be signified.§

If the rightness *did* pass away with the signifying, reflects the pupil, then the rightness of signifying so would not exist, nor could it be making any requirement. And, he grants, this is *the* rightness because of which and in accordance with which the signifying is right when what ought to be signified *is* signified. For if it were any *other* rightness, then, in its absence, there would all the same be nothing to stop the signifying from being right. We may explain this by supposing a rightness of *being polite*, for example. Suppose it vanishes, the *signifying* can still be praised for rightness, i.e. for doing what it is for, i.e. for being a signifying of what is so as being so. In the absence of this rightness, signifying cannot be signifying rightly.

> Do you not see, then, that the rightness is in the signifying, *not* because it begins to exist when what is the case is being signified as being so, but because then (when that is so) signifying is done in accord with a rightness that is from always; and it is absent from a signifying not because it dies when the signifying is not as it ought to be, or when there is *no* signifying, but because then signifying falls short of a rightness which itself does not die. … So the rightness doesn't exist through the signifying, nor does it suffer any change, no matter what happens in that way to the signifying.**

This is different from the relation of colour to the coloured body.

Thus the argument goes: Are there different kinds of rightness or truth? Do they get their different characters from the different sorts

§ *De Veritate*, c.13. [P] = pupil's response.
** *Loc.cit.*

of thing that are right and true? – No: *if* they did, and *if* they are of different kinds, then they exist and vary as the different things exist and vary and change. (Religion, for example, natural science, human prehistory and cosmology.) But rightness, truth, is not like that; it does not depend, in the case of signifying, on the occurrence of signifying; and the truth of what is true does not cease to be when the expression ceases to be true and becomes false. I mean: if the expression began by being true, and then became false (because the facts changed) the truth it had has not ceased to exist just because it itself has become false or even has ceased to exist.

It appears to me, then, that Anselm has come to the conclusion that truth is a property which something can have without existing; and, we may add, not only because it has ceased to exist, but without ever existing. I was happy to find him of this mind, for I had long thought that propositions didn't have to exist to be true.

It is indeed tempting to think that there are different kinds of truth corresponding to the different kinds of thing that are true. If we wish to maintain that, we shall have to think what to say to Anselm's argument that *if* that is so, the existence of truth depends on the existence of the thing that we call true – the bearer of truth. If we wish to resist *that*, we shall have to think what to say in reply to his argument that the rightness of a signifying of such-and-such does not require that anybody be doing any signifying at all. He generalises his conclusion; but his argument depends, apparently, on this one case. That is to say, consideration of this one case is all he offers. It would, however, be easy to extend the argument to rightness of will and action; it would take the same form. The argument seems clearly successful, as drawing a contrast between truth (rightness) on the one hand, and properties F so inherent in their subjects that the F-ness of A could not exist without A's being there to be inhered in. Thus if we want to resist Anselm's argument we must do it by attacking the first part: if truth, rightness, vary according to what kind of thing is true or right, then their existence depends on the existence of those subjects of them. That those *are* the subjects of them is mere grammar, and does not prove that they must exist in order to have those properties.

9

How can a man be free? Spinoza's thought and that of some others

I will begin with what everyone must know who has studied Spinoza a little. You will see in the end why I speak of this.

Spinoza believed that God is the sole substance, and, *qua* substance, exists necessarily because it belongs to substance to exist *per se*. Compare the Aristotelian notion that it belongs to substance to exist *not* in another thing (as shape for example is the shape of something). We might put the point by saying that it belongs to substance to exist on its own. But what does this imply, if it doesn't imply that any substance exists necessarily? The scholastic avoidance of this is found in the word 'convenit' = 'it is proper for'. It is proper for anything that would be a substance *if* it existed, to exist on its own and not in another thing. We might indeed read this into the phrase 'it belongs to', but we have then to insist that this 'belonging to' does not imply necessary existence. Unicorns don't exist, but if they did exist they'd be substances: 'unicorn' has the grammar of a substance-name.

I suppose that Descartes would have accepted this. Spinoza not. For him, the *per se* existence of substance entailed its necessary existence, and more yet, namely that there was only one substance.

He also thought that *that one* necessary being produces infinitely, so that all possibilities are 'produced in actuality' by him. He —God—is the source of the possibility of whatever is possible. So this philosopher rejects the doctrine that God, through or by an exer-

* Reprinted with the permission of Professor Josef Seifert from *Aletheia. An International Yearbook of Philosophy*, Vol.7 (2002): 21–30.

cise of freedom of will, creates the actual world, choosing from among possibilities what shall come to be.

It hangs together with this doctrine of Spinoza's that will itself is identical with intellect, at least in God: will is the *being thought of* of what we would be inclined to say is primarily thought of, and this is, *further*, itself therefore willed.

God's thoughts are all necessary because it is his nature to think of everything *logically* possible (as we would be inclined to say) and this thinking of them makes the objects of the universe actual. God's thought is thus not simply of his own existence and attributes.

This should not make us forget that according to Spinoza God is cause of himself — *causa sui*. What Spinoza frequently calls 'nature' is not among the attributes of God. He does indeed speak of God's own nature, and that nature he calls *natura naturans*, by contrast with *natura naturata*. This scholastic distinction is between the nature that 'natures', i.e. confers their natures on everything besides itself, and nature that is 'natured', i.e. has its nature conferred upon it. (Spinoza more prominently adopts this distinction in the Dutch writing 'God, Man and his Well-being'.)

When he says '*Deus sive natura*', 'God or nature', this means 'God, i.e. nature' and he is referring primarily to *natura naturans*. God's attributes are identical with him, being infinite and eternal. All other things are finite or finite† *modes* of his attributes and are *natura naturata*. The only infinite attributes of God which we can grasp (from their modes in created things) are thought and extension.

Spinoza argues that God is free in making come to be whatever else can be thought of, *not* because he acts by freedom of will, choosing e.g. among possible worlds, but because nothing can prevent and nothing can compel his action. For we must always remember that his action comprises all the infinite possibilities that there are, and is necessary from his nature.

I infer from this that God's freedom, as Spinoza understands it, is a freedom that we may also ascribe to numbers. Nothing can either compel or prevent them in the matter of their relations to other numbers; every such thing, however, that *can* be true *is* true. As for what might be called empirical facts about numbers, e.g. that such-and-such is the number of people in this room at present, this too in Spinoza's belief will have been necessary in the nature of things: but,

† The original typescript, though not the printed text, reads 'infinite' here.

while that means it could not have been prevented, also it could not have been 'compelled' either. It was *merely* necessary.

Nevertheless, this 'freedom' would hardly impress us. I suspect that this is at least partly because numbers are not substances, as God is. The necessity of his *being* and making all else that is possible also be, is a necessity on the part of a being that has infinite thought and infinite extension. The character of being a thinking being makes us readily accept that it is free in its actions even if the freedom is nothing but the impossibility of being either compelled or hindered by anything else. Numbers are not thinking beings and therefore the impossibility of any feature of them being compelled or hindered does not easily suggest that they are 'free'. But there is another aspect of the limited kind of mathematical objects that most interested Spinoza – namely geometrical objects. He thought that they ought to be defined genetically – i.e. by what makes them come to be – in the explanations of them. One might then not agree that nothing *compels* them, natural as that thought is to us.

I must, then, somewhat moderate my comparison of Spinoza's God's freedom and an analogous 'freedom' of mathematical objects. Nevertheless, everything essential about them is necessary, and *that* necessity can be compared with the necessity that attaches to everything about Spinoza's God. The necessity of his nature by which the *natura naturans* is all that he is and does all that he does – it is that very necessity, with no external source, which *is* freedom, the freedom of the divine and only substance. That substance, Spinoza says, is the only 'free cause'.

After this beginning, I can come to the subject of my talk, given in the title: 'How can a man be free?' I will not dwell on Spinoza's rather curious conception of the human mind as itself *the* idea of one's own body, interesting as that is. Nor yet upon his rather faulty way of defining the various emotions or passions. I will only remark that if you want to give a definition of, say, hate or admiration, you need to take the formula 'A hates x' or 'A admires y' and explain it in a way that brings the variables (x, y) into the definition. Spinoza gives us a lot of definitions of 'affects', but he observes no such rule. Nor can the faultiness be remedied, as someone suggested, by simply introducing as explanation of 'A loves x', 'x causes A joy' or something of that sort. Spinoza's major fault is *this*: he does not observe the distinction between the object and the cause of an emotion. Between the cause of one's admiring x, say, and the *respect* in which one admires x.

Indeed, we can say of him more generally than that, that he is dominated by an all-embracing conception of causality. And here I have an acknowledgement to make: I am *grateful* to him for giving us a single axiom in the opening of Part IV of the *Ethics*, the part with the title 'De Servitute Humana' and the subtitle offered as alternative: 'De Affectuum Viribus'. In English: 'On Human Bondage, or the Power of the Passions'. I translate the second bit like that rather than 'the Strength of the Emotions', precisely because of the connection with human servitude or bondage. We should not fail to notice that Spinoza mentions God as having *affectus*. (See e.g. Part V p.36 *Sch.*) Used of human beings, the word covers *all* the affects or emotions. But we quickly learn that Spinoza distinguishes between affects that are, and ones that are *not*, passions, *passiones*. And God is possessed by love of his own being and nature, which could not be a passion.

I will come back to this, but for the moment my interest lies in the sole axiom, which he supplies after giving a number of definitions. These are of good and bad, of the contingent and of the possible, of mutually contrary effects, of an end (an object) of action, and of virtue and power. After all this, he produces his solitary 'axiom': it is a very remarkable one. It runs: '*Nulla res singularis in rerum Natura datur, qua potentior et fortior non detur alia. Sed quacunque data datur alia potentior, a qua illa data potest destrui.*'

I translate: 'Among the objects of Nature there is none such that there is not another more powerful and stronger than it, by which it can be destroyed.'

This is offered to us to accept, as one accepts axioms. (I wonder why I should believe it.) It is put to use in the 'demonstration' of proposition 3 of this Part IV: 'The strength by which a man continues in existence is limited and the power of external causes infinitely exceeds it': '*Vis, qua homo in existentia perseverat, limitata est, et a potentia causarum infinite superatur.*' The argument from the axiom is obvious. As Spinoza puts it: 'Given any man, there is something, call it *A*, which is stronger than he is, and given *A* there is something further, call it *B*, stronger than *A* and so on *ad infinitum*: accordingly, if a man's power is defined (bounded) by the power of something else, it is *infinitely* exceeded by the total power of external causes.'

What we have here is a pretty abstract formulation of Spinoza's determinism about nature, together with a conversion of it into the particular thesis that, given any object in the realm of objects, there is always something stronger than it. We may be reminded of St Anselm's answer to Gaunilo, who treated Anselm's argument in

Proslogion 2 as an argument for something greater or better than everything else in the world; Anselm says: 'You may point to something which you think is greater than all the other things – but I can then *think* of something that would be greater still.' But, for Spinoza, what can consistently be thought of must exist, being itself a possible thing; everything possible exists necessarily, because God can cause it and he necessarily causes everything that is in his power to cause.

As a rigid, formal, determinist, Spinoza has no belief whatever in what most people would think they meant by 'freedom of the will'. Upon the whole, human beings will be dominated by those of their affects which he calls 'passions' (*'passiones'*). These are precisely the affects in which a man is moved by external causes. If he is moved in his actions by external causes, he is not an *'adequate cause'* of his actions. An 'adequate cause' is a cause such that the action it produces is produced *truly by it*: a man is an adequate cause when he acts *'ductu rationis'*, i.e. is led by reason. For an adequate cause is a cause such that the causality of its effects by it is perfectly intelligible from a consideration of its own nature.

It should not be thought that in that case a man cannot be an adequate cause of his consumption of food, for whose availability he is dependent on others. He may still be 'led by reason' in taking and eating it, and his action in doing so is intelligible as an act of reason, i.e. as in the relevant sense rendered intelligible as *being* an exercise of his rationality. (Contrast breathing.)

The understanding of this causality makes the effect 'intelligible'. Reason, or the idea of reason, is in Spinoza's view also an *adequate idea* in a rational being.

Although nothing can equal God's 'liberty' as a 'free cause', nevertheless the thought and action according to reason of a thinking being, who is as such a finite mode of God's infinite attribute of thought, comes as near as possible to the freedom attributed to God.

Here I should pause to consider the notion, so dominant in much seventeenth century philosophy, of an 'adequate idea'. I think it is clear that it is historically derivative. It is derived from the famous definition of truth as *adequatio intellectus et rei*, the mutual measuring-up of thought and thing. Or, we might more clearly translate it as 'thought and thing fitting one another'. This definition is attributed by Aquinas to the Rabbi Isaac, a philosopher of the great Jewish-Muslim period. I have heard that the Rabbi Isaac – Isaac Israeli – himself derived it from Avicenna. Be that as it may, it is certainly the source of our term 'adequate' as a term of ordinary language. In the seventeenth century we find 'adequate idea' as a frequent term used by some philosophers. It is prominent in John Locke, whose chapter on adequate ideas is far from clear – it is inadequate!

Spinoza, however, gives a definition of an *adequate idea* in terms of truth, which we may say is historically going round in a circle. The fourth definition of Part II of the *Ethics* runs: 'By "adequate idea" I understand an idea which, so far as it is considered in itself, without its relation to its object, has all the properties or intrinsic denominations of a true idea.'

The interesting thing about this definition and the thoughts connected with it is that 'idea' is mentioned as a term standing for something *possibly considered* quite apart from its object. Spinoza goes on positively to *explain* the term 'intrinsic' as applied to denominations, saying he is using it to exclude what is *extrinsic*, namely the accommodation (*convenientia*) of an idea *cum suo ideato*, i.e. with what it is an idea of. We have here an example of Spinoza's psycho-physical parallelism: ideas, considered in themselves, i.e. intrinsically, have the properties they have quite independently of their being ideas *of* anything actual.

If Spinoza is to be considered a forerunner of another philosopher, that philosopher is Hume. Hume's definition and explanation of – for example – voluntary movement clearly give only exterior relations of an *impression* with the movement of the body (or, indeed, mind) which the impression accompanies; but he cannot stop himself from saying that 'we produce' the movement in question, and that phrase really raises the whole question again.

Hume indeed puzzled much about the relation of impressions and ideas to what we nowadays call 'the external world'. His belief in the external things which they supposedly represent is decidedly sceptical. I think Spinoza did not so puzzle: he was a plain psycho-physical parallelist. We can already see this in his regarding the relation of an idea *cum suo ideato* – i.e. with what it is an idea of – as an external relation. I believe – but without much learning in the matter – that admirers of Spinoza tend to lack awareness of the problematic character of his thought at this point.

Man is essentially part of 'nature' – i.e. of the *natura naturata*; nevertheless in respect of his possible freedom – in respect of his *becoming* free, if he does – he comes as near as possible, in Spinoza's philosophy, to the freedom attributed to God.

Spinoza *rejects* any ordinary idea of free will, on the part of God or man. Here he accords with a very common opinion on the part of modern Anglo-American philosophers, at least as far as concerns man; for such philosophers usually have no belief in God. We have seen what Spinoza calls God's freedom. In the case of man, he rejects the idea of the mind as a sort of kingdom within a kingdom, i.e. not a part of law-governed nature. I think we are right to take his talk of laws here as much the same as ours when we talk of 'scientific' laws.

Spinoza despises Descartes — from the first so much admired by him — for believing that men are free in respect of their passions, that man has a sort of metaphysical control of them. 'Not at all', Spinoza says. The affects which he calls 'passions' have causes external to human minds. They exist necessarily under the influence of their external causes and in respect of them a man is therefore in a condition of bondage.

Nevertheless, there is such a thing as becoming free. Here we should note that Spinoza's Part V, entitled 'De Libertate Humana', certainly reads like the writing of one who is exhorting and encouraging human beings to think, act and live as he thinks a *free* man will. We might find this odd as he does not abandon his determinism. We ought not to do so: what happens happens necessarily, and one of the things that happen is that Spinoza in effect *exhorts to virtue*. It may also happen that his exhortation is of no effect, and it may happen that it is effectual. Its being effectual contains no implication or indication that he is wrong in his determinism, or in his belief in common human bondage.

The reason why Part V of the *Ethics* is exhortatory, in reality as well as in appearance, is that Spinoza, while far from abandoning his determinism, is all the same enthusiastic about virtue (which he identifies with power) and also about 'the intellectual love of God'.

Of this last I will say only this: his best explanation of what he calls 'the third kind of knowledge' is an example. Namely: there is a proportion between 1 and 2. What *has* that proportion to 3? One has immediate perception here. Such 'perception' is intellectual — what else? Well, it occurs with joyful pleasure. This is love. If a man has such a perception of the being and nature of God, this is joyful and is a minimal likeness to the divine life, in God's knowledge and understanding and love of his own nature and existence.

We should note that Spinoza's thought here has nothing to do with repentance or humility (or petitionary prayer). He despised repentance and humility. It is noteworthy that he shares a common view that humility is thinking yourself worse than you are. He does not consider the view that humility is truthfulness about oneself. This view is not common but exists in some thinkers.

We may find a certain sublimity in Spinoza's idea of coming as it were to share in or imitate the divine life in a way which is not given to man — is not there in him — simply *qua* thinking being. The impression lessens when we remember about the divine life in this philosophy (a) that the life *in respect of thought* is an essential attribute of the *natura naturans*; but is not the same attribute as God's infinite extension. And (b) we must remember that God, the one and only substance, cannot but be the *adequate cause* of everything else. Nothing 'can either be or be conceived without him', as Spinoza says repeatedly. This, of course, includes extension. Giving this as an infinite attribute of God probably helped Spinoza's excommunication by the leading members of Amsterdam Jewry. But God's 'adequate causation' of everything in the universe does obviously, in Spinoza, involve *extension* in God. He deals with the arguments against it which refer to extension's involving divisibility, by thinking that the infiniteness of extension in God does *not* do so. This can be supported by reflecting that half of infinity would still be infinity.

Now, as adequate cause of everything else, God is also the adequate cause of man as a thinking being. This adequate causality is reflected in the adequate causality by a man of those thoughts and actions of which his reason is an adequate cause. So far as I know, Spinoza did not believe in angels (who are invoked in his excommunication), but thought man to be the only created thinking being. Man's life and actions are on the whole little rational, certainly not guided by reason as Spinoza conceives possible. Only when he is in *this* manner guided by reason *is* he an adequate cause of his thoughts and actions. That means that upon the whole man does not act as an 'adequate cause', does not act 'according to his nature', which is a nature with reason. So his actions are not the actions properly and intelligibly proceeding from reason.

Man, *qua* rational, is not, we must say, a *mere* thinker, a haver and contemplator of thoughts. He *can* be 'led by reason' and to be so, which is for him to act according to his nature, is for him to be a minimal reflection of that adequate causality of things which is wholly given in the divine nature. When this happens there is in him also the analogue of God's love in perceiving his own existence and nature.

For man's actions to be intelligible in a way in which they are *so long as he is guided by his passions*, and is the object of infinite external causes — is human bondage.

But being guided by his essential nature, which is reason, he understands reason and loves it, and this can lead him to that intellectual perception of, and love of, truth and reason in God. This is the possible freedom and real happiness, of which no other created being is capable.

Nevertheless, a quite particular doubt arises here. We saw that there is no difference between thought and will in God. But this is especially connected with *God's* own thinking being of everything possible, which makes possible things actual. Whether or not a distinction between thought and will is also denied in man, man's 'adequate causation' cannot reflect God's in being of everything he can think of. To that extent, then, the distinction between thought and will in the man, free through being guided by reason, must be admitted.

Here we have to reflect on the connection between action and truth. We might test what some sorts of animal other than man are able to do, and conclude that chickens, for example, are able to discriminate objects, otherwise similar, which differ in colour. If the objects are eatable by chickens, we might note that the ones of green or purple colour were nevertheless eaten by a chicken which would readily eat stuff of the same kind but neither green nor purple. It is also a familiar fact that an imprisoned bird will fly against transparent glass as if it apparently gave the possibility of escape. I do not know how much some people would attribute 'practical thinking' to such a bird. One would wonder whether one could teach it as it were to understand words of warning or encouragement, reproof or satisfaction. We do know that human beings, if some few years old, are normally able to get to understand such expressions and may act accordingly.

Thinking about this, and especially about more grown-up humans, we are approaching the topic of 'practical reason'. As a first generalisation, we may readily introduce the concept of good and harm, which ought to lead us to think of desirability and undesirability, misbehaviour and 'sensible' action.

I have observed that Aristotle upon the whole thinks desirability is a key notion here. At any rate, it would seem that a 'rational' animal, i.e. a human being, will operate in getting and avoiding things with highly intelligible conceptions of good and bad. I would not claim that this supposition is obviously correct; however, if it seems to have no sense in it at all, one will think that the human behaviour one is contemplating is not worth much consideration—less, at any rate, than the behaviour of some 'inferior animals'.

I have remarked that in the writings of St John the Apostle he speaks occasionally of people whose actions, or some of them, are 'not true'. This is a more tantalising way of speaking than it is to say that someone 'does not walk in the truth'. That is fairly easy to understand, coming as it does in the writing of a Christian apostle. But how can he speak of *doing*, or *not doing* the truth? The Greek verb used is '*poiein*', which rather commonly has or includes the notion of *producing*. Some people might be very puzzled at this—do I produce (or do) truth by my actions? It sounds like nonsense.

True. But Aristotle has a different general point to make. We can ask: Was it a good idea to do such-and-such *with the purpose of getting a good reputation*?

We need not discuss this in any special detail. For Aristotle has a general view which we should look at. If you are *acting*, and that would include making something (if that is what your action is), then you must have it as an end that you should do it well. He gives us the abstract Greek word *eupraxia*—a general term for doing well. Anyone who acts (*prattei*) has that objective (unless, we may say, he is bloody-minded enough not to care). Acting well—and the Greek word *eupraxia* includes the sense of 'doing well' when we speak of someone doing well in some business or in health—this end, *eupraxia*, is the actual end of any action, at any rate of any *poiesis* (production). If it is the, or an, end of any action or behaviour supposed by the agent to be sensible or good, then Aristotle can tell us that 'doing well' is the objective of the rational life that is led by a human being.

Admittedly, the idea of production of truth does not seem to fit in very well. My own experience has led me to outrage philosophical audiences by maintaining that I can produce truth. E.g. I may say 'I am going to stand on this table', and then I produce truth in what I said by doing that. People protest: 'You can't talk like that. Truth is eternal. If you do stand on the table, it was always true (before you did it) that you would stand on the table when you did.'

I understand this impulse about truth. Nevertheless, in such a case I *do* make something true, which I had said I would do.

Aristotle apparently appeals to the fact that if you are purposefully making something, you have some sort of end in doing so. You may, as I suggested, be aiming at getting your work admired, but some purpose you must have in having *that* aim.

Thinking about this, we are approaching the topic of practical reason. Man, to be sure, is essentially part of 'nature' — i.e. of *natura naturata*, or as we might say, he is part of the created world. Nevertheless, in respect of his possible freedom — in respect of his *becoming* free, if he does — he comes as near as possible, given Spinoza's philosophy, to the freedom attributed to God. Why not, then, also in Aristotle's philosophy?

I think no conception of 'free will', as Spinoza contemptuously regards it, can seriously get in Aristotle's way.

10

Hume on causality: introductory

Hume's doctrines and reasonings on the subject of causation are comprised in or otherwise connected with three main points.

First: the relation of cause and effect is a contingent one.

Second: this relation is the sole bridge by which we may pass from present experience to belief in a world beyond such experience. 'Belief arises only from causation.'[1]

Third: there are two definitions of cause; in the first it is considered as a 'philosophical' relation, and is defined as: 'An object precedent and contiguous to another, and where all the objects resembling the former are plac'd in like relations of precedency and contiguity to those objects, that resemble the latter.' In the second it is considered as a 'natural relation' and is defined as 'An object precedent and contiguous to another, and so united with it that the idea of the one determines the mind to form the idea of the other, and the impression of the one to form a more lively idea of [that is, a *belief* in] the other.'[2]

Someone who knows that these are the principal points about Hume's doctrine knows the skeleton of it and has starting points from which he may proceed to a grasp of the whole. For it is evident that each of these needs much investigation and exposition. Hume's own exposition is so ramified that it is very difficult to comprehend

---

* From an undated, unrevised typescript corrected in the light of the two notebooks on which the text of the typescript is based. The notebooks seem not to be earlier than the 1970s.

---

[1] David Hume, *A Treatise of Human Nature*, edited by L A Selby-Bigge (Oxford: Clarendon Press, 1888), p. 107.

[2] *Op.cit.* p.170.

it. One must proceed like an anatomist correctly separating muscle from muscle and tracing the path and discerning the operation of each separate sinew and nerve.

I. *That inference from cause to effect or effect to cause is non-demonstrative.*

The first main thought which Hume has to instil into us is that which is often briefly expressed nowadays by saying: the relation of cause and effect is a *contingent* relation. Hume does not himself put it that way, nor indeed is that way of putting it quite free from objection. (We shall return to this.) Hume's first formulation is this:

> The power by which one object produces another, is never discoverable merely from their idea, [so that] 'tis evident that *cause* and *effect* are relations of which we receive information from experience, and not from any abstract reasoning and reflection.

It straightway follows, in Hume's view of the matter, that this relation, and the objects we may infer by means of it, cannot as so inferred be 'objects of knowledge and certainty'; for he restricts the concept of knowledge, and of certainty as well, to what falls under either *intuition* or *demonstration*.

What is *intuition*? It is for example the perception of resemblance, contrariety, or degrees in quality; perception how? 'Resemblance will at first strike the eye, or rather the mind', Hume says,[3] and the same will presumably hold for contrariety and for degree. 'By sense [we may emend, since not only sight is in question] or rather by the mind', then, these relations are intuited. The qualification need not be seen as an evasion; Hume is concerned with relations of ideas more than of objects of sense, and it is his thesis that any impression is attended by its correspondent idea.[4]

If I see a patch of Oxford blue and a patch of Cambridge blue simultaneously, I will also perceive that the first is darker than the second, and that at least one of the patches, or bits of ribbon, say, which are of these colours must change in colour if the relations *darker-than lighter-than* cease to hold between them. Correspondingly, if I attend to my ideas of these colours, I see that I must change my ideas if I am to suppose those relations no longer to hold. And so we have as objects of intuition not merely (if at all) sensible facts but some propositions asserting necessary relations, or, as Hume puts it,

---

[3]   *Op.cit.* p. 70.
[4]   *Op.cit.* pp. 4–5.

relations which 'depend entirely on the ideas which we compare together'; we compare them, it seems, in formulating the propositions asserting these relations.

Demonstrative reasoning, as Hume understands it, is deductive reasoning from intuitive certainties of this nature.

II. On relations, natural and philosophical.

That the notion of a relation is that of a *comparison of ideas* is to be found in Berkeley. Berkeley thought that there could be no *idea*, i.e. no impression or image of a relation, partly because the notion of a relation involves that of a comparing mind. He did not think that mind, or spirit, in a word the *subject* having ideas, could be the content of any presentation to the subject. He did not infer from this (as Hume did) that the notion of mind or spirit was illusory – chimerical, but rather that our knowledge etc., involves more than ideas, presentations to us; it involves also *notions* which are not ideas.

Thus the way of speaking of a relation as involving a comparison of ideas was a familiar starting point for Hume. Where in modern philosophy we would speak of formulating a relational proposition, Hume will speak of comparing ideas 'in a circumstance'[5] which evidently means 'in something about them' or 'in a respect'.

But Hume has a distinction, which he calls a distinction in the *sense* of the word 'relation', between 'natural' and 'philosophical' relations, and we know that this is an important point, since the two different definitions of *cause* relate to it, one as a 'philosophical', the other as a 'natural' relation.

What then is a 'philosophical' relation? It is nothing but what in modern philosophy is called a relation *simpliciter*. We are used to the thought that in relational propositions there is a more-than-one-place predicate: e.g. if we have the proposition 'A is a father' we understand that there is someone A is a father to; 'father', unlike 'square' or 'bright' is not just predicated of someone, but of someone and *to* someone. Wherever, then, we can formulate a proposition containing a predicate of this character we have a relation to consider. When Hume speaks of comparing ideas in some circumstance, this circumstance will be the relation: e.g. *distance* is a circumstance in which we may 'think proper to compare' two ideas when we say such and such is far distant from such and such. This brings out how the talk of 'comparing ideas' is no explanation of relations at all,

[5]   *Op.cit.* p. 15.

since relation has to be introduced as the circumstance in which the 'ideas' are compared.

A *natural* relation, on the other hand, is not any arbitrary relation we may care to think of: it is a quality 'by which two ideas are connected in the imagination, and the one naturally introduces the other'. This 'quality' (or property, as we should more naturally say nowadays), however, turns out to be already a relation; there are three such 'qualities': resemblance, contiguity in place or time, and cause and effect.

What are we to say here? Are there really two senses of 'relation'? In one of these senses we say 'there is no relation between *a* and *b*, they are utterly remote', and in the other '*a* is remote from *b*' expresses a relation of *a* to *b*. We may say so if we like; but the difference is not a difference at all relevant to the logical category of *relation*, to which category relations must belong, whether called 'natural' or 'philosophic'. The meaning of the connection of terms in a relational proposition is to be explicated *neither* as a natural association by which one idea leads on to another via a certain quality, *nor* as a comparison of the terms in some more arbitrary, sophisticated respect. That this is so comes out in the way both the 'quality' causing 'the association', *and* the 'circumstance' in which the comparison is made turn out to *be* relations; the character of being a relation is thus nowise explained by reference to natural association on the one hand, or comparison of terms on the other.

It is then no surprise that the 'natural' relations listed by Hume are a subset of the 'philosophical relations'. 'Philosophical relations' are simply relations; 'natural relations' are those relations an object stands in which naturally occur to one thinking of the object, so that he equally naturally thinks of their other terms.

III. *Difficulty about cause and effect as a 'natural' relation.*

There is the following difficulty about Hume's account. As a natural relation, *being cause of* or *being effect of* is a quality *by* which the mind is naturally carried from one idea to another, or from the impression of one term of the relation to the idea of the other. But what is that quality is this case? That is a question which it will turn out just cannot be answered.

By contrast, if it is said that resemblance is such a quality, we can indicate what the quality is, *independently of its having that tendency*. To be sure, we could not be struck by a resemblance between one object and another — the first present and the second absent let us say

— without thinking of the other. That is simply because the quality in question is a relation, and a relation must have another term.

But we readily think of the object that has the resemblance without thinking of the resemblance; and we can also indicate what *resemblance* is in some *other* example. We can then say that *because* that object has a certain resemblance to another, it may easily make us think of that other.

With the relation of cause and effect, on Hume's own showing, we cannot indicate what causation is in an example. Furthermore, by his *account* of the relation, explication of the 'quality' involves the fact *that* the idea or impression of one term makes us think of the other — that fact is part of the 'quality' itself.

On the first point: that we cannot 'find' or indicate the quality, we have Hume saying:

> Let us cast our eye on any two objects, which we call cause and effect, and turn them on all sides, in order to find that impression, which produces an idea of such prodigious consequence. At first sight I perceive that I must not search for it in any of the particular *qualities* of the objects [here he uses 'quality' in the more familiar, narrower sense]; since, whichever of these qualities I pitch on, I find some object that is not possest of it, and yet falls under the denomination of cause and effect. And indeed there is nothing existent, either externally or internally, which is not to be consider'd either as a cause or as an effect; tho' 'tis plain there is no one quality which universally belongs to all beings, and gives them a title to that denomination.[6]

It must be admitted that this is a bad argument. One could make the same point about resemblance. Indeed, Hume has observed something of the sort, at least something relevant, about resemblance:

> When a quality becomes very general, and is common to a great many individuals, it leads not the mind directly to any one of them; but by presenting at once too great a choice, does thereby prevent the imagination from fixing on any single object.[7]

The 'great generality' of resemblance consists in just this, that resemblances are quite different from one another; fix on a quality in a narrow sense and you can form the idea of a resembling object, but *that* quality will not be the 'quality' of resemblance.

---

[6]   *Op.cit.* p. 75.

[7]   *Op.cit.* p. 14.

Hume has not put his point well. Yet, anyone will feel that he *has* a point. For, *pace* Berkeley, resemblance can all the same be indicated: you can fix your visual attention, *see*, the resemblance between two objects. But causality, the relation of production between a cause and its effect — is that in the same way an object of sense? Surely not. Is it a *sense-content*? It is certainly not such a relation as 'larger than'; it is not experienced as is *sweet*; it is not a relation perceived *in* perceiving such more elementary properties, as is resemblance.

We have seen one way in which this matters: it creates a difficulty in understanding the 'natural relation': what is the 'quality'? But it has a greater significance for Hume's philosophy than merely this, of making a difficulty. It plays a positive part in the construction of his theory.

IV. That there is no sense impression of causality which contributes to our acquisition of the concept of cause.

We may be willing to say with Hume: there is no impression of the senses from which we derive our notion of causality.

That, indeed, is not the same thing as to say: there is no such thing as a sense-impression of causality; for there really might be such a thing. On a screen, for example, shapes might be seen to move about in various ways and at some stages they might 'give one an impression of causality'. But it may be said that such an impression is *derivative*. Some impressions after all may derive from ideas.

When we say 'There is no sense impression from which we derive our notion of causality' we are evidently making a contrast. With what? Say, with there being an impression from which we derive our notion of hot, or white, or sweet.

But are there such impressions? Hume indeed believed in such a derivation of 'simple' ideas. This involves him in believing in 'simple' impressions; a very dubious notion. Yet we do not want to plunge into a discussion of this difficult topic.

Let us say at least this: sense impressions from red objects play some contributory role in our acquisition and application of the concept 'red' if we have it as the normally sighted do. That vague and minimal claim at any rate is a reasonable one and will serve our purpose. For we may very well think: such 'impressions of causality' as we have described do not play such a part either in our acquisition or in our application of the concept 'cause'. (Why? That's another question which I don't want to answer now.)

With these considerations behind us, we can with a good con-
science agree with Hume: there is no such impression. At least we
can provisionally agree with him.

V. Why this is of such significance in Hume's philosophy.

To understand this, we have to remind ourselves of Hume's theory
of impressions and ideas; we shall do this without assenting to it or
discussing it. It forms an essential background for understanding his
definition of cause as a natural relation.

Hume has a fundamental thesis: 'All our simple ideas in their first
appearance are deriv'd from simple impressions, which are correspondent to them, and which they exactly represent.'

This thesis is not supposed to go without proof. To prove it, Hume
asserts (a) that 'every simple impression is attended with a correspondent idea and every simple idea with a correspondent impression'; and (b) that 'Such a constant conjunction, in such an infinite
number of instances, can never arise from chance'. He concludes that
there is 'a dependence of the impressions on the ideas or of the ideas
on the impressions'.[8] To determine which, he considers which come
first as a matter of experience. We find that ideas don't produce
impressions: we do not 'perceive any colour, or feel any sensation
merely upon thinking of them. On the other hand we find that any
impression of the mind or body is constantly followed by an idea
which resembles it.' 'The constant conjunction of our resembling
perceptions is a convincing proof that the one are causes of the other;
and this priority of the impressions is an equal proof that our impressions are the causes of our ideas, not our ideas of our impressions.'[9]

His fundamental thesis does not merely give the origin of our
ideas, it provides Hume with a criterion by which to determine
whether an ostensible idea is chimerical or not. The ideas of substance and of the self or person are rejected on the ground that there
is no correspondent impression.[10] The idea of necessary connection
is subjected to the same test: 'As we have no idea that is not deriv'd
from an impression, we must find some impression that gives rise to
this idea of necessity, if we assert we really have such an idea.'[11]

---

[8]   *Op.cit.* p. 4.

[9]   *Op.cit.* p. 5.

[10]   *Op.cit.* pp. 15–16, 251.

[11]   *Op.cit.* p. 155.

In these enquiries Hume is indeed somewhat cavalier even on his own principles: for might not substance, self and necessity be complex ideas? And in that case they would be derived not each from one, but from several ideas.

> [Is] the idea of substance … deriv'd from the impressions of sensation or reflexion? If it be convey'd to us by sense, I ask which of them; and after what manner? If it be perceiv'd by the eyes, it must be a colour; if by the ears a sound [etc] … the impressions of reflexion resolve themselves into our passions and emotions, none of which can possibly represent a substance. We have therefore no idea of substance, distinct from that of a collection of particular qualities.[12]

Short work!

He does not proceed so with the idea of *cause*. That he seems to treat as a complex idea. In order to understand an idea, he says, we must 'trace it up to its origin, and examine that primary impression from which it arises.'[13] If the idea is complex, and (we should add) not derived from one impression, we must then trace it to the various origins of its component parts. In the idea of an object's being a cause, Hume finds the ideas of its being prior and contiguous to the 'object' which is the effect. About these ideas he evidently feels no difficulty; he does not ask whether they are colours, sounds or tastes, as he does with substance. As we discover these relations of priority and contiguity by attentively considering e.g. motion in one body produced upon impulse by motion in another, we may suppose that they are some sort of impressions of sensation, though hardly 'simple' ones. That, however, won't matter, if only they *are* given in sense; the ideas of them are vindicated.

These relations, however, are not enough to constitute the idea of causation; there is also the idea of *necessary connection*. It plainly has no origin in any impressions of sense. If, then, it is an idea at all, it must be derived from impressions of reflection. For Hume, following Locke rather than Berkeley, thought we had impressions of e.g. will, desire, and the passions; such impressions were 'impressions of reflexion'.

The necessity which he regards as so integral a part of the notion of causality, he traces to an origin in an impression of reflection. For the experience of constant conjunction of like objects with other like

[12]   *Op.cit.* pp. 15–16.

[13]   *Op.cit.* p. 75.

objects produces a felt 'determination of the mind': the mind, as it were, feels pushed to believe in the other term of the relation of cause and effect, if it but experience one term. This felt determination of the mind is the 'model' of the idea of necessity, the primary impression to which it can be traced.[14]

Thus the fact that causation is not the content of an original sense-impression leads to Hume's second definition of 'cause'. For as he holds that ideas must always be traceable to impressions, the lack of any originating impression of sensation for the idea of necessity means that if we truly have such an idea at all, its original impression must be an 'impression of reflexion'.

VI. Is Hume guilty of a circle in definition and analysis?

The question 'Is there such an idea as cause?' is answered 'Yes' by Hume's criteria; for there are impressions that cause the ideas of temporal succession, contiguity, constant conjunction, and necessary connection. That is, Hume gives a causal analysis of the existence of the idea of causality. That is so far nothing special to causality: in *this* sense he gives and holds to be required a causal analysis in connection with every idea. When the idea in question is causality, one may suspect a circle.

Independently of that (suspected) circle, there are obvious grounds for suspecting a circle in the second definition of 'cause': 'An object precedent and contiguous to another, and so united with it, that the idea of the one determines the mind to form the idea of the other, and the impression of the one to form a more lively idea of the other.'[15] For what does 'determines' mean but 'causes'? Certainly 'determines' is not being used here in the sense in which *reason* determines anything, as when premises determine a conclusion: we know that it is a great point of Hume's that the idea of the cause does *not* in that sense determine that of the effect. No: causation is what is in question here, as in the various other expressions he uses, as of the mind 'being carried' or 'conveyed', or the one idea or impression *giving rise to* or producing the other idea, and so on.

Well, it is obvious that there is no replacing of the word 'determines' in the second definition *by* that definition of cause; the definition would never be completed, but one would go on like a stuck gramophone record: An object precedent and contiguous to another

[14] *Op.cit.* p. 165.
[15] *Op.cit.* p. 170.

and so united with it that the idea of the one is an object precedent and contiguous to another and so united with it that the idea of the one is an object precedent and contiguous to another and so united with it … (Here we see a nice illustration of the identity of a vicious circle and a vicious infinite regress. The circle is in the repetition of the defining words; the regress is back through an endless succession of *different* things referred to, for we begin with objects, move to ideas of objects, which ideas are now considered as objects, move to ideas of ideas of objects, which ideas are now considered as objects, and so on ad infinitum. Certainly if we only had the second definition we should have something circular and worthless.)

Russell, in the essay on the notion of cause in *Our Knowledge of the External World*, remarks that our experiences of constant conjunction are constantly conjoined with expectations of one term of the relation when we experience the other. So, without explicitly going into the matter, he is clearing up the charge of circularity in analysis by applying Hume's first definition of cause, where a cause is defined purely in terms of resemblance, succession, contiguity and constant conjunction. We have there in the particular case of experiences of constant conjunction and expectation — *these* are the resembling terms which are constantly conjoined. Therefore, by definition (the first definition) the experience of constant conjunction *causes* the expectation of the unexperienced item of a pair of things found in constant conjunction.

I said: we have these relations in the particular case of constant conjunction and expectation. The resemblance will be purely in respect of being experiences of constant conjunctions, and in being expectations. The experience of a given constant conjunction will be prior to the expectation of one term on the apprehension of the other: that gives us temporal precedence. But 'contiguity'? That seems to drop out or to have to be given a somewhat extended sense.[16] Contiguity of place seems inapplicable; contiguity of time false: is not my *experience* of the constant conjunction of fire and heat separated by a gap from my expectation of heat in connection with the next fire that I see? For my *last* experience of the two together was some time back, and I see no fire now.

---

[16] In the *Enquiry* Hume forgets contiguity in his definition of cause as 'an object followed by another and where all the objects similar to the first are followed by objects similar to the second'. This does indeed make things easier; but the question arises 'Followed how soon?'

The answer to this is perhaps that the causality here is indirect. The experience of constant conjunction, which Hume does not distinguish from the no-counter example and frequent experience of conjunction, *was* precedent *and* contiguous in time, in respect of its last instance, to an impression of reflection, the felt determination of the mind to pass from the one object to its usual attendant. (This, as impressions will, generated its correspondent *idea*, which is the idea of necessity. In Hume, ideas once generated are, like permanent actors, able to stroll on to the stage at any time. *This* idea—of 'necessity'—always appears when the idea of one of the terms appears. But it is mistakenly applied, not to the other idea, but to what the other idea is of.)

Since the experience of constant conjunction always is in this sense precedent and contiguous to that impression of mental determination, it can by said by definition to cause it. The impression of mental determination to pass to the idea of the other term is always of course succeeded by the idea; so it causes the idea, which may of course *also* be being caused by its own correspondent impression too. But the impression of mental determination always succeeds an idea or impression of one of the terms alone, and so is caused by it. Thus the idea or impression of one of the terms *causes*, determines, the mind to form the idea of the other. It is this last bit of causality that is mentioned in the second definition of cause, in which, note, there is no mention either of constant conjunction or of necessary connection. The constant conjunction is there implicitly in the expression 'so united that'; necessary connection, though Hume regards it as an integral part of the idea of causation, does not come in at all except genetically—*it* is an idea derived from the impression of mental determination, and, we must suppose, mistakenly applied. It is the idea of necessitation.

In this way we can exonerate Hume from the charge of a *circulus in definiendo*, by interpreting 'determines' (= 'cause') in the second definition in terms of the first definition.

However, there is the other accusation of circularity, since Hume says

> 'Tis impossible to reason justly without understanding perfectly the idea concerning which we reason, and 'tis impossible perfectly to understand an idea without tracing it up to its origins and examining that primary impression from which it arises.

May it not be argued that you *suppose* an understanding of the idea of cause in one who is doing the requisite 'tracing'? We can't reason justly without understanding the idea concerning which we reason; we can't understand the idea without tracing it to its origin; we can't trace it to its origin without already *employing* it.

Well, that is true. Here one plays a certain game of 'Let's pretend' in philosophy. Let's pretend we haven't an idea and find the explanation that properly communicates it to us. E.g. we go through the motions of giving ourselves the idea, perhaps by attending to an impression, and that proves to us, we think, that we are justified in thinking that we have such an idea.

If that is what we are doing, Hume's contention about understanding an idea 'perfectly' is that you've got to be able to say: 'Here is the impression or impressions that the idea derives from, arises from, i.e. is produced or caused by.'

But if the idea that you are playing the game about is *itself* 'causes', 'produces', 'gives rise to', then clearly you can't play that game; you can't offer an explanation containing the word 'cause' or some equivalent to a mind that by supposition has not yet got the corresponding idea. (The same point would obviously hold for 'impression'.)

That, then, is the criticism: by Hume's account, you have got to have the idea in order to obtain the idea.

We could and should reply on his behalf: you may *trace* an idea to its correspondent impression just by going to the impression — attending to or thinking of the impression. That *is* tracing it. You don't have to think the thought: the idea *derives* from this impression. We saw indeed that Hume actually *argues* that it does derive, on the ground of the constant arise[†] of resembling ideas when we have impressions (and not the other way).

In that place, indeed, it was said 'Constant conjunction can't be all there is to it; there must be another connection — a causal connection'! This now turns out quite empty. For it now turns out that the causal connection *is* nothing but the constant conjunction.

There is, of course, in his genetic account, the impression of being determined. Now what is that impression? Is it an impression *of the mind's being determined by* a constant conjuction, or one term of it, to pass to the idea of the other?

---

† The person who produced the typescript version of the text was baffled by the author's handwriting at this point and simply left a gap. The word 'arise', odd though it is, is the best shot at decipherment of the notebook text that the present editor can manage.

Hume says:

> ... the *observation* of this resemblance [in the several resembling
> instances, which give rise to the idea of power] produces a new
> impression *in the mind*, which is its [sc. the idea of power's] real
> model. For after we have observ'd the resemblance in a sufficient
> number of instances, we immediately feel a determination of the
> mind to pass from one object to its usual attendant. This determi-
> nation is the only effect of the resemblance; and therefore must be
> the same with power or efficacy, whose idea is deriv'd from the
> resemblance.[17]

I cannot find that he says 'We feel a determination *by* the constant
conjunction or *by* the previous impression'; he says not that but just:
after experience of constant conjunction we feel a determination,
like: we feel compelled. One can feel *compelled* without feeling *compelled by*.

Further, he says: 'The uniting principle among our internal
impressions is as unintelligible as that among external objects, and is
not known to us any other way than by experience.'[18] An impression
of determination *by* one impression to pass to another would be a
uniting principle, and would I suppose be 'intelligible' just by our
having the impression—*impressions* can't be 'unintelligible'. The
uniting principle's being unintelligible must mean: we can form no
conception of it.

In brief: Hume does not speak of a feeling of *being determined by*;
and it looks as if he would quite reject the idea of such a feeling.

To sum up, then: the causality mentioned in the second definition
—the idea of the one *determining* the mind to form the idea of the
other—not merely *can*, to avoid a *regressus in infinitum*, but *must*, in
accordance with Hume's own account, be explained in terms of the
first definition. That is to say, the 'determines' of the second definition, which is definitely a relational expression—*something* determines *the mind*—is *not* a word for any impression, and when
'determination' is used as the name of an impression it is not the
determination meant by the second definition and is not *determination by*.

---

[17] *Op.cit.* p. 165.
[18] *Op.cit.* p. 169.

VII. Hume's discussion of 'Whatever has a beginning of existence must have a cause'.

At the end of Section II [of Part III of Book I of the *Treatise*] Hume distinguishes two questions, the one: Why a beginning of existence must necessarily always have a cause? and the other: Why such particular causes must always have such particular effects, and what is the nature of the inference from the one to the other?

Note that not only are these distinct questions, but that a person might consistently hold that a beginning of existence must always have a cause, without holding that 'such particular causes must have such particular effects'.

Let us consider Hume's treatment of the proposition that every beginning of existence must have a cause. Having distinguished this at the end of Section II from the proposition that 'such particular causes must have such particular effects', at the end of Section III he proposes to sink consideration of grounds for belief in the first into consideration of grounds for belief in the second. Section III is devoted to refuting the thesis that 'Whatever begins to exist must have a cause of existence' is intuitively or demonstratively certain, i.e. is what would nowadays be called a proposition whose truth is logically necessary.

What Hume calls 'intuitively certain' is a proposition whose truth is discoverable purely from examining the ideas contained in it, and what he calls 'demonstratively certain' is apparently a proposition which follows from something intuitively certain.

He first produces a 'proof', which we shall soon examine, that that first 'principle of causality' cannot possibly be intuitively or demonstrably certain, and he devotes the rest of the section to disposing of such arguments as he knows purporting to demonstrate it. He considers four arguments, of which he is able to refute three with complete ease; indeed they do not deserve attention. One says that something that came into existence without a cause must produce itself, which is impossible; another, that it is produced by *nothing*, which is incapable of producing anything. As Hume says, these arguments assume the very thing that they set out to prove, and so can hardly prove it. This is not 'just reasoning'. The point is obvious indeed. Not that the arguments are exactly invalid, but they cannot prove the conclusion except to someone who already accepts it. Another argument he reasonably calls still more frivolous: every effect must have a cause since cause and effect are relative terms. As Hume says, this does not show that every beginning of existence must be an effect, any more than the truth that every husband must have a wife shows that every man must be married. We shall see that his making this point is of some importance for our understanding of his positive argument that this 'principle of causality' cannot possibly be intuitively or demonstrably certain. So much for the second, third and fourth arguments which he considers.

The *first* argument, however, is obscure and is dealt with rather sketchily. It is that

> All the points of time and space, say some philosophers [Mr Hobbes], in which we can suppose any object to begin to exist, are in themselves equal; and unless there be some cause, which is peculiar to one time and to one place, and which by that means determines and fixes the existence, it must remain in eternal suspence.[19]

Hume replies:

> Is there any more difficulty in supposing the time and place to be fix'd without a cause, than to suppose the existence to be determin'd in that manner? The first question that occurs on this subject is always, *whether* the object shall exist or not: The next, *when* and *where* it shall begin to exist. If the removal of a cause be intuitively absurd in the one case, it must be so in the other: And if that absurdity be not clear without a proof in the one case, it will equally require one in the other. The absurdity, then, of the one supposition can never be a proof of that of the other; since they are both upon the same footing and must stand or fall by the same reasoning.[20]

This hardly seems satisfactory. Before going into it, however, let us pause to ask why he says 'The first question is *whether* an object shall exist'. This seems to consider the matter from the point of view of a creator. This indicates that Hume is consciously in Leibniz country; for Leibniz argues for the identity of indiscernibles on the ground that God must have a reason for putting A here and now, B there and then, which there could not be unless something distinguished A from B. Yet Hume doesn't consider this. It seems reasonable to suggest an amendment, for his argument would not be affected except, for improved clarity, by not raising this puzzling question, if we rewrote it 'The first question must be, *whether* an object can exist or not, the next, *when* and *where* it can begin to exist'.

---

[19]   *Op.cit.* p. 80.

[20]   *Ibid.*

But what is Hume's argument? He is saying: You cannot argue to the absurdity of *p* from the fact that it entails *q*, which is absurd, for if someone saw no difficulty in *p*, he'd see no difficulty in *q*. (Rather as if the argument were a shaggy dog story.) This is somewhat cavalier. The arguer is not saying 'There is no absurdity in *p*' but rather 'There is *this* absurdity in *p*, that it entails *q*, which is absurd.'

Hume is saying 'But why should I find *q* absurd if I don't *already* find *p* absurd?' And to this there may well be an answer in this case. It is not fair to say: you *cannot* argue like that, because you are initially supposing that *p* is not absurd. I am not initially supposing anything of the sort! Well, Hume says, by producing an argument instead of simply saying *p* is absurd, you are conceding it is not intuitively absurd; now *if* it is not intuitively absurd, then neither is *q*. Well, even that is not clear; but anyway, perhaps *q* is not 'intuitively' absurd but there are further arguments to show that *q* is absurd. And this is indeed the case. Without existing at a definite place and time, a particular finite and non-eternal thing won't exist at all. Hobbes' argument, as cited by Hume, seems to go on as follows: Antecedently to a thing's existence at a place and in a time nothing can connect it with that time and place more than with any other, unless something already existent *makes* that the time and place of the thing's existence. This argument indeed seems very uncertain. Hume could say: the thing is connected with the time and place by the brute fact of existing at it: you can think of that without invoking something that *makes* it exist at that time and place. But the argument suggests another one, namely: Space and time are relative; that is, antecedently to a thing's existence at a place and time, there can be no distinction of that place and time from any other unless something *else* distinguishes them. In this passage, Hume writes as if the place and time for a thing's existence could be specified independently of its existence. The argument that he is considering assumes that too; and also it is the truth. Since, then, space and time are relative, this specifiability requires a determinant other than the thing which is to exist or have existed in the place and at the time. That is the argument, and Hume does not deal with the questions suggested by the argument he cites, which give rise to this one; he has apparently not seen that the question arises what the requisite specification of place and time could mean without a prior existence; or at least *some* other existence, for it might be posterior. Thus we might specify a time as *n* years ago. This is not to give a cause; but the requirement of other existences by which to specify time and place does falsify Hume's great principle 'That there is nothing in any object, consider'd in itself, which can afford us a reason for drawing a conclusion beyond it'.[21] If he should say: 'consider'd in itself' includes 'considered as existing at a given time and place', then, since a thing that comes into existence must come into existence at a given time and place, considered in itself it can't be considered as coming into existence at all. But as soon as you consider it as existing at a given time and place, the question arises as to how that time and place could be specified.

This is a very obscure topic, and we will leave it, with the observation that Hume has hardly done it justice. Let us now attend to the argument, already given by him, to show that a beginning of existence without a cause is not demonstrably absurd. It is an argument from imagination:

> As all distinct ideas are separable from each other, and as the ideas of cause and effect are evidently distinct, 'twill be easy for us to conceive any object to be non-existent this moment, and existent the next, without conjoining to it the distinct idea of a cause or productive principle. The separation, therefore, of the idea of a cause from that of a beginning of existence is plainly possible for the imagination; and consequently the actual separation of these objects is so far possible, that it implies no contradiction or absurdity.[22]

This argument from imagination is uneasily prolix, more so, even, than my quotation shows. Let us set it out proposition by proposition:

1.   All distinct ideas are separable.

2.   The ideas of cause and effect are distinct.

3.   Therefore it will be easy to think of an object's coming into existence without thinking of a cause.

So far, so good: 'separable' presumably means 'such that one can think of one without *eo ipso* thinking of the other'.

We might query (2) on the ground that cause and effect are relative, like husband and wife. But from Hume's giving an example of an effect in (3), and especially in view of his calling 'frivolous' the argument that the ideas of cause and effect are correlative, we must, I think, take him to mean that the ideas of whatever objects are causes

[21] *Op.cit.* p. 139.

[22] *Op.cit.* pp. 79–80.

and effects are distinct from one another. The next step is the crucial one:

4.   Therefore the separation of the idea of a cause from that of a beginning of existence is possible for the imagination.

What does this mean? There are two possibilities: that it is possible to imagine a beginning of existence without imagining a cause, and that it is possible to imagine a beginning of existence without a cause. The first certainly follows from (3) but is too close to it in sense for us seriously to suppose it is what Hume means. He must, then, mean the second, so we have

4(a) It is possible to imagine something's beginning to exist without a cause.

From this he draws the conclusion:

5.   Therefore the actual separation of these objects is so far possible that it implies no contradiction or absurdity.

This makes one ask 'What objects?' The answer, as far as concerns one of them, is plain: it is 'A beginning of existence'. For example, I imagine a star or a rabbit beginning to exist. To supply such a particular case is both reasonable and conformable to Hume's doctrine of abstract ideas; for neither in reality nor according to Hume can there be a bare image of a beginning of existence which is not the beginning of existence of anything in particular. But what is the other 'object'? The only answer we have is 'a cause'. Now we can go two ways. We can either forsake the doctrine of abstract ideas and say that it is to be a sufficient description of our image in the particular case, or we can, as we did with 'a beginning of existence', supply a specific cause, as another rabbit or the cohesion of nebulous material. And here arises the difficulty. For the argument from imaginability to possibility has a good deal of force on the second interpretation: let me imagine any event, say the boiling of a kettle, and any particular cause of it, say the heat of a fire, and not only can I imagine the one's happening without the other, but the imaginability convinces me of the possibility in the sense of implying no contradiction or absurdity. 'I know what it would be like to find the kettle boiled without a fire', I say. Similarly, I know what it would be like to find a rabbit coming into being *not* from a parent rabbit. So here the argument from imagination is sound. But this sound argument does not yield the desired conclusion. Let it hold for any particular causes I care to introduce, then I can say

6. From any beginning (or modification) of existence E and any particular cause C, I can imagine E's happening without C,

and infer from this

7. From any beginning (or modification) of existence E, and any particular cause C, E can be supposed to happen without C: i.e. there is no contradiction or absurdity in the supposition.

But the first proposition does not give me the possibility of imagining an effect without any cause at all. That is, it does not give me

8. I can imagine this: there is a beginning of (or modification) of existence without any cause

For quite generally from 'For *any*, it is possible that ...' there does not follow 'It is possible that for *none*...'; or again, from:

'For *any* colour, I can imagine that a rose is not that colour'

it does not follow

'I can imagine that a rose has no colour'.

Nor does (6), the possible exclusion of any particular cause in the imagination, or what follows from it, (7), the possibility of a beginning of existence without any given cause, yield

9. A beginning of existence can *happen* without any cause, i.e. this supposition is without contradiction or absurdity.

So if we go this way we have a sound argument from imagination, 'This can be imagined, therefore this is possible', but the *this* is not the desired conclusion that the effect can occur without any particular cause which you have imagined it without.

We must, then, try the other track, in which we forget Hume's doctrine of abstract ideas, and accept that the second 'object' is just 'a cause' and no more. Then the argument is simply:

We can imagine something's coming into existence without a cause. Therefore it is possible (i.e. there is no contradiction in supposing) that something comes into existence without a cause.

If this is the right interpretation, one wonders why Hume did not give the argument straight in this form. The trouble about it is that it is very unconvincing. For if I say I can imagine a rabbit coming into being without a parent rabbit, well and good: I imagine a rabbit coming into being and our observing that there is no parent rabbit about. But what am I to imagine if I imagine a rabbit coming into being without a cause? Well, I just imagine a rabbit coming into being. That this *is* the imagination of a rabbit coming into being without a cause is nothing but, as it were, the *title* of the picture. Indeed I can form an image and give my picture that title. But from my being able to do *that*, nothing whatever follows about what is possible to suppose without contradiction or absurdity in reality.

At the end of Section III Hume abandons the question why a cause is always necessary. Having satisfied himself that the opinion of the necessity of a cause cannot arise from 'knowledge or any scientific reasoning', he concludes it must arise from observation and experience. The question 'how experience gives rise to such a principle' he proposes to sink in the question (the second one mentioned at the end of Section II): why we conclude that such particular causes must have such particular effects, and why we form an inference from one to the other? He thinks that it will 'perhaps be found in the end, that the same answer will serve for both questions'. We may note that Hume does not himself revert to the first question or try to show that his answer to the second serves to give an answer to the first. He probably thought it was obvious that, and how, it did. Not only is it not obvious; it is impossible. We think that such and such a cause must have such and such an effect, and such and such an effect such and such a cause, according to Hume, because we constantly experience their conjunction, so as to expect the presence of the 'usual attendant' of whatever term of such a constantly experienced conjunction we are currently perceiving or remembering. Even if every beginning or modification of existence had in our experience had such a 'usual attendant', that would only lead us, on his account, to the constant expectation of such particular usual attendants upon repeated experience of such particular beginnings or modifications of existence. The transition to the general, unspecified proposition 'Every beginning of existence has a cause' is unexplained.

For example, we believe in mother rabbits—we believe *that* a rabbit we may see had a beginning of existence, and that this had a cause: it came from its mother. Suppose we say that this is because of our experience of the constant conjunction between rabbits and a having come into existence of the same, and of the coming to be of a new rabbit with the contiguous being of a mother rabbit. It is instructive and amusing to note *how* untrue the former is. How many of us have witnessed the birth of even a single rabbit? And of those who have, will it not be true that they have perceived *many* more rabbits than births of rabbits. However, let that pass: there has been a constant conjunction between the coming to be of new rabbits (so far as we have experienced this) and the presence of mother rabbits; suppose we claim that this constant (i.e. no counter example) experience of the conjunction between the coming to be of a rabbit and the presence of a mother rabbit is enough to lead us to our expectation that every rabbit that came to be will have had a mother — how does this and similar examples for other species lead us to expect *a cause* for *any beginning of existence*? It would seem, if they do, that the examples are examples of more than their own generalisations: *new rabbits come from mother rabbits* will be *one* generalisation, and *beginnings of existence come from prior causes* a different one. We do not get what we need: an account of how the specific generalisations lead us on to the more generic ones.

VIII. Causes and belief in what is not present to the senses or memory.

For several sections now, Hume is concerned with the nature of belief in anything beyond what is present to the senses or memory. ''Tis only causation', he had said in Section II, 'which produces such a connexion, as to give us assurance from the existence or action of one object, that 'twas follow'd or preceded by any other existence or action.'[23] And this belief of his determines some of his arguments about the correct account to give of cause and effect. For example, he dismisses the move of saying that constant conjunction suggests a power in the cause to produce the effect: the suggestion is useless, for how do we know that the cause will go on having the power? [24] To be sure, he considers this move in the context of discussion of the 'inference from the impression [sc. of one thing] to the idea [sc. of another thing]'; but the discussion of this topic (in Section VI) furthers his analysis of causality: the relation of cause and effect is thought of as essentially a principle of association of ideas whereby such inferences are made. That is: it being such a principle is treated implicitly as part of the account to be given of the very notion of cause.

Section VI is interesting but confused, as Hume speaks of reasonings from causes to effects when he seems really to mean reasonings from effects to causes. The presentation also turns out to be very elliptical.

---

[23] *Op.cit.* pp. 73–74.
[24] See *op.cit.* pp. 90–91.

> When we infer effects from causes, we must establish the exis-
> tence of these causes ... either by an immediate perception of our
> memory or senses, or by an inference from other causes; which
> causes again we must ascertain in the same manner, either by a
> present impression, or by an inference from *their* causes, and so
> on, till we arrive at some object, which we see or remember. 'Tis
> impossible for us to carry on our inferences *in infinitum*; and the
> only thing that can stop them, is an impression of the memory or
> senses, beyond which there is no room for doubt or enquiry.[25]

Inferring effects from causes, which are themselves effects from
causes ... etc, until we come to some cause which is seen or remembered, would seem to be *prognoses* from what is seen or remembered.
But in illustration Hume invites us

> to chuse any point of history, and consider for what reason we
> either believe or reject it. Thus we believe that CAESAR was
> kill'd in the senate-house on the *ides* of *March*; and that because
> this fact is establish'd on the unanimous testimony of historians
> ... Here are certain characters and letters ... the signs of certain
> ideas, and these ideas were either in the minds of such as were
> immediately present at that action ...; or they were deriv'd from
> the testimony of others, and that again from another testimony
> ... till we arrive at those who were eye-witnesses and spectators
> of the event.

This line of thought does indeed sound like deriving the effect, our
perception of certain characters and letters, from an original cause
which was an object of (someone's) direct perception. But the trouble is that that original cause is not an object that *we, now*, see or
remember. If this were to be taken as inferring effects from a cause
which 'we' see, then 'we' is mankind, represented by the original
witnesses. Hume must have been aware of some difficulty at this
point, though he does not sort it out. Rather he goes on: "Tis obvious
all this chain of argument or connexion of causes and effects is at
first founded on those characters or letters which are seen or
remember'd.' But this is not to infer effects from causes, i.e. to believe
in effects on grounds of belief in the causes, but rather to infer causes
from effects.

   The confused presentation at first sight seems unnecessary. Surely
it was of no real importance to Hume to call this an instance of inferring effects from causes rather than causes from effects? The confusion perhaps rests on a certain ambiguity in the expression 'inferring

[25] *Op.cit.* pp. 82–83.

effects from causes'. One might call it inferring an effect from a cause if one suggested *that the effect was derived* from a certain cause. But in that sense the effect is not what one comes to believe in because the cause is given in perception or memory.

Let us then assume a correction of the passage, thus: 'When we infer effects from causes, or causes from effects, we must establish the existence of those causes, or of those effects (as the case may be).' The historical example could then be presented as an inference of the original cause from its remote effect, the present memory or perception of 'certain characters or letters'. Though this would be consistent and coherent, it must be admitted that it loses something in convincingness; for there is *something* right about the picture of the information *deriving from* the original eyewitness. Only it will not suit Hume's purpose; so it seems we must charitably adopt the impoverished but at least coherent amended version I have proposed.

Taking this as the right re-construe, then, the argument is fairly straightforward: we believe in the killing of Caesar in the Senate House because we infer it as ultimate cause in a chain of causality terminating in our perception of 'certain characters and letters'. Waiving the question (to be considered later) whether this is a reasonable account of belief in historical testimony, we may grant there *is* a chain of causality terminating in that perception, and that it is because of our perception of sentences telling us of that event that we believe it.

But, now, what has become of Hume's argument about the impossibility of an infinite chain? The *end* of the chain is the death of Caesar or the perception of it by eyewitnesses, *not* our perception; *that* was surely the beginning of the inference! So after all there was reason to conceive the chain running the other way. But then how do we justify the starting point? Our charitable reconstruction has misfired.

We must suppose ourselves to start with the familiar idea, merely as idea, of Caesar having been killed. Now if we ask why we believe it we shall, as Hume does, point to historical testimony (the 'characters and letters'), which doesn't at this point figure as what stops inference going on *ad infinitum*. However, if we want to explain the connection we shall form the idea of Caesar's death being recorded by eyewitnesses; and these records having been received by others, who transmitted an account ... etc. Here we really are arguing from the *idea* of an original cause to the *idea* of an effect; we *are* 'inferring effects from causes', though only in the sense of passing from the idea of the cause to the idea of the effect.

Now what is the force of Hume's saying: "Tis impossible for us to carry on our inferences *in infinitum*; and the only thing that can stop them, is an impression of the memory or senses'? Why is it impossible for us to carry on our inferences *in infinitum*? Is it just that we are unequal to it? No: for in that case the inferences would stop from sheer inanition; Hume would not invoke an impression of the memory or senses as 'the only thing that can stop them'.

I said: 'we really *are* inferring effects from causes' — when, that is, we start from the idea of Caesar's death and then think of eyewitness reports and records made from them and records made from them, etc. Now there really is no difficulty about going on *ad infinitum*, or at any rate about saying 'and so on *ad infinitum*', if the 'inferring' is simply deriving the idea of the effect from that of the cause. But the inferring is more than that — it is *believing*. It is in connection with *this* that Hume is saying 'this chain can't go on for ever'.

Let *p* be 'Caesar was killed in the Senate'; and *q* be 'There were eyewitness reports of Caesar's killing'; and *r* be 'There were records made which derived from the eyewitness reports'; and *s* be 'There were records made which derived from records made which derived from eyewitness reports'. Suppose that in justification of my belief I say 'If *p*, *q*, and if *q*, *r*, and if *r*, *s*.' This chain does not give me belief unless it terminates in a consequent *t*, which I can affirm, and then return from, saying: if *t*, then *s*, and if *s* then *r*, and if *r* then *q*, and if *q* then *p*.

The point at which there comes the argument "Tis impossible … to carry on inferences *in infinitum*' is thus in the middle, where we said 'The chain does not give belief unless it terminates'!

Hume was not thinking of a series of implications, '*If p*, then *q*', but of a series of inferences '*Since p*, then *q* etc' and he is saying: *this* chain of inferences cannot go on for ever. The 'Since *p*' could not express belief in *p* if the chain did not terminate. He would, I suppose, have no objection to a chain of purely hypothetical reasonings going on for ever (or being rounded off with 'and so on *ad infinitum*'). But there is 'in them neither any present impression, nor belief of a real existence'.

His argument then falls into two parts. First, a chain 'Since *p*, *q*, etc' in which *p* gives a believed-in (*not* perceived) cause and *q* an inferred effect, cannot go on for ever but must terminate in a proposition that is believed without inferring any consequences from it; and from this proposition we then work back in reverse order to p.[26]

This is a particular form of a familiar argument that not everything can be argued from something else, that is: that it cannot be the case that everything *is* argued from something else. I believe p because I believe q because I believe r because I believe s – *this cannot go on for ever; it must end in something which I believe, not* because I believe something else. This argument appears to be correct. Proofs must have unproved starting points; definitions be in undefined terms, explanations must come to an end somewhere. For circular proofs, definitions, and explanations fail to prove, define, or explain to someone not yet convinced, not yet instructed in meanings, not yet understanding. So significant proof, definition and explanation cannot be circular; and until a terminus is reached, we do not know what the proof, definition or explanation amounts to.

Hume's second point is that not merely must the chain that he is concerned with come to an end somewhere, but its terminus must be of a different kind from the other members.

> … without the authority either of the memory or the senses our whole reasonings wou'd be chimerical and without foundation. Every link of the chain wou'd in that case hang upon another; but there wou'd not be anything fix'd to one end of it, capable of sustaining the whole; and consequently there wou'd be no belief or evidence.[27]

The picture is that of a chain which must be nailed by and to something different from the links of which it is composed. As the picture swims before the imagination, the chain even so hangs forlornly down – one remembers that hint of a *nailing* at the other end, where there were eyewitnesses of Caesar's assassination. But Hume cannot give us *that* picture. For the picture that he can give us, the ordinary idea of a dangling chain is unfortunate: that of a cantilever would be more satisfying. And no doubt the supported structure in a cantile-

---

[26] The whole passage is very curious; if one does not consider it quite closely and attentively, its incoherence, its need of emendation, quite escapes one's notice. Upon examination, we note the curious fact that there is not here any explanation of our originally forming the idea of, say, Caesar's death in the Senate. It is only if we *have* that idea already that we can argue 'from causes to effects', which the argument really does require us to do in that very example, for only taken in that direction is there a chain which 'must terminate' in an impression of our own memory or sense.

[27] *Op.cit.* p. 83.

ver construction could consist of a succession of blocks each of which interlocked rigidly with its predecessor.

But the other end *ought* to be nailed. That is, *historical testimony* is no use unless it derives in the end from witnesses. So there is after all a 'this can't go on *ad infinitum*' in the other direction too. Yet on Hume's view, the very necessary witnessing at the other end of the chain must itself be only the far end of what is supported by the present 'characters and letters'.

The second part of his argument, which says that the terminus must be of a different character from the links of the chain, is more doubtful than the first part which only says there must be a terminus. Hume does not think that I have to have a present perception (of memory or sense) in connection with my belief that Caesar was killed in the Senate House: we can 'reason upon our past conclusions and principles, without having recourse to those impressions from which they first arose.' The convictions, however, must have been *produced* by impressions, and 'all reasonings concerning causes and effects are originally deriv'd from some impression'.[28] It is indeed rather convenient *not* to have recourse to impressions! So, we do not have to be more than vague about the origination of the convictions, do not have to show how the impressions have it in them to generate the convictions. For in Hume's psychology his principle that anything may cause anything plays a part: the *content* of the impressions matters for the *ideas* they can give rise to.

No doubt I could not have my present conviction that Plato wrote philosophical dialogues without having had a good many relevant sense perceptions — I mean, among others, sense perceptions such as one has when one hears the word 'Plato'. But that 'the belief is derived from those sense impressions' — that is a more doubtful, indeed a thoroughly obscure statement. The most we can be confident of is that the perception of sentences about Plato is a *sine qua non* of a man's now having any beliefs about Plato. But to say that these beliefs are reached by inference from those perceptions is to say far more.

How could it be justified? Echoing Hume, we say: Here are certain sounds, characters or letters which we remember to have been used as signs of certain ideas. Reverting to the example of Caesar's death, a single episode and so easier to deal with, we may suppose the perceptions to be of various passages in various books. What does it mean to say 'We remember them to have been used as signs of cer-

[28] *Op.cit.* p. 84.

tain ideas'? That is a crucial step: that gives us the association in experience between an A and a B which is the basis for later supposing a B when we experience an A. The type A here is *such and such letters and characters*; the type B is *use as signs of such and such ideas*.

Use by whom, ourselves or others? If by ourselves, the memory is intelligible, but the use of it to infer a use by others (essential to a claim of record) seems unjustified. If by others, then we need an account of how we originally recognised that someone else was using a character as the sign of an idea. It ought to be something experienced if it can then be remembered, but how on Hume's view can 'we' experience *someone else's using a character as sign of an idea*? Remember that Hume denies that we perceive causation. How then can he suppose we perceive *this*?

This is an example of what happens many times with Hume. His analysis in one area depends on his saying things which, from his analysis in another area, it is not at all clear he can say; or, at any rate, it is not at all clear what they would amount to on application of his doctrines.

Let us note, but pass over, this difficulty. Those who find Hume broadly right will at this point vaguely sketch in their minds a theory of other minds within which there is an account of finding certain characters used as signs of certain ideas, and of the vast extension of this to create and apply the ideas of historical records extending to past ages. To others it will be one more objection, of a particular pattern, to Hume's whole system; again and again they will remember and half echo Schopenhauer's 'He must be forsaken by all the gods who dreams that the world we see outside of us ... should stand there ... and thereupon through the instrumentality of mere sensation should enter our head.' Schopenhauer was arguing for Kantian idealism against the idea of an independent objective reality: the objective world, he thinks, must be the *creation* of the understanding. But his complaint stands equally against Hume, who would account for our knowledge of history by our sensations and certain associative habits.

To my mind the interest of Hume lies primarily in the problems he consciously or unconsciously discovers to us. Here there is a problem unconsciously raised. For Hume judges that we believe Caesar was killed in the Senate House from the testimony of historians. (Is that *testimony*?) And he thinks that this belief is explained as our reasoning from our perception of 'certain characters and letters', through successive steps referring to intermediate records, back to the perception of eyewitnesses and through that to the event. He supposes that the record before our eyes is our reason for believing in the intermediate records, which are in turn our reason for believing in the eyewitness report, which in turn is our reason for believing in the original event. He must suppose this, otherwise it would not be possible for him, however confusedly, to cite the chain of record back to the eyewitnesses as an illustration of the chain of causes and effects with which we cannot run up *in infinitum*, but must eventually bring to an end with our present perception or memory of written documents.

But it is not like this at all. If the written records that we see are our grounds for belief, they are first and foremost grounds for belief in the original event, and then our belief in the original event is a ground for belief in the intermediate transmission. For let us ask: why do we believe there *were* eyewitnesses? Certainly because we believe that the event happened. Therefore the belief in the event is not based on belief that there were eyewitnesses. I have heard that the Rabbis hold that the six hundred thousand witnesses to the crossing of the Red Sea must be credited; 600,000 witnesses — that is *very sure* witness! And now let us ask: why do they *believe* there were 600,000? Because they *believe* 600,000 passed through.

There is an interesting comparison to be made here with our belief in the spatio-temporal continuity of the existence of a man we recognise now and identify as a man we saw last week. We do not believe this is the man we saw last week because we observe the spatio-temporal continuity of the human pattern from the man last week to the man we see now. Rather, we believe in the spatio-temporal continuity of a body of this kind from then and there to now and here because we believe this is the same man. What *is* true is that proof of a break in the continuity — a proof that this man was in New York in between, while that man was not — would destroy our belief in the identity. And the same holds for the chain of tradition of record.

Our belief in recorded history is a belief *that there has been* a chain of tradition of reports and records: it is not a belief in the historical facts *through* the links of such a chain. At most, that can *very seldom* be the case.

The interesting problem that arises, then, is why the things we are told and the writings that we see *are* the starting points for our belief in the far distant events and so in the intermediate chain of record. This is a question of vast importance. But the consideration of it would take us far away from that investigation of Hume on cause which has been our present business. I take it as sufficiently demonstrated that Hume's account is wrong. (One may be convinced of that without thinking that one has an alternative account.)

Not only is Hume's account wrong, but it is irremediable within his system of philosophy. More narrowly, it is irremediable within his philosophy of belief. The reasoning would have to be as he describes it, if his account of the relation of cause and effect, and the relation of that relation to belief, were correct.[*]

---

[*] The discussion of Hume ends half way through the second notebook referred to in the first editorial footnote. The remainder of that notebook is taken up with Anscombe's own analysis of beliefs about the past. There are directions in her handwriting that the typescript about Hume should end where the present text ends.

PART 2

RECENT &

CONTEMPORARY

11

Frege, Wittgenstein and Platonism

When people call Frege a Platonist, one thing they have in mind is that he believed that numbers are objects. Some, ignorant of his writings more than I am, think that he believed that concepts were objects too. He is famous for having said 'The concept horse is not a concept'; less famous for having thought the matter out further and written to the effect that e.g. 'is what "horse" means' is equivalent to 'is a horse'. The essay didn't get published, it just got a rejection slip.

I draw attention now to part of one of his greatest lectures, published as an article in 1891, 'Funktion und Begriff'. He tells us there what was originally understood in mathematics by the word 'function'. He remarks:

> To this question one may well get as answer: 'By a function of x was understood a mathematical expression containing x, a formula which includes the letter x.' According to this explanation, for example, the expression
>
> $2.x^3 + x$
>
> would be a function of x, and
>
> $2.2^3 + 2$
>
> a function of 2. This answer cannot do, because in it form and content, sign and signified are not distinguished, an error which is often found in mathematical writings, even in celebrated authors, at the present day.

Referrring to his *Grundlagen der Arithmetik*, he says he has already

---

* From an undated manuscript without title. Title supplied.

pointed to the lack of viable formal theories in arithmetic. Signs with no content, and which aren't supposed to have any never-theless have properties attributed to them which can intelligibly attach only to the content of a sign. So here: a mere expression, the form for a content, cannot be the essence of the matter: only the content can be that. Now what is the content, the meaning of '$2.2^3 + 2$'? The same as of '18' or of '3.6'.

All these expressions stand for — *bedeuten* — the same thing.
Frege says he must set his face against

the opinion that for example 2 + 5 and 3 + 4, while equal, are not the same. In this opinion again, at bottom, resides that same con-fusion of form and content, of sign and signified. It's like saying that the sweet smelling violet and *viola odorata* are different because the names sound different. Difference of designation by itself is insufficient to ground a difference in what is designated. Here the matter is less transparent *only* because the meaning of the numeral 7 isn't anything perceptible to the senses. The pres-ent widespread inclination to acknowledge nothing as an object that cannot be perceived by the senses tempts in this case to take the numerals *themselves* for the numbers, for the proper objects of consideration, and then of course 7 and 2 + 5 would be different. But such a conception is untenable, because it is quite impossible to speak of any arithmetical properties of numbers without going back to the meaning [the *Bedeutung*] of the numerals. The prop-erty that 1, for example, yields itself when multiplied by itself, would be a mere fantasy: however far you carry a microscopic examination or chemical investigation, you could never discover *this* property in the innocent character that we call the numeral 'one'. Perhaps a definition is spoken of — but *no* definition is cre-ative in such a way as to be able to impart properties to a thing which it hasn't got, apart from the one property of expressing and signifying what the definition introduces it as a sign of.

I am reminded of the passage where Frege, discussing the views of someone who said numbers *were* numerals, and who spoke of a number as getting constantly smaller, said 'I see what you mean' and printed a row of sevens, smaller and smaller across the page. I am reminded again of how Frege, in discussing people who explain numbers in terms of units, asks whether the units in 1 + 1 = 2 are the same or different — if the same, how can one say 'one and one'? Can one say 'The moon and the moon'? *What* is going on? And if they are different, what is it all about? And I am reminded of Socrates in the *Phaedo* saying he can't understand how addition and division (both) are supposed to turn one into two. When I read the introduction to Frege's *Grundlagen* my spirit bounded with the recognition of a brother to Socrates as so depicted by Plato.

Returning to 'Funktion und Begriff': a bit further on, Frege remarks that

$(1+1) + (1+1) + (1+1) = 6$, and so $(1+1)$ is the number designated by 6:3.

The different expressions correspond to different *conceptions* and *aspects* but still always to the same thing. Otherwise the equation $x^2 = 4$ would not just have the roots 2 and –2 but also 1+1 and innumerable others, distinct from one another though similar in a certain respect. In acknowledging that there are just two real roots one is *rejecting* the opinion that the equals sign means not a perfect co-incidence but only a *partial* agreement. Hanging on to this, we see that the expressions

'$2.1^3 + 1$'

'$2.2^3 + 2$'

'$2.4^3 + 4$'

mean numbers, namely 3, 18 and 132. If a function were really the meaning of a mathematical expression a function would just *be* a number, and nothing new would have been attained for arithmetic. Of course in connection with the word 'function' one usually has in mind expressions in which a number is only indefinitely indicated by the letter x, e.g.

'$2.x^3 + x$'

but that doesn't make any difference; for this whole expression too indicates a number only indefinitely, and whether I write down this expression or just x makes no essential difference.

All the same [he goes on], this fact about the indefinite indication by 'x' does lead us in the right direction. That indefinite indicator 'x' is called the argument of the function and we recognise the same function, but with distinct different arguments in

'$2.1^3 + 1$'

'$2.4^3 + 4$'

'$2.5^3 + 5$'

Here the arguments are 1, 4 and 5. From this we can see that the proper essence of the function resides in what is common to these expressions, that is to say, in what is present in

'$2.x^3 + x$'

apart from the letter x — which we might also write as follows

'$2.(\ )^3 + (\ )$'

Frege 'wants to show that the argument doesn't belong with the function as part of it but *together with* the function forms a complete whole'.

What, stopping here, can we learn from these considerations of Frege's? Two things spring out. First, a similarity of form of expression does not necessarily betoken a similarity of what is expressed. Example: understood as expression of a function

'$2.x^3 + x$'

is quite different in meaning from

'$2.2^3 + 2$'

Secondly, a function need not be signified by a sign which is to be found in every expression in which that function is expressed. The function was the same in

$2.1^3 + 1$

and $2.4^3 + 4$

and $2.5^3 + 5$

not because of a particular sign designating the function, but because of what is common to those expressions. The fact that we might define φ as a function sign such that

$\varphi(4) =_{\text{Def.}} (2.4^3) + 4$

or more generally

$\varphi(x) =_{\text{Def.}} (2.x^3) + x$

does not mean that anything false has been said in identifying this function as what, beyond (x), is common to expressions of that form. Supplied with arguments they give *values* of that function, which are numbers.

Let me sum up these two lessons thus:

> the first is a principle of the possible non-identity of mode of signification of expressions which look and are significantly similar.

> The second is a principle of identities being possibly visible only to the intellect.

I don't mean that Frege started out from these principles as premises; rather he exhibited their truth in his reasoning. They will have been clear to him from when he wrote *Begriffschrift*.

Frege works through in the same article to the conclusion that a concept is a function from objects to truth-values. Here I am not especially concerned with this part of his work for my topic here is Wittgenstein. I have shown what I think there is in calling Frege a Platonist. This is for me the interest of the question: is Wittgenstein anti-Platonist and more particularly anti-essentialist? It might be thought that he was anti-Platonist from the story he told of asking Frege 'Don't you see any difficulty in calling numbers objects?' To which Frege replied: 'Sometimes I seem to see a difficulty, and then again I don't see it'. Wittgenstein thought that this was a typical expression of a certain sort of thing that happens to one in doing philosophy. He was not excluding himself from this generalisation.

Frege reaches the account of a concept as a function from objects to truth-values via his addition of =, > and < to the functions +, −, exponentiation, ÷, etc. that he has been considering. The values of these functions are of course numerical; the values of the new functions are truth and falsehood, and so he introduces the terminology of truth-values (which comes from him) so he comes to functions, which he calls concepts, that often are not numerical at all.

His conception was rich and fruitful. Wittgenstein could not be supposed to object to the material I have been expounding up to *this* point about concepts; but here there is certainly a break. Frege's conception involves regarding sentences as complex names of truth-values; it also involves a certain equality on the part of the two truth values: it is as if they were there to be designated independently of the construction of their designations. Whatever one may say about truth this appears highly objectionable about falsehood. Already in the *Tractatus Logico-Philosophicus* Wittgenstein had objected to both of these things — explicitly to Frege's taking a sentence to be a complex name, but also in rejecting the notion that truth and falsehood are *equally justified* relations between signs and what is signified. Not that he is there assuming that the 'signified' in the case of propositions are the two truth-values; it is the equality of justification between truth and falsehood that he objects to. He objects to this *whatever* is thought to be signified by sentences.

However the part of Frege's work in 'Funktion und Begriff' which I have identified as Platonist — that stands. So far as I know, the only places where Wittgenstein considers the expression itself to be *what it expresses* are *aesthetic*. A musical phrase, a bed of violets: such things may strongly give one the impression that they *tell* one something. What is it that they tell one? They tell one *themselves*, not something else.

At the beginning of the *Philosophische Untersuchungen* Wittgenstein describes a simple proceeding in the use of words. I ask a greengrocer for five red apples; I give him a slip of paper with these words so written on it. The shopkeeper

> opens the drawer marked 'apples'; then he looks at a colour table for the word 'red' and finds a colour sample by it; now he utters the series of cardinal numbers (he knows them by heart) up to the word 'five', and at each numeral he takes an apple out of the drawer whose colour is that of the colour sample. … How does he know where to look up the word 'red' and what to do with the word 'five'? — Well, I assume he *acts* as I have described. Explanations come to an end somewhere. — But what is the meaning of the word 'five'? — No such thing came into the matter; only how the word 'five' gets used.†

I take it we should say: gets used *in such* and *similar* cases. If we are counting how many prime numbers come before twenty, *one* which we shall count is the number five. It has to be the *number* which is counted, for the property of being prime, Frege surely showed us, cannot belong to the *numeral*. Is 5 an object here, then, though no such object made its appearance in the transaction with the greengrocer?

I would say that Wittgenstein never — so far as I can tell — got that question really sorted out. In the *Philosophische Grammatik* he compares the feeling that Three is an object with the feeling or conviction that understanding is a *process*. But so far as I know he does not anywhere *show* that it is a grammatical illusion, as he does succeed in doing about understanding being a process.

The words 'Five red apples' are each of a different category. One learns the word 'red' as name of a colour, yet things one calls 'red' aren't all in every sense the same colour. But in counting one doesn't *call* anything 'five', say. If one were teaching a child to count, using oranges and pears as objects to be counted, and the child said 'But last time you called that pear "one", why are you calling an orange "one" now and that pear "three"?' he would not have so much as *begun* to grasp the grammar, the technique of application, of numer-

---

† *Philosophical Investigations*, §1.

als in counting. When one counts prime numbers one utters numerals and might be thought to be counting the numerals standing for prime numbers, as when one counts distinct printed words. But if one includes 'nine' one has made a mistake which can only be shown by considering the number: '9', it will be said, 'is not prime, it is 3×3'. Evidently one is not talking about the numeral, which cannot be said to have the property of being prime or of having factors.

'Essence', Wittgenstein said, 'is expressed by grammar'. It's been supposed that he meant something different by the word 'grammar' from what is ordinarily meant. Well, for what it is worth, I can testify that he claimed not to mean anything different. I heard him in class saying 'What I mean by "grammar" is what you mean by it, what you heard lessons in at school'. Now at school the grammar we learned, if it was not Latin declensions and conjugations and what cases are taken by this or that preposition, and what genders various nouns are, and if it was not syntax, was an exercise called 'parsing'. You learned what to call nouns and verbs and participles and conjunctions and adjectives and adverbs and to say what 'governed' what in a sentence, and you were given sentences which you had to parse – that is, say what was subject, what predicate, what direct or indirect object, what was an adjective attaching to what or used attributively, and so on. It was mildly interesting but it didn't go very far. I knew a child, who had been taught that an *adjective* was a word describing what something is like; encountering a sentence which had the phrase 'two boys' in it, she wondered what part of speech to call the word 'two'; it surely didn't say anything about what the boys were like. So she asked her teacher, who simply said 'Call it an adjective'. The grammar she was being exercised in was very superficial, of course. Being intelligent in her difficulty, it was no wonder that she took to philosophy later on. Plato was about the first grammarian (unless the Sanskrit grammarian Panini was earlier than he, which I think he wasn't quite; but anyway there is no connection between them). Plato in the *Sophist* invented the distinction between a noun and a verb or predicate – what you are talking about and what your sentence is saying about it: ὄνομα and ρημα. He had earlier come to think that a sentence, a λογος, is a complex, a complex of names, συμπλοκη ὀνοματων. There are exceptions to this like a shout of 'Fire!' But it was a big advance in philosophy to see the essential complexity of most λογοι.

Now a really serious and comprehensive book of grammar would treat *numerals* in a separate chapter. Here the more important part would be the *grammar* which expresses the essence of what we call, say, the natural numbers. Frege's remark that a numeral can't have the property of yielding itself when multiplied by itself is a grammatical remark; the child's observation that 'two boys' doesn't profess to say what any boys are *like* was a grammatical observation. It was in this way that Wittgenstein spoke of grammar and it is clearly an extension of the grammar you learn — if you learn any these days — as school children.

Now why is the assumption that 'to understand' stands for a process a grammatical illusion? Why should it be thought to be a process? May it not at least be an *event*? 'I suddenly understood' we may say. And don't we also say 'I began to gradually understand what he was talking about'? That *sounds* like a process, just as the other *sounds* like an event. But consider the following: 'What are you doing? What's going on here?' Answer: 'I'm working out the square root of 1729'; and compare it with: 'What's going on here? What are you doing?' Answer: 'Understanding the rules of chess'. That won't do: one would have to say 'getting to understand'. *That* takes time.

Lewis Carroll makes Alice say: 'You can't believe the impossible' and the Red Queen reply: 'With practice you can. With practice I can believe six impossible things before breakfast every day.' This is a grammatical joke, a deep one, because it is about the depth grammar of the verb 'to believe'.

The novelist Charles Dickens makes a contribution to the depth grammar of the verb 'to mean'. Harold Skimpole orders lamb chops from his butcher to whom he owes a lot of money. The butcher sighs and says 'I wish I meant chops the way you mean pounds'. 'Oh, but you can't', says Skimpole. 'You can't mean chops and not give me them, because you've *got* chops. But I can mean pounds and not pay you pounds because I haven't got any pounds.'

Now what is the grammatical illusion in regarding numbers as objects? People call Frege a Platonist partly for this view, and it's not unreasonable to do so. The word in Greek would be οὐσίαι which Plato said the forms are; Aristotle stole the word for his philosophy and it became the Greek we translate mostly as 'substance'. Cabbages and cats and men are substances in that philosophy; Plato didn't think they were οὐσίαι — really real beings. Those were forms and though we learn that the Platonists didn't think there was a form of *number* it is certain that Socrates is represented as thinking there was a form of two, three, four, etc.

That we speak of numbers, not numerals, when we say e.g. '2 is the only even prime' is perfectly clear: Frege made it so, or re-established its clarity in what I have quoted. Are there essences expressed by the grammar of numerals? Surely. It belongs to the grammar of the *term* 'numeral' that a numeral names, designates, but is not, a number. Or if you prefer: is a sign *for* a number. And what is the essence expressed by the grammar of 'Three'? Well, what it is a sign for has the property of being odd, not even; and this property does not change. That there is a procedure called 'taking two away from it' which we teach children and which leaves *one*. That it is the first number of the natural numbers such that a group of that number can be called 'several'. That it therefore can be called the number of a group of things whose number can be seen and counted.

Several of the features of the grammar of 'Three' are common to many numbers, and sometimes what I have said sounds as if Three were indeed an object, — e.g. when I spoke of 'taking two away from *it*'; doesn't the 'it' suggest an object? Yes, it does — as a matter of superficial grammar. But when we think of the procedure and what a remarkable thing we teach a child to do, which we call 'taking *x* away from *y*', does it not appear that the initial appearance of an 'it' that one has done something to, is a sort of grammatical hallucination? I think it does and that *this* appearance is no illusion.

If the grammar of certain terms expresses essences, the mastery of their grammar is an indication of a grasp of essences, and essences can never be grasped except by intellect.

Now: was Wittgenstein an 'essentialist'? To the extent that I have described, yes. But he toyed with the idea of peoples — tribes — whose languages contained expressions of *different* concepts from ours — colour-shape concepts, for example, without concepts of colour or of shape. Would they be *missing* something? Well, he remarks that you don't always have a word for something just because you can see it. They'd be missing a hunk of language, but that doesn't mean they'd be colour blind. Are *we* missing something because we don't have colour-shape concepts? In this sort of questioning there is a suggestion that essences *depend* on grammar. He did not say: Essences 'are created by grammar', only 'are expressed by grammar'. What is implied for my question I have to leave unanswered.

12

On Russell's Theory
of Descriptions

I shall argue

1. that Russell's Theory of Descriptions, definite and indefinite, is correct in the sense that the analysis he offers of propositions containing denoting phrases in subject-positions is right and useful at least outside the foundations of mathematics;

2. that he is wrong in that conception of 'logically proper names' which demands the existence of a logically guaranteed bearer for every real proper name;

3. that he is wrong in his belief that propositions cannot change their truth-value.

I shall argue for these positions in the reverse order to that in which I have given them.

I

In *The Principles of Mathematics* Russell explains 'Change is the difference, in respect of truth or falsehood, between a proposition concerning an entity and a time T and a proposition concerning an entity and another time T', provided that the two propositions differ only by the fact that T occurs in the one where T' occurs in the other.' It is clear what he means: if and only if, given a proposition 'φ (*a*) at t' and another 'φ (*a*) at t'', one true and the other false, there is no other difference between them, then a change has taken place or is taking place or will take place. We ought to concede that certain differences

---

* From an undated typescript with the author's handwritten insertions and corrections. It appears to date from the 1950s. The explicit argument of the paper applies to definite descriptions only; to indefinite ones by implication.

between propositions would be irrelevant — e.g. that one was to be found (stated) at one place in a book and another at another; for these differences most often do not express anything and we may suppose that they do not here.

I do not unreservedly accept Russell's account; it seems to suggest that there can only be change where there is a nameable individual which persists through the change, the change consisting in something's holding of that individual at one time which does not hold at another time; and this seems doubtful. But let us accept it for the moment.

A time specification such as is needed for Russell's explanation must give a stage in a process which is used as a clock; most usually it would give a stage in the nth period from some point of origin. The point of origin would be so many periods ago; thus all time specifications will depend in some way on 'now'.

Disregarding this, however, let the clock we actually use be the 'entity' of which Russell speaks in his account of change. Let our clock be e.g. the sun, and the sentence 'The sun is in the middle of the sky' be a specification of time, like 'It's two o'clock'. If we consider the proposition 'The sun is in the middle of the sky' we must say that it is sometimes true and sometimes false. We could find another clock to give a time at which it was true and at which it was false, but certainly do not need to do so in order to state the change that takes place. Russell would say that 'The sun is in the middle of the sky', if it is a complete proposition, means 'The sun is in the middle of the sky now'; and that this is a different proposition at each time it is said; or again, he would say that 'now' means 'the time of this', 'this' being used as a name of something different every time it is used; for its only constant feature is its relation to its user.

Now it is possible that someone may want to attack Russell, on the ground that 'now' and 'this' are not names. But the following formulation of Russell's point might be accepted by such a critic: 'the word "now" is used to *refer* to a different time every (relevantly) different time it is used'; and 'the word "this" is constantly used to *refer to* different objects'.

This formulation is not to my mind importantly different from Russell's. I should contend that in such statements the word 'reference' is being used in a way that wavers between an argumentative (and incorrect) application of its ordinary sense, and a technical sense in which it ought to be restricted to proper names. Russell's formulation is more clear cut.

'Refer', like 'mention', in ordinary language is a thoroughly vague word. This can be seen from the following example. In a conversation it might be said 'He turned very red'; and someone who was checking reports of the conversation might ask 'Was any reference made to the colour of his face?' and get the answer 'Yes', because of that remark.

Similarly, it might be asked 'Was there any mention of the time at which he was in England?' and answered 'Yes, Mr. N. made some reference to that — I think he said something about its having been in the first week of July'.

On the strength of this vague use of 'refer' it might be said that a date could be used to refer to a time; and if we speak of a proper name as being used to refer to, say, a place or person, and also of a demonstrative pronoun as being used to refer to a person etc., then by an easy transition of thought, we may speak of 'now' as being used to refer to a time; for 'now' is rather to a date as 'this' is to a proper name or definite description of an object. But in ordinary usage it would not be said that a time had been referred to because someone had said 'I think I had better be going now'.

I do not think the ordinary usage of 'refer' is of interest, except for the part it is apt to play in aiding the movement of thought I have just described.

What is of the greatest interest is a *technical* sense of 'refer' in which we may say that a proper name refers to its bearer. That is to say, the term 'refer' has been used for the relation between a proper name and its bearer. But the relation in question has been variously taken not to be restricted to ordinary proper names and their bearers. For Frege, a predicate — i.e. what is left of a sentence if you remove at least one proper name from it — also has reference: the reference of a predicate is a concept, not an object. He also held that a non-vacuous definite description referred to the object it described, and that whole sentences containing non-vacuous proper names and definite descriptions referred to the objects *true* and *false*. He held that definite descriptions and sentences of the kind described *were* proper names; so this part of his theory is not an extension of the notion of 'reference' beyond proper names but only of that of proper names beyond what are ordinarily so called; but he did not hold that predicates were proper names, so in this part of the theory there is an extension of the notion of reference itself. So far as I know, he does not discuss demonstratives, 'now', or personal pronouns. Russell holds that designating or naming is done by what he calls 'real'

proper names and words for ego-centric particulars but not by definite descriptions or sentences or predicates; others, that 'referring' is
done by means of all the candidates except predicates and sentences.
Exactly *what* it is that is done when referring is done is also a disputed matter; as also, what does the referring—a word, or only a person using a word. I.e. is referring in the soul alone, or also in the
grammar of sentences?

It seems fairly clear that proper names are at the centre of this
topic; for there is a relation between proper names and their bearers,
which is variously conceived by various philosophers and is also
variously conceived to hold between other expressions and various
kinds of thing. For Russell, it is not the relation between what are
usually called proper names and their bearers, but that is a rather
coarse, macroscopic indication of it. This is because the main feature
of a proper name is that it refers to a single thing of some sort or
other; but for Russell a thing like an individual man or city falls short
of really being a single object.

The most common view is that the technical sense of 'referring' or
'designating' in which we are interested is one in which only *individuals* are referred to or designated. But 'individual' and 'particular'
are rather problematic terms. Hence one wants to speak of 'an individual person' or 'a particular place' or 'a single object' or 'a particular event' (I am using Mr Strawson's list) and so on, in order to
explain what one is driving at. But don't we need a specification of
what sort of general term can come after the word 'a single ...' or 'a
particular ...' or 'an individual ...'? A particular constellation, such
as Orion, would seem to qualify; 'a particular colour' perhaps not—
but why not?; and how about 'a particular time', e.g. 'the eighth year
of the French Revolution'? If 'a particular time' qualifies, then is
'now' just like 'this', a word used to 'refer uniquely'? If so, then since
it can hardly fail to have reference, it presents us with a real example
of a 'logically proper name' in Russell's sense. But perhaps a particular time is *not* something that expressions can be used to 'refer to
uniquely'; in that case we need an account of the restrictions on the
kinds, particular ones of which can be made the objects of unique
reference.

I want to argue that neither Russell, nor anyone—if there is
anyone—who would reformulate Russell's point by saying that
different times are referred to by different uses of 'now', is right. The
appearance that 'now' refers to a time is produced as follows: the
question 'When is "now"?' has a good sense when asked in connec-

tion with an old letter, say, containing the sentence 'Such and such is happening now'. We find the date when the letter was written in order to know when the things it describes happened if what it says is true. Hence, in a quite non-technical way, we can say that the letter, the sentences and the words in it, refer to or relate to a particular time; the nature of the 'relating to' is not indicated in such a remark. It is quite another thing to say that the word 'now' in the letter refers to a particular time in a sharp, technical sense of 'refer'.

There are two possible views to this effect: according to both 'now' means 'the time of this'; according to one 'this' is to be explained as a token reflexive, and according to the other it is to be considered as naming anything the speaker likes to make his object of attention.

The token reflexive substitutions for 'now' are not wrong, and yet the associated explanation of the word 'now' cannot be correct; its persuasiveness derives from the fact that vocal utterances of the kind brought forward are of very short duration; they last no longer than the time required to take them in. On the token reflexive view, an ancient inscription running 'Say, O stranger, if you can, the date of my inscribing' raises a similar question for the traveller who is looking at it to the question of someone who approaches him and says 'What's the time, please?'.

The other explanation — that 'now' means 'the time of this' and 'this' is to be considered as naming anything the speaker is attending to — is faulty because he may be thinking of something in the distant past or future. However, someone who held this view would probably deny that, say, Aristotle can be an object of attention for me; he would say that only such things as an image of Aristotle or a page of Aristotle can be so. Leaving the difficult problems involved in such a dispute, let us reformulate the position by saying that 'now' means 'the time of this' when 'this' is used to name some object of sense-perception. Even if it is an antique temple, still it has to be admitted that its time includes the present if I can see it now.

This consideration brings out how much nearer to the truth the token reflexive view of 'now' is than this one; indeed on this view we cannot understand the word 'now' at all except when we are saying or hearing it used in relation to the time at which we are saying or hearing it; or else we have to bring in token reflexiveness to explain our general understanding of it, or our understanding of it in an old letter.

On the token reflexive view, 'What time is it now?' means 'What is the time at which these words are uttered?'; this question, however, is like the inscription's challenge — but seems not to be, because of the short duration of the utterance, which is simultaneous with its being taken in; this enables the hearer to accept the present tense of 'these words are uttered' as true. But on the token-reflexive view the 'are' here is not really a tense: it is a purely logical word.

The hearer of a speech containing 'as I utter these words' could tell himself 'he says he is uttering them — and so he is!' But that is accidental; if I get a letter saying 'Even as I write these words the children are starting another fight', I can't say to myself 'She says she's writing the words — and so she is'; and yet there is nothing misleading about the letter. The sentence in the letter has indeed just the same meaning as if it had run 'The children are now starting a fight'; and that is what is correct about the token reflexive view. But since 'now' could be replaced by 'the time of this', 'this' being understood token reflexively wherever it occurs in the relevant sense, I need the additional information that the time of the token's production is now if I am to understand a sentence containing 'now' to relate to now. The sentence itself cannot include this information in what it says. The procedures adopted by the traveller to answer the question posed by the inscription and to tell the enquirer the time are wholly different; for the inscription he tries to find a date, he does not look up the date for the time being in his calendar; in reply to the enquirer he looks at his watch straight away.

We must say 'now' always means the same, but a sentence containing the word 'now' does not say that what it says to be the case is the case now, unless it is uttered now. Sentences containing 'now' are uttered at various times; and we need to know when 'now' is or was being said in order to determine the truth of what is or was being said. And one answer to this question — which would hardly ever be asked when it was the answer — may be 'it is being said now'. (It might be the answer when the question was asked about a piece of ticker tape.) Only if it is said now does the truth of a sentence *p* whose tense is significantly present imply that *p*. This pronouncement relates to things said now. It can be generalised thus: at any time, this can be truly said: 'Only if it is said now, does the truth of a sentence *p* whose tense is significantly present imply that *p*.'

This shows the sense in which propositions cannot change their truth-value. If the expression 'The truth-value of a significantly tensed proposition' means: 'The truth-value of a proposition at the time of its being stated, when that time is relevant to the question as to the truth-speaking of the sayer', then that truth-value cannot change; and so also, when the specification of a date is included in a proposition, what it describes ceases to be significantly tensed; if the sentence is still significantly tensed, as in 'The third world war will break out on October 1st, 1962', it divides up into the dated, tenseless proposition 'Outbreak of third world was, October 1st, 1962' and 'October 1st, 1962, is yet to come'.

Reichenbach† says that quoted 'token reflexives' are not used 'token reflexively', which is correct. But unless hearing and understanding are considered to involve either a *token reflexive use of what is heard or understood,* or a *quotation of a token reflexive,* as the case may be, the point does not enable us to succeed, by an analysis of 'now' as token reflexive, in getting rid of propositions whose truth-value changes. Those who are convinced that the analysis does succeed in doing this are possibly influenced by a feeling of what it is to *mean* 'now'. One can be tempted to say to oneself 'Said *now,* 'now' means *now!*' The temptation arises partly from the idea that we can see what a word means by considering what we mean when we attentively go through the performance of *meaning* it; and partly from a supposition that it must be something meant by the isolated word 'now' that constitutes the meaning of a significantly tensed sentence whose time is the present. For it is quite correct to say 'Only if it is said now, does the truth of a significantly present-tensed sentence *p* imply that *p*'.

If something was the case at a certain time, then at that time anyone who said of the thing in question 'It is the case now' would have been speaking truly. This is one reason for the pre-eminent role of the present tense. It means nothing to suppose that something was the case or is going to be the case, and to exclude 'It is the case now' from having been or from going to be the truth. There might seem to be an analogue to this for the past and future tenses: if something is the case, then 'It will be the case' was true to say, and 'It was the case' will be true to say. But here we can ask 'When?', to which a reply '*Then!*' would raise the question 'When is then?'. It makes no sense to ask 'When is now?' except (a) to ask the time or date it now is, or (b) using 'now' in quotes in connection, say, with an old letter in which 'now' occurs.

Propositions about changeable things are variable in truth-value, because in order to explain the sense in which they are invariable in

---

† The reference presumably is to Hans Reichenbach, *Elements of Symbolic Logic* (New York: Free Press, 1947). [Ed.]

truth-value, either you must give an incorrect account of 'now' and the present tense, or you must introduce the idea of 'the truth value of a proposition at a time'; but that is to admit variability of truth-value. The invariability of the truth-value of a proposition is the trivial fact that a dated proposition cannot vary in truth-value. When I say that the truth-value of a proposition at the time of its being stated (supposing that to be relevant) cannot change, I only say that if it has a certain truth-value at the time of its being stated, it cannot come to have had a different one at that time; I do not say that it cannot cease to have the truth-value that it has at that time. On the contrary, if the time at which it is stated has any relevance to its truth-value, then it can come to have a different one. The universal denial of the variability of the truth-value of propositions is tantamount to a denial of change.

My account of 'now' may seem very slightly different — if at all — from Reichenbach's: it is not clear that a single sentence I have written conflicts with what he says. It comes out that there is a difference of view involved if we consider a principle which he puts forward elsewhere in his book: 'Two propositions have the same meaning if they obtain the same verification, as true or false, for all possible observations'. This is intended as an explanation of identity of meaning for propositions. I am saying that two propositions can be identical in every way, and hence one be merely the repetition of the other, and yet get different verifications as true and false.

Now since I should not call two identical sentences[1] *therefore* identical propositions, I have to give some account of propositional identity. Two identical sentences may not be identical propositions because, for example, identical names of different people might occur in them. This would make a difference of meaning, and hence, I should say, a difference of proposition. The view of 'now', and of tenses generally, that I have been attacking, is one in which two identical sentences containing tenses or 'now' have different meanings when said at different times; the difference being of the same kind as that between the differences of meaning between identical sentences containing a name 'John' when 'John' names a different man in each. That is to say, the difference is supposed to be a difference of reference in a sharp, technical, and very important sense of reference.

---

[1]   i.e. two propositional signs which are identical from the printer's point of view. This is a rough indication of something that can and need be only roughly indicated. Handwriting, different fonts, etc., do not count against this identity.

I do not have or desire any general account of the identity of propositions where the sentences to be considered are different. But
where the sentences are the same, I should say that the propositions
were the same so long as any proper name referred to the same bearers and the other words had the same meanings. Context may affect
meaning — it is indeed context that shows which the bearer of a name
is — but not just difference of time.

II

I now come to my second thesis: that a real proper name does not
have to have a logically guaranteed bearer.

Russell's idea of 'logical proper names' has a long history behind
it; it will help us to understand it if we go back to Locke and Mill.
Their views are very tangled, but of very great historical importance.
Taking Mill first, we recall his doctrine that proper names have no
connotation, only denotation, while predicates have both. Mill
explains that the bearer of a proper name is its denotation; the denotation of a predicate is the list of things that it applies to. He cannot
have it both ways; if the bearer is the denotation of a proper name,
then the list of things that it applies to is not the denotation of a predicate; for these are the things that the predicate is true of, and a proper
name is not anything that is true of its bearer; that, indeed, is a great
part of the point of insisting that proper names have no connotation.
And indeed in another place Mill inconsistently says that the denotation of a predicate is what it predicates of the things it is applied to.
Now if proper names have *only* denotation, that is, only bearers, then
it is natural to argue that when they have no bearers they must be
without significance.

To this we should add the idea that a predicate, if it has application, would seem to demand the existence of things it is true of; for
'having application' = 'being true of', what Mill misleadingly called
the denotation of the predicate. These things, that the predicate is
true of, must in the end be signified by words which are not themselves in turn predicates, for if they are signified by words that are
still predicates, these predicates in turn must have both connotation
and 'denotation'; and we shall only reach what predicates are true of
when we give words that have only denotation. Why, one may ask,
can one not name the things that a predicate is true of by means of a
predicate? as e.g. in '*Men* are mortal' and 'I met *a man*'. There are several reasons against making this the end of the matter; in the first
place, it is natural and surely correct to think that such propositions

are true only in virtue of the holding of propositions of the form 'φa', i.e. in virtue of something's holding of individuals who are named and *not* described; in the second place, these examples at any rate are examples of generality, which is best explained by using quantification; we need some account of the difference between 'a man' in 'I met a man' and 'Each soldier killed a man'. It is a constant kind of difference, not a peculiar idiom; it is best set forth by using quantification; but the account we give using quantification will contain the function 'x is a man', and this is a pattern for the formation of propositions containing proper names — never predicates — where we put 'x'.

I spoke also of a comparison between Russell and Locke. This comes out if we consider the following aspect of Russell's ideas. He holds that

> there are words which are only significant because there is something that they mean, and if there were not this something, they would be empty noises, not words. There must be such words if language is to have any relation to fact. The necessity for such words is made obvious by the process of ostensive definition. How do we know what is meant by such words as 'red' and 'blue'? We cannot know what such words mean unless we have seen red and seen blue. If there were no red and no blue in our experience we might perhaps invent some elaborate description which we could substitute for the word 'red' as for the word 'blue'. Any description which a blind man could understand would have to be in terms of words expressing experiences which he had not. Unless fundamental words in the individual's vocabulary had this kind of direct relation to fact, language in general could have no such relation.

This is not like Mill's terminology of connotation and denotation, because (a) Mill ascribes denotation to words that have connotation, but we can cut that out, having found fault with it, and simply say having connotation is the same thing as being a predicate, and (b) for Mill, 'red' has connotation, for it is a predicate. But the disagreement is then only about what 'red' is, not about the way words have meaning. For Russell says that he does not regard 'red' as a predicate for purposes of philosophical analysis. He prefers a language in which 'red' is a subject, i.e. a proper name. The predicates attaching to this subject would be descriptions of positions in space and time.

We can understand this better, I think, if we remember the things that Locke said about the names of simple ideas: that they 'intimate some real existence, from which was derived their original pattern' and that they 'signify always the real as well as nominal essence of their species'. Any 'essence' according to Locke is an idea; real essence is the being of anything, whereby it is what it is; nominal essence would be given by the list of properties which give anything a right to a name; but since simple ideas have no definition, the list would only have one item, and that the name of the simple idea itself; the real and the nominal essence are one, and that one is given by the real existence which is the original pattern.

Individuals, such as John Locke, have according to Locke no nominal essence. If we compare Locke's doctrine with Mill's, we may at first sight be tempted to think that the names of individuals according to Locke are the very same as Mill's 'words which have only denotation and no connotation'. That is to take 'connotation' as partly involving the notion of 'content'. But this would be wrong; for if we look at Mill again, we find him asserting that the abstract forms 'whiteness', 'virtue', 'length' are also words which have denotation and no connotation.

But it is absurd to speak of any name at all without a nominal essence; if a name can be without a nominal essence, there can be no right or wrong about its repeated use. Hence we can see why for Russell Locke's simple ideas should assume the position of designata of real proper names. Russell might indeed give 'this' as an example of a name which does not have to have a nominal essence — and what goes with this is that for 'this' it does hold that it cannot be a misnomer and so not a correct 'nomer' either. But even if we accepted Russell's view of 'this', a proposition running 'This this this here now' would seem profoundly unsatisfactory; we want some names with some content; and such words as 'red' would seem to satisfy our demand.

Although Russell's ideas are more clear-cut than Locke's or Mill's, it is clear that there is a certain family resemblance among them all.

Locke's thesis that proper names have no nominal essence attached to them is, as we have seen, not identical with Mill's view that they have only denotation, since for Mill 'having only denotation' is not the same thing as 'having no content' (or nominal essence); but so far as Mill's thesis about denotation concerns proper names it is fairly close to Locke's; and attempts to make the same point are still to be found in many authors, who either repeat Mill's formula, or say that in some sense proper names have no meaning. We are likely to be told, for example, that nothing about a proper name tells you what object it is a name of — as if anything about the word 'blue' told you what *it* meant! The following passage from Basson and O'Connor[†] is fairly typical:

> If we require some further insight into the difference between a proper name and a description, we may consider the following example. The word 'Palumbo' is a proper name. But if you knew you were going to see Palumbo tomorrow, you would not know at all what to expect. It might be a man, a horse, a dog, a mountain, a river, a city, or numberless other things. The name 'Palumbo' does not give you the smallest clue as to the nature of the thing named. In other words it is not descriptive.

Compare with this:

> The word 'closh' is a descriptive term. If you knew you were going to see something closh tomorrow, you would of course know exactly what to expect. The word 'closh' gives you all the clues you need as to the nature of the thing so called. In other words, it is descriptive.

Locke, explaining himself to the Bishop of Worcester, who had futilely protested against him 'Peter, James and John are all true and real men' said:

> I beseech your lordship to consider whether ... by naming them Peter, James and John ... your lordship does not first suppose them men ... But if I should ask your lordship whether Wewena, Chuckery and Cousheda were true and real men or no, your lordship would not be able to tell me until I have pointed out to your lordship the individuals called by those names, your lordship, by examining whether they had in them those sensible qualities which your lordship has combined into that complex idea to which you give the specific name 'man', determined ... them to be of the species which you call 'man'.[§]

In this passage Locke shows that he supposes it to be understandable what individuals are called Wewena, Chuckery and Cousheda without its yet being determined whether these are proper names of men or what. To point and say 'That is Wewena — and I mean that "Wewena" is the proper name of that' should prompt the question 'That *what* is Wewena?' Or, what comes to the same thing: 'And how

---

† A H Basson and D J O'Connor, *Introduction to Symbolic Logic* (London: University Tutorial Press, 1957).

§ John Locke, *An Essay concerning Human Understanding*, Bk.III, c.3, Note to section 11.

am I to go on using the name Wewena?' Locke writes as if an intelligible reply would be 'so long as it is the same individual'. And hence the question which often concerns philosophers: 'What is an individual? What is a particular?'

That a word is a proper name is some information as to its meaning: it means that it has a very special kind of use; this is parallel to the information that a word is the name of a colour. The further enquiry 'What kind of thing is it a proper name of?' should elicit an answer such as 'a city', 'a river', 'a man', 'a trumpet', which we may reasonably say gives the full meaning, or connotation of the word. Thus Mill would have been nearer the truth if he had said that proper names have both denotation and connotation, but predicates only connotation. A small boy gave a moving spot of light that appeared in his room the proper name 'Tommy Noddy'. Locke writes as if one could know what individual Tommy Noddy was without knowing that this was the proper name of a spot of light. To see the mistake in this, imagine that someone who had grasped that 'Tommy Noddy' was a proper name, asked to have Tommy Noddy pointed out to him. The child points to Tommy Noddy at a time when the spot of light is on a human being.

That is to say, with every proper name there is associated a predicate x, such that when a proper name is assigned to an x, the proper name is rightly used for the future to name the same x. The information 'Tommy Noddy is the name of a spot of light' thus gives the *sense* (meaning, connotation) of the proper name; and the difference which authors have striven to express between proper and common names is this: if you know the sense of a common name and are presented with that to which it applies you can apply it straight away; whereas you can know the sense of a proper name and be confronted with the individual whose name it is, and not know it is his name: you have to be introduced.

But what do I mean 'to *name* the same x'? The explanation I have just given is very inadequate. To see this, consider that with 'square' there is associated a predicate 'shape', such that the word 'square' is rightly used always to name the same shape. But that does not turn 'square' into a proper name.

In order to explain what a proper name is, I therefore first introduce the notion of an 'identifying predicate': I shall henceforth use this expression in a technical sense. To be an 'identifying' predicate, a predicate φ must satisfy two conditions.

(1) The instruction 'Count the φs' must be a straightforwardly intelligible one: i.e. one which in ordinary circumstances does not stand in need of elucidation to someone familiar with the application of the predicate φ . To give a few specimens, the following predicates tend to satisfy this condition:

> Human being.
>
> Stroke of a gong.
>
> Day.
>
> Chess (token) piece.
>
> Chess (type) piece.
>
> Word (as spoken of by a printer or editor).
>
> Prime number.

For most usually, the instruction to count the humans in a certain place, or the strokes of a gong on a certain occasion, or the days until such and such happens, etc., is straightforwardly intelligible. One would count chess (type) pieces that there were in a certain place by counting chess pieces, but not counting any of a type one had already counted. On the other hand the following predicates do not satisfy the condition:

> Human.
>
> Gold.
>
> Red.
>
> Dust.
>
> Bigger than.

For 'Count the xs such that x is human', '... red', '... dust', or '... gold', or '... that there is a y such that x is bigger than y' is an instruction that would normally require elucidation if one was to do anything in obedience to it. Circumstances can be imagined in which the stage is so set, that e.g. 'Count how many red things there are here' has an obvious application — on a page of a picture book showing a number of toys some of which are red all over. That is because in this case there is an obvious predicate — 'pictured toys' — satisfying the condition, such that only things of which this predicate is true are red. No negative of a predicate yields an intelligible instruction 'Count the not-φs', except under conditions similar to those holding for 'red'.

One can count the φs when one knows what counts as one, what as two φs. Thus in ordinary circumstances the instruction to count human beings is straightforward; it belongs to the technique of use of the word 'human being' to yield instances of the technique of applied counting. (I say 'applied' as opposed to counting 'in the abstract'; counting in the abstract is when nothing is counted but the number series is gone over.) 'Count what is human', on the other hand is in ordinary circumstances an instruction that would need *ad hoc* elucidation. Is a human being and human skin one or two human things, and are a human footprint and a human cry to be counted one, two …?

This, then, which I will call 'countability' for short, is the first requirement which a predicate must satisfy to be an identifying predicate. Note that it is not necessary, in order for a predicate φ to satisfy this requirement, that it should be impossible to find border-line and problematic cases, or to imagine circumstances in which we should not know how to count φ s. (It is impossible that this should be impossible — except conceivably in mathematics: the 'countability' of prime numbers, say, is not something in connection with which I find it possible to conceive of borderline or problematic cases — but that may just be lack of knowledge and imaginative power on my part.)

Countables (i.e. φs, or *x*s such that φ*x* where φ is a countable predicate) seem to correspond to the possible substituends for individual variables in symbolic logic. I will call the individual signs for the substituends *quasi-names*. But for the identifying predicates associated with proper names and so for a quasi-name to be a proper name there is a further requirement. Let φ be a countable predicate. Then in some cases the expression 'the same φ' is so used that we can speak of the same φ as now ψ, now not ψ. E.g. we can speak of the same day as now sunny and now not sunny, the same proposition as now true, now false; and so on. Now in these cases the identity of the φ that is and then is not ψ is formal. If a day is first sunny and then not, it is one part of the day that is sunny and another that is not, and the day is sunny and then not sunny because *the parts constitute the day*. An identifying predicate is a countable predicate whose application is such that the identity in question is not formal. E.g. 'man', 'spot of light', 'hurricane', 'city'.

For Russell the identity associated with such predicates is formal; for a φ of this sort is part of space-time that falls, so to speak, within a certain outline within space-time and a φ will be first ψ and then not ψ because a part within this whole part of space-time that constitutes the φ in question is ψ, and another part not ψ. Suppose we have a proposition ψ*a* where *a* is a quasi-name whose countable predicate is φ, then if we have ψ*a* and then not ψ*a*, on Russell's view ψ*a* and not ψ*a* will not be complete propositions but propositional functions, just as '*x* is bald' is a propositional function and not a proposition. The proposition is only completely specified by putting in the *time* at which ψ*a* and not ψ*a*: with the time specification in, the proposition will, if true, give a description of a cross-section of the four dimensional worm that is, say, a man. Thus the possibility of such a view stands or falls with the correctness of his account of the invariability of the truth-values of propositions, and hence with the correctness of his account of 'now'.

A proper name is a word associated in the way I have described with an identifying predicate. If, as often happens, the same word has two associations of the kind in question with the same identifying predicate — e.g. if two men have the same name — there is no mistake; for the assignation is arbitrary, and the only sort of mistake occurring in connection with a proper name is misidentification: i.e. one makes a mistake in calling something John Smith if this implicitly goes with a mistake in the application of 'the same man'.

Now it is possible to see in what sense a proper name logically demands the existence of a bearer. Suppose a sentence contains what appears to have the role of a proper name in it. This is partly a matter of grammar — i.e. that the word is in a place where a proper name might be, and partly a matter of words sounding like proper names. Consider the sentence 'Enough is as good as a feast', which someone ignorant of English might construe like 'Bernhardt is as good as a feast'. Now, if we have such a sentence, then it is true if what its predicate means holds of a φ named by that name in the sentence, φ being an identifying predicate. Now the condition for a word to name a φ is that it shall have been assigned to a φ and is used in predications about the same φ. If there has not been any such assignment, there can be no predications about the same φ as the word was assigned to — for it never was assigned; there can however be a pretence of there having been such an assignment, i.e. a proceeding as if there had been such an assignment, as far as concerns the purpose of constructing narrative sentences; or again a mistaken conviction that such an assignment has been made. The first case is that of fictitious proper names, the second that of mistakes like those of the astronomers who thought there was an extra planet, which they called Vulcan, between Mercury and the sun. In such cases no real predications are made, for if predications appear to be made in connection with an ostensible proper name, the subject of predication is the thing named; hence if there is no such thing, since the name never received an assignment, we have no predications and so nothing either true or false, but pretense-predications or would-be predications. How is it, then, that such sentences could serve the purpose of explaining the notions of 'subject', 'proper name' and 'predicate'? They can serve it as counterfeit money or toy money could be used in explaining the notions of buying and selling. On the other hand, if the fiction runs 'Once there was a man called John, and John did so-and-so and such-and-such', then the sentences of the story have a truth-value — they are most likely false, but since they are not supposed to be true, the question as to their truth does not engage our attention.

Now we readily become confused by the following facts: (a) *any* fiction could be cast into the form: once there was a man (fairy, god, etc) and this man did so and so and the same man did such and such …; (b) the fact that people utter sentences under a mistaken conviction that an assignment of a proper name in it has been made, could be explained by saying e.g. 'They think that there is a planet (which they call 'Vulcan') which is between Mercury and the sun, and that this planet was observed on such-and-such an occasion and the same planet was observed on such-and-such another occasion'; (c) an historical narrative might begin 'In the third century B.C. there was a king, of such-and-such a state, called so-and-so, who …' When we look at these three point (a), (b), (c), we can see how natural it is to suppose that the existence propositions (true or false) that we can associate with every ordinary ostensible proper name as it occurs in ostensible predications, stand to these proper names as similar existence propositions stand to descriptions (definite and indefinite in the Russellian theory). If, then, the form (φa) in some sense stands behind every proposition of the form $(\exists x) (\varphi x)$, we can see why it should seem that the names 'Vulcan' (the non-existent planet), 'Churchill' (the former prime minister), 'Themistocles' (the Athenian statesman), 'Pickwick' (the fictitious character), could none of them be the *real* proper names, for *they* must all receive the same treatment, and propositions in which they occur can be represented as true and false propositions beginning 'There is (or was) a …'. So the form (φa) which is fundamental to propositions of the form $(\exists x)$ (φx) is not truly represented by examples like φ Churchill, precisely because these have to be explained away as existential. In particular, any distinction between legendary and historical proper names is hard to make; for it is a disputed matter, in some cases, whether something is legend or history.

I fear the correct reply to this may seem to muddy the clear waters of logic; but that may be an illusion, and at any rate I have no doubt it is correct. We should distinguish between a formal and a real assignment of a proper name. The assignment is formal when it is simply an assignment to a bound variable in the narrative. King Arthur is a character of uncertain historicity: thus 'There was a man—and only one—who was King in Britain such that the stories of the Arthurian cycle derive from or are embroideries on stories about him' may be true, but it is not certain; and the assignment of the proper name is a formal assignment to the variable in 'an x such that x was a man who was King etc'. (In ordinary language the bound variable is represented by 'who', 'which' and the personal pronouns when they have e.g. 'someone', 'anything', 'no one' as antecedents.) But when such narratives are (a) certain, (b) secondary to the use of the proper name itself, as in 'There was a man called Churchill who was Prime Minister in England for the greater part of the Second World War', then the assignment of the proper name is real and not formal and is prior to the existential narrative. An historical assignment can be real and not formal when we have the proper name by tradition from those who used it of its bearer.

Where the assignment, necessary for an ostensible proper name to be a real one, is real, then the proposition containing that proper name (or any sub-clause containing that proper name) is a genuine predication and is true or false if the predication makes sense for φs, where φ is the identifying predicate associated with the proper name. Where the assignment is pretended or clearly only formal, then there is no genuine predication (except within the scope of the existential quantifier) and no proposition either true or false. When the assignment is neither pretended nor real we can say that we do not know if a genuine predication has been made; and that an analysis of the proposition will show the relevant formal assignment.

Now when we turn to descriptions, so long as they do not contain any proper names lacking real assignment, the position is completely different. This is because propositions containing such descriptions set forth the situation they describe without any ambiguity beyond any that may be involved in the grammatical predicate. If it is under debate whether Themistocles was bald, we know of what man it is disputed whether he was bald. If it is asked 'Was

King Arthur (*really*) bald?' it is reasonable to reply that we don't yet know about whom the question is being asked. Analysis of the origin of the stories might reveal that we could not adhere to any distinct conception of what we meant, in this context, by a story's being derived from or being an embroidery on stories about a particular man. It is, I suggest, a mark of (not certainly fictitious) proper names lacking real assignment, that the existential propositions, which must be true if the ostensible predications about the bearers of those ostensible names are to be true or false, have this kind of indeterminate character. And yet these existential propositions are all we can offer by way of an explanation of the *supposed* application of the ostensible proper name.

Now with descriptions it is quite otherwise: 'The only son of the King of Saudi Arabia is bald' is perfectly determinate in meaning, just as determinate as 'Themistocles was bald at the end of his life'. But unlike such a proposition as 'Themistocles is bald', it has an external as well as an internal negation: 'It is not the case that the only son of the King of Saudi Arabia is bald' and 'The only son of the King of Saudi Arabia is not bald'. The latter proposition shares some truth conditions with 'The only son of the King of Saudi Arabia is bald' and hence is not its contradictory.

What Russell's analysis does for us is to remove the first impression that here, as in the case of a genuine proper name, we have a predication of a subject which is named, designated, referred to — whatever expression you prefer, it expresses the important relation of proper name to bearer. This relation is important in this way: if a genuine proper name is removed from a sentence (or sub-clause), what is left can be considered as a predicate expressing something affirmatively or negatively predicated of the bearer of the name. That is to say, we have here a distinctive and important form of proposition. Not the only form, nor yet necessarily the one fundamental form; it is not necessarily the case that all others (e.g. '2 x 2 = 4'; 'The probability of p in the light of q is such-and-such') are to be explained in terms of it; but certainly an important form. And the theory of descriptions shows how propositions containing definite descriptions in subject-positions (argument places) are not of this form.

13

Ludwig Wittgenstein

Ludwig Wittgenstein was born in 1889, son of parents of Jewish
extraction but not Jewish religion. Asked how his family came by the
name 'Wittgenstein' Ludwig said they had been court Jews to the
princely family and so had taken the name when Jews were required
by law to have European-style names. The father, Karl, was a
Protestant, the mother a Catholic. The Jewish blood was sufficient to
bring the family later on into danger under Hitler's Nuremberg
Laws. They did not think of themselves as Jews or belong to the
Jewish community in Vienna. The children were brought up sort-of
Catholic though so far as I know only the eldest, Hermine, towards
the end of her life, took this seriously and made a profession of faith
before friends and household. At 9 years of age Ludwig and Paul, a
year or two older than Ludwig, talked together and decided that
their religion was all nonsense. Paul became a pianist of some fame,
but soon after his debut in Vienna he became a wounded prisoner on
the Russian front and his arm was lopped off by a surgeon who did
not know he was a pianist. Their father, Karl, who died in 1913,
thought the only proper career for a son of his was that of a civil engi-
neer. He had himself started the Austrian iron and steel industry and
become immensely rich. Two of his sons committed suicide, one
upon the armistice in 1918. Ludwig was sent to Berlin before the war
to study engineering. He went from there to Manchester for the same
purpose and while there got extremely interested in explaining the
mathematics that he was studying. He also flew kites and invented a
jet engine for an aeroplane. He was told that if the questions about

* First published in *Philosophy* 70 (1995): 395–407 and reprinted by permission of
the publishers, Cambridge University Press. Originally delivered as a lecture in
Cambridge in 1991 as part of a series of lectures on Cambridge philosophers. Mis-
prints in the original printed version corrected in the light of the author's final
typescript.

mathematics that he seemed so concerned with were truly his interest, he should go to Cambridge and study with Bertrand Russell. This he did. As I heard the story, it was Russell who drew his attention to Frege. He read and went to see Frege. They had a discussion, of which Wittgenstein said 'He wiped the floor with me'. He was very delighted that Frege said he should come again. Frege wrote him some letters during the War expressing a remarkable respect for him. Later he received a copy of the *Logisch-Philosophische Abhandlung* (pretty universally known as the *Tractatus Logico-Philosophicus*, a title proposed by G.E. Moore).[1] Frege said he could make nothing of it.

It is a book that stands, one might say, halfway between Frege and Russell — at least in some ways.

A principal concern of the *Tractatus* is the relations of sense to reality — truth and falsehood. Only propositions have sense, and if the structure of a sentence is permissible and the sentence — the proposition — doesn't make sense, this must be because no *meaning* has been given to some sign or signs as they occur in it. 'Meaning' — the translation of Frege's *Bedeutung* and also a word constantly used by Russell for *standing-for* — belongs to names, which have meaning only in the context of propositions.

A significant proposition — *sinnvoller Satz* — would prove on final analysis to be a kind of arrangement of names of simple objects, or a truth-function of several such, or indeed of all possible such arrangements.

The arrangement of names in what is (simply) such an arrangement is called its structure.

The question arises, how the propositional connection comes into existence. Wittgenstein mentions this question but does not answer it.

The possibility of the structure is called the form of representation.

---

[1]   The works of Wittgenstein referred to here are as follows: *Tractatus Logico-Philosophicus*, tr. Frank Ramsey, ed. C.K. Ogden (London: Kegan Paul; New York: Harcourt Brace, 1922); *Remarks on the Foundations of Mathematics*, ed. G.H. von Wright, R. Rhees, and G.E.M. Anscombe (Oxford: Blackwell, revised edition, 1978); *Philosophical Investigations*, tr. G.E.M. Anscombe (Oxford: Blackwell, 1953); *Philosophical Remarks*, ed. R. Rhees (Oxford: Blackwell, 1964); *Last Writings on Philosophy and Psychology*, ed. G.H. von Wright and H. Nyman (Oxford: Blackwell, 1982); *Zettel*, ed. G.H. von Wright and G.E.M. Anscombe (second edition, Oxford: Blackwell, 1981).

The form of representation is also the possibility that the simple objects *named* by the names – which are guaranteed to name permanent simples – are arranged *as* the names are in the proposition.

Thus the possibility of the structure *is* the possibility of the arrangement *of the simple objects which are named* in the significant proposition.

This is the possibility of the fact expressed by the significant proposition.

It will also be possible that the objects named in the proposition are *not* so arranged. Then the significant proposition will be false. If – as at present – we are speaking of arrangement, then the propositions we are considering are *elementary – atomic –* and the non-arrangement of the objects as their names are arranged is falsehood and will be the non-existence of elementary, or atomic, facts. (The expression 'atomic fact' used by Ramsey was taken from Russell.)

If you had the totality of elementary propositions you could express the sense of any one of them by putting it down as a conjunct with all the huge array of disjuncts of the remaining elementary propositions and their negations, e.g. thus: p & q v $-q$ & r v $-r$ & s v $-s$ & t v $-t$ ... and so on. This would be a significant proposition and could be offered to illustrate the thesis that all logical constants are already somehow present in the compoundedness of any proposition. (5.47) Any significant proposition thus reaches through the whole of logical space.

I once mentioned to Wittgenstein that I had come across the philosopher Proclus saying that a *name* is a logical image of its object. I hesitated to say 'logical picture' because the *Tractatus* doctrine that *propositions* are logical pictures of (possible) facts was so famous, but he at once responded 'I have so often had that thought' – the thought, namely, that a name *is* a logical picture of what it names. I was slow to realise that I had been wrong in assuming that the objects, the simples, spoken of in the *Tractatus*, were uniform characterless atoms, whose arrangement alone produced the characters of familiar things. (These characters indeed Wittgenstein called 'external'.) The assumption was absurd – the internal characters of objects are not of the same logical form (2.0233) – in fact, it looks as if their logical form and their internal character were the same thing. The possibility of a given fact must be 'prejudged' in the things that *can* occur in such a fact. (2.012) This at least suggests that it is not possible for every simple object to occur in just any fact. Rather, as holders of their names too, the objects can only enter into certain compositions. We cannot illustrate this with elementary propositions, as we do not know any, but we might construct analogues, using only the sorts of names we do know; we may note that 'Mount Everest chased Napoleon to Cairo' does not express a possible fact — unless we change the meaning of, say, 'Mount Everest'.

That the simple *objects* of the *Tractatus* are diverse in logical form is actually quite obvious. For example, we are told 'Its possibility of occurring in elementary facts (*Sachverhalte*) is the *form* of an object.' (2.0141) And 'Space, time and colour are forms of objects.' (2.0251) These thoughts are quite near to 'Names are (logical) pictures of objects' if you grant the character of a name only to names of simples — even though you cannot produce an example of such a name.

This truth — that for the *Tractatus* there is a diversity of *forms of object* — allows a corresponding diversity in the characters of names, even of simple objects. Such names would be the elements of a 'fully analysed' proposition — a sprinkle of names on a logical network, as Wittgenstein put it later on. Remember that he calls a proposition a logical picture of a (possible) fact. This means that there isn't a problem arising from the 'isomorphism' between language, thought and reality, as many — including myself — have felt there is for the *Tractatus* theory. The problem was constituted by the isomorphism's being two-way. If a figure x is isomorphic with a figure y. then equally y is isomorphic with x. So how does x's isomorphism with y show that x is a picture of y any more than y is a picture of x?

In some cases we must make the admission: *which* is a picture of *which* is not determined. If you have a simple spatial picture of another spatial arrangement, and you exhibit the correlations by lines of projection, then the second spatial arrangement is as much a projection of the first as the first is of it. Similarly with arrangements of colours. But here the forms of representation are not purely logical; they include the forms signified by the terms 'spatial' and 'coloured'. If you have a tune, with a temporal order of notes, and you see this represented by a line of musical notation which is spatial, there is no form of representation *other* than the logical form connecting the two things — the tune and the line of notation. (These considerations help us to understand the remark 'Space, time and colour are forms of objects'.) The pattern in the tune and in the line of notation is also, Wittgenstein says, in the grooves of the gramophone record of the tune and the sound waves. That need not concern us. The marks belonging to the line of notation signify the notes of the tune and not the other way round. You have to understand such and such a mark as the sign (name) of a *note* in order to know what these marks are coordinated with. And similarly, if you wanted to say: a fact declared by a proposition was just as much a picture of the proposition as the proposition was of the fact, you would have to call the objects in the fact 'names of *names*' — for it is only *as names* that certain elements of the propositional sign are elements of the picture of the fact. But you could not make out what the elements of the picture were independently of its being a picture. No *such* difficulty arises about the elements of the fact which the picture presents. Thus the argument from isomorphism's being two-way fails — except in cases where it is harmless and either structure may be used as a picture of the other.

Let us return to the relation between structure and form of representation. The structure of a picture is the way its elements combine, the way they relate to one another. The form of representation is both the possibility of the structure *and* the possibility that the objects in the reality being represented are related to one another in the same way as the elements of the picture.

In what way do the elements of a proposition, an elementary proposition, relate to one another? It is composed only of names of simples. They are connected together in a *'logical'* arrangement.

If that is so, then the simples in the corresponding fact (if the proposition is true) are connected together also in a 'logical' arrangement — the same 'logical' arrangement as that of the names. We ought to be amazed.

This announcement makes the connection between thought and a thinkable reality. The possibility that the elements of the reality combine as they do equals, i.e. is identical with, the possibility of the logical picture's elements combining as they do. The picture's very form of representation is identical with the (logical) possibility of things combining in the way its elements do. And the possibility of *things* combining in the way that would constitute the actual fact, is *its* form. (2.033)

So much for the *Tractatus* on simples and pictures. Let us however think again of Proclus' remark: The name is a logical picture of its object. As the *Tractatus* lays down what 'logical picture' is to mean, that will not have been true of *its* names and objects. One might, as I did, translate Proclus' phrase by 'logical image' — the Greek will have been *icon logike*. But whatever we do, and even if we follow the *Tractatus*, there is something about names and their objects which is not a matter of a simple relation effected arbitrarily in the manner assumed by John Locke and John Stuart Mill. Mill said that *proper* names have only denotation, not connotation. Wittgenstein, as I heard him in his classes, denounced this. 'It is a great deal of information about a word that it is a proper name, and still more, what kind of thing it is a proper name of – a man, a battle, a place, etc., etc.' In the *Tractatus*, names being restricted to simple objects, we can't say what their objects are, only give propositions presenting configurations of them. 'A proposition cannot say *what* a thing is, only *how* it is.' In his later work, Wittgenstein certainly gave up his simple objects. But even they had logical forms, which would have come out in the propositions that could have been formed out of their names – if we could in fact have named them. And propositions were descriptions of possible elementary facts *by their internal properties*.

This has not simply died in the later work. Earlier, he had spoken of structure; later he spoke of grammar, and said 'Essence is expressed in grammar'. This, we may say, was made clear in the first place by Frege in the case of the essence connected with the general notion of an arithmetical function. Of course, Frege did not produce that sentence about 'essence'. I am inclined to say that he laid an egg, in such writings as *Funktion und Begriff* and *Was ist eine Funktion?*,[2] an egg which Wittgenstein hatched. In *Funktion und Begriff*, Frege pointed to the difference between, say, $2 + x^4$ and $2 + 3^4$. The former is an expression of a numerical function of which the latter is an example. The first has no numerical value, the second has one:

$$2 + 3^4 = 83$$

The difference of meaning between the expressions of *instances* of a numerical function – in this case e.g. $2 + 1^4$, $2 + 5^4$, $2 + 10^4$, etc – and the expression of a numerical function is not an example of equivocation like 'John gave three rings', when it was a door-bell he is described as ringing, and 'John gave three rings', when it was a present of rings for the fingers. The difference between $2 + x^4$ and $2 + 3^4$ is highly significant because the point of the former is to signify the form of such expressions as the latter. This is a grammatical difference, as can be clearly seen in the joke about the teacher who says 'Suppose there are x pounds of sugar in a box' and the pupil who

[2]   Translated as 'Function and Concept' and 'What is a Function?' respectively in *Translations from the Philosophical Writings of Gottlob Frege*, tr. P.T. Geach and M. Black (Oxford: Blackwell, 1952).

puts up his hand and says 'But sir, suppose there aren't?' The pupil hasn't yet grasped the grammar of x used as it is in expressions of a function for example — or he is making a cheeky joke. Even so, it would be a grammatical joke.

That essence is expressed in grammar was clear enough in the case: *arithmetical* function. But it is also clear in most cases of familiar concepts of substances and kinds of stuff. Examples: acid, wood, metal, milk, animal, plant, peacock, man, flea, banana-tree. N.B. that when we come to plants and animals the identity of an individual is of a different kind from the identity of a lump of lead, say. Here I have been mentioning 'substantial' terms. The notion of essence is certainly not confined to those, as the example of numerical functions shows. Let us consider another example of a mathematical essence. It occurs in Plato's *Meno*: a square.

One which is twice the area of a given square is the square of its diagonal. I once undertook to demonstrate Plato's point in the *Meno* with a nine year old girl who, like Meno's slave, had never learned any geometry. I began as Socrates did, drawing a rough square and asking: how long will the side be of a square twice as big? To my astonishment and pleasure she answered *just* as the slave did, and we proceeded just as the dialogue did, because she always said the next thing that the slave did. I became convinced that this famous bit of the dialogue is no fiction.

What did she end up knowing? One might say: *if* I drew the squares etc. quite accurately, she ended up knowing that *this* square and *this* one (the first and the second guesses) weren't twice the original square, but this last one was. But, first, I wasn't being accurate in my drawing, and second, we could ask how she knew what we are saying she ended up knowing. Was it by the way they looked? If so, would she have any reason to suppose it would look the same another time? You might say it would have to. But suppose another time I drew them in a different colour and a different size. 'Oh', you might say, 'we don't mean "look the same" in *those* ways.' What way of 'looking the same' *do* we mean? 'The same, in that square on the diagonal *was* (and so at least roughly *looked*) twice the size of the original square.' But how will it look twice the size? You reply 'By being composed of triangles, each being half the size of the original square, and a quarter of the new one.'

If you don't draw it so, or at least ask questions which the child answers so, then I am not asking about the geometrical proposition. (For this, accurate drawing doesn't matter.)

What I am eliciting by my questions – which are not 'leading questions' containing the wished for answers – is an essence, part at any rate of the essence of a plane square.

Wittgenstein says in Part I of the book *Remarks on the Foundations of Mathematics*, remark 32, that mathematicians *produce* essences. We can see what he means in the examples: numerical function and plane square. Functions emerged, as a mathematical topic, I believe, in the seventeenth century. I didn't say that Frege 'produced' such essences, but only that he showed what they were, and how to avoid confusing sign and thing signified. The square of Euclidean geometry was an essence produced many centuries before.

Mathematicians have 'produced' such essences by using a grammar; the first formulator of the geometrical notion of a square was presumably extending and adding to a grammar already in use. It is a curious thing that people can build grammar without knowing what they are doing. There is a remark something like this in the *Tractatus* at 4.002: 'man possesses the capacity of building languages in which any sense can be expressed, without any idea how and what each word means. – And one speaks, without knowing how the individual sounds are produced.'

This may be verified, up to a point, in examples of mathematical concepts, and in a host of others. That language as such was a human invention seems enormously doubtful, as does the expression 'build languages in which *any* sense can be expressed'. Languages don't fail to be languages because they need to be built onto in order to express physics in its present state. There may be in this remark about expressing *any* sense a sign of conviction that anything that is a language can say anything sayable. The later Wittgenstein, like Descartes, rather makes a comparison with an old city, the centre full of narrow twisty streets and odd corners, while the suburbs are all straight wide streets.

However, I am more interested in the similarities than the differences. And I put it forward that 'grammar' hasn't got a special new sense, it is only more extensive than the rather thin grammar children learn at our schools. And grammar, as Wittgenstein considers it, corresponds to the 'structure' of pictures, of which he wrote in the *Tractatus*. In that book, maybe we can say objects have essences, if we are allowed to say anything about objects; Wittgenstein speaks not of essences there but rather of logical forms, and there is little about *them*. What have essences rather are propositions and elementary facts; and this fits in well with the analogue of structure to grammar.

We might truly observe that the *Tractatus* has a sort of simplicity. It offers a strange and rather powerful theory of sense, truth and falsehood for what it calls 'significant propositions'; and a rather simplistic conception of mathematics as consisting of nothing but equations. (This I do not understand, so I won't dwell on it.) It also gives an account of propositions of logic, or logically true propositions, which makes them non-significant though not nonsensical. They are not significant, because they can't be true *or* false like 'significant propositions'. This doctrine, together with the special meaning Wittgenstein invented for 'tautology', has been widely embraced. According to it, $p \vee -p$ is not significant, because it excludes nothing. Equally, the contradictory $p \ \& \ -p$ is not significant, because it excludes everything. Still, neither tautology nor contradiction are nonsensical, *'unsinnig'* in German; they have a role to play in logical exposition.

Having said that much, I can characterise Wittgenstein's latest period — not his middle period or periods — as marked by the realisation consequent upon the middle work, that 'it's not as simple as all that'. Much in the *Tractatus* remains valuable and the book fascinates people like me, who do not *believe* a lot of it; I believe the valuable stuff so far as I can identify it, but remain fascinated by much I cannot discern as valuable. However, noting the excessive simplicity of the central picture of sense, truth and falsehood, I also note what the book does *not* cover, even though it covers astonishingly much. It shows a half belief that experimental psychology is a natural science. The observation 'Theory of knowledge is philosophy of psychology' I think indicates this — along with the statement that psychology is no nearer philosophy than is any other natural science. When he was writing one of the short pieces which we put at the end of Part II of *Philosophical Investigations* (for it had no definite place given it by Wittgenstein in his MS of that work) he wrote that experimental psychology is marked by experimental methods and *conceptual confusion*. He called it analogous to set theory, which he said was marked by conceptual confusion and methods of proof.

However, the observation that theory of knowledge is philosophy of psychology can be taken in a more sophisticated sense than I have given it. Once in conversation with Wittgenstein I asked how he'd describe the difference he had made — I meant, and he understood me — in his later work. His answer indeed fits the *Tractatus* too, from which I have taken the remark about theory of knowledge. He said in answer to me, that if you looked at the titles of most of the famous works of philosophy in recent centuries, you found that they tended either to contain the word 'principles' or some reference to the human mind. This last is correct enough even of Hume's title *A Treatise of Human Nature*, no less than of Locke's *Essay*. Reflecting on the matter, I reminded myself that for the centuries since Descartes, theory of knowledge has been queen in philosophy — as metaphysics had been in earlier centuries.

Now let us consider some principal features of this phenomenon. One is that extraordinary leap by which Descartes turned so many successors into believers in the certainty only of immediate experience. In his second Meditation he asks what he attributed to the soul. His answer includes nutrition. I am always surprised that this doesn't bring people up with a jolt. Why nutrition? The answer is simple; he had something of an Aristotelian training at La Flèche. Nutrition is one of the marks of the vegetative soul. Two pages later, Descartes is reciting what he knows, which includes 'I see'. But he remembers his method of doubt, and corrects it to 'I seem to see' and then says that that's what seeing really is.

Contrast with this Wittgenstein's late investigation into the difference of category between two different 'objects' of sight: first, 'I see *this*' I assert and offer a description, 'a sleeping cat', say, or I draw a picture. Second, 'I've suddenly seen a likeness between this face and that'. A new aspect, which the man I say this to does not see. In the *Tractatus* Wittgenstein had regarded the two ways of seeing a cube as seeing 'two different facts'. Is one really just *seeing*, which is all one thing; or is one's seeing partly *thought*? We remember ruefully what all Descartes was willing to call *thoughts*.

And later philosophers were worse. At least Descartes did not count knowledge and memory among his *cogitationes*. Early twentieth century philosophers sometimes did make just that mistake. Whether Descartes thought an act of will — simply of the will itself — was involved as an immediate precedent to a voluntary or intentional action I don't remember; John Stuart Mill certainly did, and I could recite twentieth century philosophers who do so treat voluntariness, and even intention. It is not that they think there can be an act of resolution sometimes involved in bringing yourself to do something; it is that they think that it is essential to the performance of a voluntary act. But voluntariness doesn't require any such thing. Wittgenstein was clearly as subject to temptation here as any of us. '*Doing* itself seems not to have any volume of experience. It seems like an extensionless point, the point of a needle. This point seems to be the real agent ...' Yet ' 'I do' seems to have a definite sense, separate from all experience'. (*Philosophical Investigations*, 1.620) Again he asks 'when I raise my arm, ... are the kinaesthetic sensations my willing?'

There is a little book, probably little known, called *The Practice of the Presence of God*. It is mostly records of what was said to people who came to visit him by a Carmelite friar, a lay-brother of little 'education' who worked in the kitchen of his monastery. If that phrase was his, what did he mean by it? Reading what he said to people, it is clear that he meant often speaking to God in prayer in the course of his work. But suppose he was having to concentrate on some tricky job? Did this involve an intermission in his 'practice'? I should judge not; that he thought the practice should be *all* the time. Was he all the time imagining God observing him all the time while he was busy? After some reflection I realised that I was still the victim of a Cartesian type of assumption — it must be a constant state of consciousness, and that must have been a continuous Cartesian *cogitatio*. I then saw that no such thing was necessary. What one is doing in one's activity, the reasons one has for what one does, may, as Wittgenstein occasionally observed, be merely elicited from one by a question. 'Why did you pull that cord?' — 'To change the notice on the door' — 'Did you notice the notice?' — 'No, I always change it, round about now'. 'But isn't there an act "peculiar to the will" which is nothing but a turning towards doing something, an act which proceeds from an interior starting point of cognition?' How is one supposed to learn there is such a thing? What one knows, what one mentions to explain one's action, may not have been 'in one's consciousness' at all. And suppose one's action is inaction — in some situations one votes by doing nothing, saying nothing, making no movement of the hand, for example. One knows this, but does not have to be thinking of it so to vote. Indeed one did *learn* about it at some time; one was told and one would probably give it in explanation if someone asked.

To say this is not to say there is no such thing as an event of thinking of something and being 'therefore just about to' do what one does. The mistake is to think that there must always be some such thing.

Even when there is such an antecedent to a voluntary action, it may itself consist in different things on different occasions. It may for example be a memory or a reminder, which 'prompts' a behaviour; sometimes it may be a catching sight of something, sometimes a thought which struck one. The 'interior act of will' is invoked because of the *being prompted* which one refers to in the explanation of one's movement which one truthfully gives: it is not necessarily an experience, but it resides in the 'because' of such explanations.

There is a similar mistake that threatens us when we seek to explain what suddenly understanding something is.

In the sense in which there are experiences characteristic of understanding, Wittgenstein remarks, understanding is not an experience. Further, it is the circumstances in which one has an experience characteristic of understanding that justify taking the experience as one of 'understanding'.

An intelligent logician once responded to my speaking of an explanation as sometimes being 'elicited' after the event, by calling it then a 'rationalisation'. That it might on occasion be that I would of course not deny; that it *must* be that, if it was not present in the consciousness of the person at the moment of the action that he is explaining, is a thought showing a powerful 'Cartesian' influence.

There are things in the early Wittgenstein which he never gave up: for example, the equivalence of p and 'It is true that p'. And some things which lasted with him for a long time: 'To be able to say: 'p' is true (or false) I must have determined in what circumstances I call 'p' true, and with that I determine the sense of the proposition.' (*Tractatus* 4.063) Much later, when someone mentioned the 'verification principle' at the Moral Science Club, Wittgenstein asked who invented it, and having it attributed to himself, explained 'Who? *Me*?' in a tone of outrage. I do not know what was the formulation given. But it seems to me that he must have forgotten something he had written in the work *Philosophical Remarks*, which was published after his death: 'A proposition (*Satz*) is a draft upon a verification'. He wrote that book around 1930 and at some time gave it to Moore, indicating that he didn't think it was particularly good. Nevertheless, that remark does seem to be related to the 'verification principle'. When he wrote the *Philosophical Investigations*, he wrote: 'Asking about the kind and possibility of the verification of a proposition is only a special form of the question 'How d'you mean?' The answer is a contribution to the grammar of the proposition.' (I, §353)

The equivalence of 'p' and 'It is true that p' must of course be understood as confined to where '"p" is true' makes surface-grammatical sense. 'Oh damn!' would not be a substitution instance. On the other hand, cases like 'I've got a pain' where 'there is no distinction between truth and truthfulness' as Wittgenstein put it in *Philo-*

sophical Investigations Part II, *would* be examples of the equivalence. At a very early stage (in *Last Writings on the Philosophy of Psychology*, Volume II) he mentioned the thought that belief in the existence of God is 'an attitude' with the comment that one who believed in God might say that if *that* was what someone thought, then he did *not* believe in God.

One thing I have observed among people who have been influenced by Wittgenstein: a certain tendency to think that *if* such and such a 'language game is played' that fact is justification of it. First, I deprecate talk of language games except where the speaker is able to describe them – that is, to describe the procedure into which words are woven in a certain fashion. But, more importantly, it should not be supposed that when a certain language game is played – i.e. when there is a certain use of words – that constitutes a title so to use the words. In *Zettel* 608–610 we have a passage where Wittgenstein says: 'No supposition seems to me more natural than that there is no process in the brain correlated with associating or with thinking', and further on asks 'Why should there not be psychological regularity to which *no* physiological regularity corresponds?' He remarks: 'If this upsets our concepts of causality, then it is high time they were upset.' One could not refute this comment by saying 'But we *do* play these language games with "causality" and explanation'.

To come to an end: I once heard someone ask Wittgenstein what it all came to, what was, so to speak, the upshot of the philosophy he was teaching in the 1940s. He did not answer. I am disposed to think that there wasn't an answer he could give. That, namely, he did not think out a total position as in writing his first book; that, rather, he was constantly enquiring; some things he was pretty sure of, but much was in a state of enquiry. I therefore deprecate attempts to expound Wittgenstein's thought as a finished thing. He himself in his classes sometimes said he was as it were giving examples of 'five-finger exercises' in thinking. These were certainly not limited in number like the set a piano teacher might employ, and were not like automatic formulae of investigation. Predictions of 'what Wittgenstein would say' about some question one thought of were never correct.

14

The simplicity of the Tractatus

Let us begin by remembering the most central doctrine of the *Tractatus Logico-Philosophicus*.

Objects — which are simples — combine into elementary situations. The kind of way they hang together in such a situation is its *Structure*. *Form* is the possibility of the structure. Not all possible structures are actual: one that is actual is an 'elementary fact'. We form pictures of facts, of possible facts indeed, but some of them are actual too. A picture consists in *its* elements combining in a particular kind of way. Their doing so presents the objects named by them as combined in just that way. The combination of the elements of the picture — the presenting combination — is called *its* structure and its possibility the form of representation of the picture.

This 'form of representation' is the possibility that things are combined as are the elements of the picture.

Note, then, that the possibility of the structure of a picture *is* the possibility that the objects to which its elements correspond are combined as are the elements of the picture.

This resolves a problem apparently raised by the 'isomorphism' of the *Tractatus*. Propositions are pictures. If this means that there is a projective relation between propositions and possible or actual facts, must not the fact presented by a proposition, if it *is* actual, be as much a picture of the proposition as the proposition is of it? Projective relations can be seen as going in both directions. So isn't the reality as much a picture of a possible proposition — which, if actual, is itself

---

* The text is based on a copy of the printed version from *Critica. Revista Hispanoamericana de Filosofía* Vol.XXI/No.63 (diciembre 1989): 2–16, to which the author made 64 handwritten alterations/corrections.

also a fact — as *it* is of the reality? The answer to this objection is that the elements of a proposition (completely analysed) are *names*. So if the reality represented by a true proposition were a *picture* of that proposition, the simple objects of which that reality was composed would have to stand for names. Now, that some object is a name is not to be seen by looking at the object — the mark on paper or the bit of furniture or whatever is doing duty as a name. You have to understand the configuration of those objects as a logical configuration of *names* in order to understand it as a proposition.

I don't mean that every picture is a proposition; its form of representation may be spatial and it a picture of a spatial arrangement somewhere; or temporal and a picture of a temporal arrangement. But *every* picture, according to the *Tractatus*, is at any rate *also* a logical picture and propositions are *only* logical pictures. This is so even though they represent by means of a spatial arrangement. A representation by a spatial arrangement — a musical score — can be a representation of something temporal, as here it is of a succession of sounds. But here the 'form of representation' is not the spatial form, because it isn't a representation of anything spatial; there is no form of representation in question except the logical form.

I have set forth the doctrine of the *Tractatus* to be found in numbers 2 to 2.22, in order to bring out Wittgenstein's solution to the ancient problem of the connection between language or thought and reality. Thoughts (we learn from a letter to Russell)† consist ultimately of elements, just as propositions consist ultimately of simple names: these are sprinkled on a logical network — so Wittgenstein described his earlier doctrine in a later notebook. The ancient *problem* is solved by the thesis of the *identity* of the possibility of the structure of a proposition and the possibility of the structure of a fact.

We can derive from this the astonishing thesis that the structures of realities are logical structures. See 2.18. 'What any picture, of whatever form, must have in common with reality in order to be able to represent it truly or falsely, is the logical form, that is, *the* form of the reality.'

What I have set forth is enough to explain, or at least to adumbrate, the *Tractatus* doctrines about tautology and contradiction, about propositions of logic and proofs of them, about psychological propo-

---

† See R.37 in Ludwig Wittgenstein, *Letters to Russell, Keynes and Moore*, edited with an Introduction by G. H. von Wright assisted by B F McGuinness (Oxford: Basil Blackwell, 1974), pp. 71–3, at p. 72.

sitions and, finally, about ethics and the mystical. Before approaching this last, I will call attention to 4.221: 'It is obvious', Wittgenstein says, 'that in analysing propositions we must come to elementary propositions which consist of names in immediate combination.' He goes on: 'The question arises here, how the propositional connexion comes to be.'

To this question, which obviously does arise, Wittgenstein offers no hint at all of an answer. I assume he did not think of anything worthwhile to say about it. He had already said at 3.3 'Only a proposition has *sense*, only in the context of a proposition does a name have *meaning*'. (By 'meaning' he means what Russell meant, and what Frege meant by '*Bedeutung*', namely, the object a word stands for.) Then the question he speaks of at 4.221 would not be how names – already there – get connected into propositions, but how names – connected into propositions as they must be to be names – come into existence at all. This is a question about the origin of language, which knowledgeable intelligent people have banned as a topic of investigation. Wittgenstein once said to me 'Why shouldn't men have been created ploughing and sowing?' It would seem to me *difficult* to give *any* reason why not. And equally if you add speaking to the list. Upon the whole, then, I applaud Wittgenstein for not offering any suggestion of an answer to the question 'how did the *Satzverband* come about?'

However, for the moment I have a further purpose in reminding you of the doctrine of the *Tractatus* that the things that are the *case*, the *facts*, whatever they might be, have logical structures. Lots of people, including myself at one time, would protest that logical structure and logical connections are features of the linguistic and of thought about this-and-that-being-the-case. We know from Wittgenstein's letter to Bertrand Russell, that he was sure that such thoughts must be composed of elements just as in the end a fully analysed proposition would turn out to consist of simple names in a logical pattern: he did not know, he said, *what* elements thoughts were composed of – it would be the business of psychology to find that out. Here he displayed a naïf belief in experimental psychology as one of the natural sciences which he certainly did not retain – remember what he says in what we put as the last fragment of Part II of the *Philosophische Untersuchungen* (for it was a loose sheet in the MS of that writing). There he characterised the foundations of mathematics, or set theory, as *methods* of proof together with conceptual *confusion;* and experimental psychology as *experimental methods* also together with conceptual confusion. But in 1919 and in the *Tractatus* itself, he manifested a sort of belief in experimental psychology *as a natural science:* 'Philosophy is no closer to psychology', he said, 'than to any other natural science', and indeed after that: 'Theory of knowledge is philosophy of psychology'. The latter observation is indeed a valuable one, if we take it as meaning, not anything about experimental psychology as a natural science (as Wittgenstein intended the phrase there) but as about what we call psychological matters, e.g. the mind and its acts: belief, guessing, hoping, trying; and also will and the emotions. That theory of knowledge is *part* of philosophy of psychology in *this* sense has some truth in it, except for this, that 'to know' is *not* a psychological verb, even though it has some of the aspects of one. It is, I think, much to the credit of Descartes that he did not count either knowing or remembering among what he called *cogitationes,* though the empiricist side of the watershed that he caused did in effect think that about knowledge and memory.

However, back to my purpose: the *Tractatus*'s conceptions of propositions and facts and the world exclude from being possible propositions any sentences about what Wittgenstein called 'the ethical' or anything religious. This immediately follows from the character of *significant* propositions as being propositions that can be straightforwardly true or false: tautology and contradiction are not 'significant propositions', because, as can be seen in a truth table, one, e.g. $p \, \& \, p \supset q \, . \supset . \, q$ excludes *no* possible truth-values of its argument, and the other, e.g. $p \, \& \, \text{-}p$ excludes *all* of them. Neither therefore can determine anything as being so, with other things *not* so. Further, this is supposed to be a proper account of logical necessity and impossibility, and there is no other kind of necessity or impossibility. Significant propositions, when true, are merely a matter of this or that being the case and they are all on a par — '*gleichwertig*'. We learn from Wittgenstein's later 'Lecture on Ethics' *circa* 1930,[†] that 'Palmer was a murderer' (this is my example) may well be a fact, but, being a mere *fact* it does not have the kind of weight or value that an *ethical* proposition would, if there were such a thing. Or, as he said in the *Tractatus* 'The *facts* all belong to the exercise' — that is to say, the exercise set one as a school teacher sets homework for his pupils — and not to the answer; or, as Ramsey translated the sentence 'the facts all

† Published as 'Wittgenstein's Lecture on Ethics' in *The Philosophical Review,* 74 (1965): 3–12.

belong to the task and not the performance'. The rendering is partly good. It does not bring out the meaning of '*Aufgabe*' as an exercise set, or of '*Lösung*' as a solution of a problem. I don't know how to give a translation with the merits of Ramsey's, but which does *also* bring out the association of the German words. *That* life sets us *a task*, and 'the facts' are relevant to the task, but our execution of our task can't be given as among the facts of which the world is made up — this is evidently Wittgenstein's thought here. But it is not the sort of thought that fits his account of the truth and falsehood of significant propositions which just give or purport to give information about the perfectly indifferent facts going to constitute 'the world'. This explains his letter to Ficker, in which he says that the *point* of his book is to characterise the ethical *from inside*. What he meant by that is made clear if you think that the description of a body, of its shape, gives you the shape of the space surrounding it; the surface of the body is the inner surface of the space where it is.

And now I come to the penultimate proposition of the *Tractatus*. I think it has not been translated well. I give you what I think is a more accurate translation thus: 'My sentences are illuminating in the following way: one who understands me rejects them as nonsensical if, using them as steps, he has climbed out over them. He must as it were throw away the ladder after he has climbed it. Then he sees the world rightly.'

Notice that this does not say that someone who rejects the sentences of the *Tractatus* as strictly nonsensical understands Wittgenstein. There is a condition: the rejection as nonsense depends on the process of using the propositions of the *Tractatus*, i.e. climbing on them as on the steps of a ladder; *if* the climber *so* climbs out over them and *so* comes to recognise them as nonsensical then they have been enlightening to him. Note that the word I translate 'nonsensical' is '*unsinnig*', i.e. *absurd*, not '*sinnlos*': *this* is a characteristic of tautology and contradiction, and relates to that contrast with 'significant propositions', '*sinnvolle Sätze*' which I have tried to explain. Wittgenstein's own propositions in the *Tractatus* are characterised as nonsense, as absurd, just because they are *neither 'sinnvolle Sätze' nor 'sinnlos'* like tautology and contradiction. We may infer from number 7: 'Whereof there cannot be discourse, thereon there should be silence', that in teaching philosophy it would have been strictly correct, as he also said, to teach *only* by uttering true significant propositions, the totality of which Wittgenstein calls 'the totality of the natural sciences' — and then when someone tried to say something metaphysical, to show him that he had given no meaning to some of the words he used, i.e. that he was not using them as standing for any things.

About this I would comment: in his belief that the totality of true propositions is the totality of the natural sciences, I really do have the impression, as nowhere else in the book, that his feet have left the ground. *Either* he thought that e.g. 'Napoleon came from Corsica' was a proposition derivable from, and so part of, the contents of a complete natural science, *or* he forgot all about such humble true propositions as that one.

Second, consider '*Propositions* cannot express what is higher' and 'God does not reveal himself *in* the world' and 'People to whom the sense of life becomes clear have not been able to say what it was'. This last is somewhat laughable, as many people of whom it is plausible to say that the sense of life has become clear to them have done quite a lot of saying what it was. Such people may sometimes have been silent, whether they have lacked the ability to express themselves or for some other reason. And some have deserved Samuel Johnson's stricture on Boehme: 'Sir, if Boehme saw the unutterable, he should not have tried to utter it.' But plenty have spoken without doing what offended Johnson. Augustine, for example: 'Thou hast made us for thyself, and our hearts are restless until they find their rest in thee.'

Did Wittgenstein mean that they were unable to say anything significant in the sense of the 'significant propositions', the *sinnvolle Sätze* as spoken of in the *Tractatus*?

If so, one might say: so much the worse for the *Tractatus* conception of the '*sinnvolle*'; so much the worse, to put it in English, for that sense of 'significant'.

Remember, however, what he said in his preface: part of the worth of the book is that it shows how little has been done when the problems it solves have been solved.

Consider the other two examples I gave ('God does not reveal himself *within* the world', and 'propositions can't express what is higher'). How was it that Wittgenstein so much as possessed the words 'what is higher', 'God', 'the ineffable' except that these words *belong in human languages*? One wonders wildly: if we were not a fallen race, greatly given to talking rubbish, would our race have stated verbally only the things that Wittgenstein called significant propositions, descriptions of this and that supposedly in the world, but have *lived* in consciousness of the ineffable, with the seriousness he seems to indicate, but *never* speaking of such things?

Reading the 'Lecture on Ethics', which is *extremely* 'Tractatussy', one would not think so. There he speaks of thoughts, propositions if you like, which do *not* 'have a sense' but which instance something in the human spirit which he has the greatest respect for and would not for anything mock at. One example: conviction or feeling that it doesn't matter what happens; one is absolutely safe. It doesn't mean anything like a conviction that one's bank account will always be in funds because an oil-rich Arab is taking care of it. I also remember the story of Wittgenstein, as a schoolmaster in a poor village, bringing the children back from an expedition he had taken them on; the getting back had some difficulty — it was dark — and perhaps even a bit of danger; and he told them not to be frightened but to think of God. He once said to his friend Rush Rhees, a sighing man, not to repine and blame himself for something in himself: 'That's God's fault, not yours'. He greatly admired the prayers of Samuel Johnson. He loved the utterance of a certain cricketer who had become a missionary and said in his preaching 'What God wants is a heart — any old turnip will do for a head'. I could go on but these are enough. There is a clue in his liking for something Bismarck once said. Someone quoted something to him and asked what he thought of it. Bismarck replied: 'Tell me who said it and I'll tell you what I think of it'.

What Wittgenstein rejected was the idea of a theory — a *Lehre* — of ethics, of theology. He disliked it. That is there already in the *Tractatus* at the final remark, which I think might be better represented by: 'What there cannot be significant propositions about we should not discourse about', though that lacks the fine rhetorical flavour of: 'What cannot be spoken of — on that there should be silence'.

Now what about the much later Wittgenstein? Did he come to think that the *Tractatus* not merely contained serious mistakes, but was just rubbish? — Some people think so. But it is not true: it is well known that he said 'It isn't like a bag of junk — rather it is like a clock that doesn't tell the time right'. A good deal of what he said in the *Tractatus* is extremely solid stuff: the theory of truth-functions and the use of truth-tables in expounding it; the conception of some things *showing*, though you can't state them; that '*A* thinks that *p*' does not state the existence of a certain relation between a person, *A*, and a proposition *p*; that identity is not properly speaking a relation, which, as it happens, everything has to itself. One can find many such examples of very useful thoughts in the *Tractatus*.

It would be accurate to say that the book offers a strange and powerful account of meaningfulness, truth and falsehood. It would, I think, also be correct to say that the more Wittgenstein worked — and he worked immensely hard — when he resumed philosophical investigation, the more he came to see: *It's not as simple as all that*. One of the powerful attractions of the *Tractatus* is a sort of simplicity. This *partly* accounts for the fascination that it exercises on some people, like me, who do not believe: *This is the truth*, the *true* account of the system of the world and of language and of how language is significant.

That facts in the world have logical structures — which is the thought that makes Wittgenstein speak of logic as 'world-mirroring' — this has not been refuted and, if correct, *would* be a solution to one of the deepest problems of philosophy.

One thing Wittgenstein showed in his later work, however, is that many concepts are of human invention. He said 'Mathematicians produce essences', and *that* is something it is easy to justify in some examples. Also, it appears to me — I have argued this elsewhere* — that there is a 'sort of' essence expressed in the grammar of the term 'element', even though the grammar has partly altered since the Greeks, and with that what we *call* elements are different from what they did. And I have argued that this 'sort-of-essence' *is* a human invention. But I would never suppose that all the essences expressed in the grammars of the words of common speech were human inventions. It belongs to human nature that there is speech, so they cannot be. Nor do I think that Wittgenstein in the end thought that they were human inventions, keen as he was on suggesting and exploring the possibility of some other tribe of men *not* having certain very common concepts that *we* have. I don't mean technical ones, but e.g. colour-concepts. Other tribes might have different ones: he often suggested 'colour-shape' concepts.

I mentioned earlier how Wittgenstein said in the *Tractatus* 'The question arises here, how the propositional connection comes to be' — and does *nothing* to answer it. At a later date, would he have rejected the notion, of *the* propositional connection? Yes, apparently, by a development of what he already had thought, namely that the outer form of a sentence may be deceptive as to its actual logical form: he praised Russell — and might also have praised Frege — for drawing *attention* to this. At a later time he would contrast the 'sur-

---

* 'Elementos y essencias', in *Annuario Filosofico*, 22 (1989): 9-16.

face grammar' with the 'depth grammar' of an expression, and held that we were often deeply deceived by surface grammars. He almost certainly rejected the *Tractatus* idea that there is such a thing as *the most general form of proposition*, which all propositions share. Indeed the actual representation of the general form in the *Tractatus* $[\overline{p}, \xi, N, (\xi)]$, he *must* have rejected, for there is no sign of his always continuing to believe in 'elementary propositions' and 'elementary possible facts'.

That the general concept of a proposition is prominent in our speech and that the *thing* is important by its very *commonness*, he positively asserted, only discounting some thoughts about it by comparing them to attributing to seen objects the shape of the spectacles we see them through. He also firmly adhered to the equation 'p is true = p'.

The *Tractatus* question about the *Satz* turns into a question: how does something's *saying that* something *is so* come about? And what account of it can we give? The first is answered, if it can be, by the judgment that men were created with speech. The second is a pretty serious problem, a present area of dispute.

It may be that some readers have formed the impression that Wittgenstein came to think that concepts were uncriticisable. This tribe has these, another perhaps different ones. Neither is right, *or* wrong.

This would, I think, make of him in his later work a *trivialiser*. It is false, as may be seen from his considerations about physiology in connection with sense perception and speech: he objects to the idea that there must here be a system continuing right into and out of the brain; as also to the idea of a memory mechanism. He remarks on the possibility that we might *only* be able to distinguish seeds by knowing which different plants they *come* from: there might be no here-and-now difference between them discoverable by examination.

And about these possibilities he says: if this upsets our concepts of causation, well it's high time they were upset.

It would be a worthy task to explore what of that first great work was not, and what was, rejected, gradually or suddenly, and to fill out my sketch of Wittgenstein as in effect coming to say 'It's all *more complicated* than that'. This task would require consideration of topics not treated in the *Tractatus*, not even mentioned, topics like what Wittgenstein later called the *motley of mathematics*; in the *Tractatus* he had said that all mathematical propositions were really equations. And of topics which *are* spoken of in the *Tractatus*, like the regularity of the world: 'We could not say of an irregular world, what it would be like'. And such topics as *understanding*: 'I understood what you said' surely sounds like a report of an event but *that* betrays a deception through the surface grammar. And historical propositions: in one of his pre-*Tractatus* notebooks he wrote: 'What is history to me? Mine is the first and only world'. He didn't say that in the *Tractatus*, but his remark about the totality of true propositions, which I have quoted, shows a curious unnoticingness of history on his part. Certainty is narrowly conceived and so no adequate account of it is even suggested in the *Tractatus*.

These are but pointers—hints—of what such a work as I have suggested would have to include. It would also, and this perhaps be hard, give what important thoughts, true or false, remained. With that I will close.

15

Wittgenstein's 'two cuts' in the history of philosophy

Wittgenstein is extraordinary among philosophers for having made two epochs, or cuts, in the history of philosophy. I take the idea of a cut from Wolniewicz.† He explained it like this: a philosopher makes a cut if he makes a difference to the way philosophy is done: philosophy after the cut cannot be the same as before. Thus, as I was told once by an Austrian philosopher, the effect of Wittgenstein's *Tractatus* was cataclysmic. Long established professors of philosophy threw away their old books. The task now was to do philosophy in the manner indicated by the *Tractatus*. And of course the first task was to understand that book. For the fact that you have been overwhelmingly convinced by a book or an approach does not mean that you have really grasped it and its implications. And here you have to make a distinction. The distinction is between the things you know you don't understand yet, and the things that you don't understand, but without realising that that is so. You bring prejudices to the new study, without realising that they are prejudices and that the philosopher you are studying does not share them. One instance of this for the *Tractatus* was the assumption of 'basic propositions' — what Carnap called 'Protokollsätze' — used to interpret Wittgenstein's

---

* Originally published under the title 'Opening Address' in W Leinfellner, E Kraemer and J Schenk (eds) *Language and Ontology. Proceedings of the 6th International Wittgenstein Symposium* (Vienna: Holder-Pichler-Tempsky, 1982), pp. 26–28.

† Boguslaw Wolniewicz (b. 1927), Polish philosopher, friend of Peter Geach and Elizabeth Anscombe.

concept of elementary propositions. This wished upon Wittgenstein a kind of Russellian or even Humean epistemology, which pervaded the philosophy of logical positivism, though it didn't always take the same form. I do not mean that there was absolutely no ground that could be offered for taking this line. What sentences were the *Erläuterungen* mentioned in the *Tractatus*? 'Die Bedeutungen von Urzeichen können durch Erläuterungen erklärt werden. Erläuterungen sind Sätze, welche die Urzeichen enthalten. Sie können also nur verstanden werden, wenn die Bedeutungen dieser Zeichen bereits bekannt sind.' (3.263)§ Someone might think this looks very like a form of Russell's 'knowledge by acquaintance', which contrasts with 'knowledge by description' in a way to which one might want to assimilate the contrast between elementary and complex propositions in the *Tractatus*. And didn't Wittgenstein himself say of the 'simples' of the *Theaetetus*, which 'can only be named: their names are all they have': 'these simples were my "objects" and Russell's "individuals".'[1] There is certainly a problem of interpretation here. I don't know if anyone has tackled it successfully. But the mere assumption which I have mentioned did prevent people from trying. Note that the passage in Plato does not speak of the primary elements as 'given': they are characterised as the elements 'out of which we and everything else are composed'.

Bringing prejudices, unrecognised as such, to the study of a philosopher often leads either to misunderstandings or to finding the philosopher dreadfully difficult. However, although the interpretation of the *Tractatus* is still work to do, yet the fact remains that it made a 'cut' and that it has had an enormous influence. A lot of philosophers who perhaps would not seriously try to read it nevertheless have it in their bloodstream. This is interestingly attested by the constant reference of the American philosopher Wilfred Sellars to 'Tractarian' views, attitudes and conceptions: he is not saying anything that depends on a correct exegesis of the *Tractatus*; it depends rather on what has got into people's philosophical bloodstream because of the *Tractatus*.

§ In the Ramsey-Ogden translation: 'The meanings of primitive signs can be explained by elucidations. Elucidations are propositions which contain the primitive signs. They can, therefore, only be understood when the meanings of these signs are already known.'

[1]   *Philosophical Investigations*, §46.

There is a process of exegesis, however, and of making clear what we got out of that book, which has gone on, sometimes stupidly and sometimes interestingly.

With the second 'cut', effected by the *Philosophical Investigations*, the analogous process has, I think, barely begun. Although things were very much changed by the impact of this philosophy, there is, I think, more resentment about the fact. If my informant was correct, the old professors joyfully threw away their old books when they got hold of the *Tractatus*. But except for the aficionados who want simply to imitate Wittgenstein of the *Investigations*, there are rather few philosophers who welcome the effect of that work, or who manifest in their way of going on that problems have changed their aspects, or that some rather standard positions in philosophy can no longer be taken.

This arises, I think, from the immense and yet unperceived difficulty of the work. The *Tractatus* looked difficult where it was difficult. With the *Investigations* we are rather in the situation of one who listens to a lecturer and can understand each thing that is said, but does not know where it is getting to. But there is a trap which it is easy to fall into. Bringing to the text assumptions which your author does *not* share, assumptions indeed which he attacks, you put crude interpretations on what he says, and then you either are obviously at a great distance from him, or you get into difficulties. Thus the famous sentence: 'Ein "innerer Vorgang" bedarf äußerer Kriterien' [An 'inner process' stands in need of outward criteria; *PI* I, §580] has been cited as proof that Wittgenstein's theory was that at least there *could not* be any mental occurrence without any outward phenomena to mark it. Similarly the assumption that the *Philosophical Investigations* presents us with a theory of language—a theory, say, of how sounds become significant speech—will quickly place us at a distance from the very questions which Wittgenstein is occupied with. E.g. 'Ist der Ruf "Platte" im Beispiel (2) ein Satz oder ein Wort?' When, for example, I shout 'Fire!' is that really short for 'Something's on fire that ought not to be!' Ought my shout to be analysed, unpacked, or rather expanded so as to be a description? 'Eine Beschreibung ist eine Abbildung einer Verteilung in einem Raum' [A description is a representation of a distribution in space] Wittgenstein says in Part II of *Philosophical Investigations* (ix). That makes it difficult to call the shout 'Fire!' a description—or is that dictum not true? Or does the concept of description hoax us?

If we consider carefully the questions which Wittgenstein does ask we may quickly find ourselves considering things which we have not thought were the interest of philosophy *at all*. And that indeed is *one* of the known reactions to *Philosophical Investigations* and not one of the most stupid ones. At least it doesn't involve forcing this thinking into a mould which it doesn't fit at all.

I don't know if anyone has really been cured, by studying Wittgenstein, of the following inclination: the desire for necessary explanations, necessary connections. This is illustrated by discussions of personal identity. Some people think that the identity of a human person is the identity of a living human body. That's reasonable. But they also think that the identity of the living human body must have its criterion in 'spatio-temporal continuity'. Perhaps they can be persuaded that they must mean the spatio-temporal continuity of a human form in the flow of matter. But even so, things are unsatisfactory. How can this or any other suggested criterion meet the demand *that it not be logically possible* for *two* later people both to satisfy the criterion? In fact, this enquiry has got things the wrong way round: in this life, identity is our criterion for the relevant spatio-temporal continuity, and not vice versa. We *recognise* people we know, for the most part. But mightn't there be two alike? Yes, there *can* be; and then we fall back on other things — what this person knows, what his memories are, and other people's claims about him, and so on. — But isn't it still *logically* possible that two might satisfy whatever criteria we propose? Well, and what of it? Why do we want something that there *could* not be a counter-example to, and not merely something that there has not, or not normally, been any counter-example to? In a different world, things might be different. What of it?

We say a picture is a picture of an old man climbing a hill with a stick. We may say we *saw* such a thing in a brief, a momentary, glimpse. In quite other surroundings the picture might be that of someone sliding downhill. How do we *know* what we see? — Asked in that fashion, the question reveals a demand which we ought to scrutinize. And one thing that is implicit in the demand is the demand for something that gives us necessities. Professional philosophy is to a great extent a huge factory for the manufacture of necessities — only necessities give us mental peace. It is no wonder that Wittgenstein arouses a certain hatred among us. He's out to deprive us of our factory jobs.

The detailed description of the distribution of colour-patches on a canvas does not reveal to us the picture that is on it, though if you say: 'But there is *also* the picture. *What does it consist in*? There *must* be something else besides paint on canvas' — you are embarking on an illusory search. The vast number of things that we know and do and are concerned with are like the picture on the canvas. The facts about our knowing, our doing, and our concerns are enormously interesting; but necessities of an absolute *a priori* kind cannot be found to justify our assertions. And the regions where necessity of a more harmless kind does play a part are specialised, like the necessity that the triangle is the plane rectilinear figure with the smallest number of sides.

The contrast between a harmless and a delusive concept of necessity is especially noteworthy — and, perhaps, difficult to grasp — in the case of the development of a series or working out the value of y for a given value of x in a formula. We do use the expression 'The steps are determined by the formula ...'. We use it for example in distinguishing between a formula that does and one that does not determine just one value of y for a given value of x. Learning to handle such formulae and recognising such a distinction comes into learning algebra, at an elementary stage. But, given a formula which does determine the value of y for a given value of x, obviously, or one for which we can prove it is such a formula, we may then want to say 'It does *determine* it; it does determine the whole series, the series is actually there, determined, and in calculating we are only as it were inking over the part of the series which we calculate.' Here we are not exactly manufacturing a necessity, but trying to formulate the ideal of a necessity which is being imitated by the calculations when they are of results which in the harmless sense are determined. And here there are indeed deep problems, problems about the nature of mathematics. Just what they are is the first task of someone who wants to understand Wittgenstein or the foundations of mathematics.

But he also said that the question about the right way to continue the series 2, 4, 6, 8, 10, ... and so on, or indeed 2, 2, 2, 2, 2, 2, ... and so on, was the same as the question about going on with the word 'red'. And this claim is not too difficult to understand. For here too there lurks the idea that there is a 'must' about the future application and that you grasp this 'must' in grasping the meaning of the word. Here we are not so much tempted to invent or manufacture necessities, as to rest content with the ones we think we have already in our grasp — until someone disturbs us with the question: 'And when you think you are applying the word to the same thing—must you be right?' This is a sceptical question only to those who assume that *their* assumptions are irrefragably correct and are the basis of meaning and truth. They are angry at being disturbed—if they feel the disturbance at all.

What I would like to say, however, is something that I find it very difficult to express. The things which Wittgenstein attacks—these are impediments to a true conception, or to true conceptions. It is an impediment to looking at the picture, if you are struck with the conviction that you must either extract the picture from the description of the colour of each colour patch in a fine grid laid upon it, or that you must have a theory of what the picture *is* apart from what that description describes. If you forswear both inclinations you may get to look at the picture, and doing so you may find yourself full of amazement. Or, as Wittgenstein once put it, you may find yourself 'walking on a mountain of wonders'.

16

On the form of Wittgenstein's writing

Wittgenstein once said to me in the course of a conversation that he had asked himself the question whether he was a second-rate artist. He added by way of illustration that Longfellow's discovery of the Hiawatha metre must have seemed a great thing to him; and he said, or implied, that under the influence of such an impression it would have been difficult or impossible for Longfellow to perceive — what we could easily see — that *he* was a second-rate artist.

I have often thought about this since Wittgenstein's death and since I have worked on the translation of some of his writings. I have supposed that what corresponded to the Hiawatha metre was the use he makes of separate *'Bemerkungen'*. A *Bemerkung* might be a single short sentence, or might be over a page long; it might itself be divided into several paragraphs. It is the form in which Wittgenstein composed most of what he himself wrote.

Contrast the *Blue Book* which was composed by dictation to his class at Cambridge. This was done without notes; the dictation was not continuous, but he would discuss for a while and then say, 'Now there's something you can take down' and dictate, then break off the dictation for further discussion and so on. The product is more like a regular piece of philosophic writing than anything else of his yet published; or, I think, than anything of any length that he wrote in the last twenty years of his life.

* Originally published in Raymond Klibansky (ed) *Contemporary Philosophy. A Survey/La Philosophie Contemporaine. Chroniques* (Florence: La Nuova Italia Editrice, 1969), pp. 373–378.

Philosophical Investigations sometimes makes on someone glancing through it the impression of being a more or less haphazard arrangement of fragmentary short bits of writing, and I have heard people refer to Wittgenstein's writings as 'Notes'. Some such idea may seem to be supported by Wittgenstein's own observations in the preface to *Philosophical Investigations*. For there he says that he found he could not succeed in sticking to a single direction in his writing, or weld his '*Bemerkungen*' into a whole in which 'the thoughts advanced from one subject-matter to another in a natural order and without breaks'; that the best he could produce would always be 'only remarks'; that the book was 'only an album'. And at the end of the preface he says 'I should have liked to write a good book. It has not turned out so.'

If these observations do give readers the impression that he would have liked to emerge in the end with an *Investigations* in the literary manner of the *Blue Book*, but found that he could not do it and so left only an arrangement of notes or fragments which were like preliminary jottings for such a composition, then they have been misleading. There was never any question of his writing the *Investigations* except in the form of just such discrete chunks as we have there.

Was the 'failure to write a good book', of which he speaks, simply the failure to have thoughts 'advance from one subject to another in a natural order without breaks'? If so, it was a failure to accomplish an impossibility, for he went on to say 'This hung together with the very nature of the investigation. For it compels us to traverse a wide field of thought criss-cross in all directions.'

What can be said is this: Wittgenstein would have liked to write a book that was as great a work of art as his *Tractatus*. As the *Investigations*—composed, as it would have been in any case, of discrete remarks—fell short of that ideal, he called it 'only remarks'.

The *Tractatus* too is composed of discrete remarks. Like the *Investigations* it too was a selection from a much greater mass of material—all written in the same style as itself—and a careful arrangement of what was chosen. In spite of the misgivings which the author expressed in the preface to that work too, it gives the impression of completely realising his intention: of being a perfected whole. (We may note that the dissatisfaction he expressed there did not concern the arrangement; it was a matter of 'hitting the nail on the head' less than might have been done.) The topics considered and the point of view from which they are considered seem, after the event, to make this perfection more attainable than the analogous one would have been for the *Investigations*. For one thing, the *Tractatus* really does have a 'natural order of advance from one topic to another, without breaks'. But if the failure that Wittgenstein accuses the *Investigations* of was a failure of unity and order, at any rate it could not have been *that* kind of unity and order that would have given it its unattained perfection.

But we shouldn't assume that the *Investigations* lacks a coherent and intelligible order. On the contrary; nor is that implied by the remarks of the preface, about the wide field of thought traversed criss-cross in every direction: the same, or nearly the same, point being approached along different paths. It is not that there are points of jerky disconnection with what has gone just before, either. Examine the transitions — say, from the investigation of 'obeying a rule' in §§ 143–242 to the destructive criticism of private ostensive definition of words for sensations and sensible qualities in §§ 243–315; from that to the discussion of thinking §§ 316–362 and imagining §§ 363-398 and back to sensations §§ 398–410 and consciousness §§ 410–428; in every case the transition is natural, and the general plan of the book is not difficult to describe. One is much more likely to be jolted and puzzled by a transition from one *Bemerkung* to the next, both being on the very same point, than by the transition to a different subject matter — and in such cases, puzzlement can usually be resolved by philosophical reflection.

What the *Tractatus* has, and the *Investigations* lacks in this matter of order, is completeness of treatment of each matter before moving on to the next. The *Investigations* does not finish with a topic; it zigzags back to old themes in the context of new subject matter. The discussion of thinking in §§ 316-362, for example, reverts to 'Now I can go on!' which was one of the main topics of the big discussion of obeying a rule. It does so quite naturally, *via* a consideration of 'flashes of thought' and 'sudden understanding'. This new cropping up of what has been discussed before, in just such a way, is quite typical.

It is only in about the last 150 *Bemerkungen* that I find some jerky transitions of topic: for example, the introduction at § 547 of 'negation as mental activity' occurs by a break from the previous topic of words etc. being 'charged' with feeling or meaning. In these last 150 *Bemerkungen* one has the impression that the author had sought the best arrangement he could make of these materials *rather* than that he was traversing zigzag paths because this was *the* journey through the 'wide field of thought' that he wanted to lead us on. And indeed he expressed a particular dissatisfaction to me in Dublin in 1949 with this part of the book. 'I would like my whole book, if it could be, to be only so thick!' he added, holding his finger and thumb about a quarter of an inch apart.

Someone learning the story with which I opened, and remembering those comments from the preface to *Philosophical Investigations*, might suppose that Wittgenstein had already answered his own question: it wasn't 'a good book' and so he was a 'second-rate artist'. But this would be stupidity. The artist who failed to produce the work as he dreamt it should be is not therefore, and need not therefore in the least think he is, second-rate. The doubt, I should judge, did not concern the accomplishment of the ideal, but whether the method and technique and manner were so good, and capable of producing so great a work, as it seemed to him they were. He remarked further that he thought it a question that he must leave alone; being épris with them, as he supposed Longfellow was with his metre, he could not get a view of it from outside, but it occurred to him as a possibility that *such* a view would reveal the art as second-rate. (Here I am not quoting words which I remember exactly, my memory is merely a rough impression that he thought it no good trying to answer the question for that sort of reason, but I don't remember just how he framed the reason. I should add, perhaps, that there is nothing authoritative about my interpretation of his remarks, which I didn't ask him to explain further and which occupied only a minute or two of a conversation during a walk in which we talked about a lot of different things.)

The false impression I have spoken of is in any case belied by his account of the *Investigations* as being like a photograph album. It is an unusual sort of album that he compares it to (this too is in the preface), for which large numbers of snapshots of a landscape have been taken, often of the same spot but from different positions, and the decent ones have been cut down and arrayed in such a way as to give a good idea of the whole landscape. This suggests the very careful organisation which in fact characterises the book.

It is an astonishing fact that after completing *Philosophical Investigations* Part I, and without apparently any intention of superseding it, Wittgenstein spent many months making two quite different alternative arrangements, consisting for the most part of most of the *Investigations* material.

This brings us to the question what his separate *Bemerkungen* are. A great many of them are separate in the sense that one could read each of them without looking before or after; and someone who heard that the author made two quite different arrangements of a lot of the same material might guess that they were all like that. But that is far from being the case. There is very often a necessary connection between one remark and its predecessor, say in the form of a demonstrative whose reference is, or is given in, the predecessor. Whatever the arrangement of the material as a whole, such connections were preserved. So that the building blocks for the different structures are *not* quite generally the separate *Bemerkungen*, but may be these or may be short runs of them. (But not such lengthy runs as may be found devoted to a single subject matter.) Whether a sentence or set of sentences or paragraphs form one whole *Bemerkung* or only part of one is thus not a matter of whether it is independent of its immediate surroundings. In looking at Wittgenstein's MSS I do not recall hesitations on whether something was a separate remark or not. This is noteworthy as the MSS are full of second thoughts in the way of expression — there are endless variant readings — far more often than not quite insignificant, as far as concerns the content.

A typical example of a non-independent *Bemerkung* comes from *Zettel* 646-7. I give only the tail-end of 646:

> 646 … There is of course a close tie-up of these language-games; but a resemblance? — Bits of one resemble bits of the other, but the resembling bits are not homologous.

> 647. I could imagine something similar for actual games.

We could easily imagine 647 appearing in parenthesis at the end of 646. So the separation seems to be a matter of rhetoric. The separate *Bemerkung* here, though its content can't be grasped without reading its predecessor, has a content which when once ascertained can be dwelt on, worked on, discussed as to its truth or falsity and its consequences, by itself. The rhetorical device of separation commands a peculiar attention.

It is the assemblage of many *Bemerkungen*, together constituting a multifarious and ramified attack on the problems of philosophy, that produces the effect that is intended. If then I am right, what corresponds to the Hiawatha metre is not the single *Bemerkung*, but the use of many such separate *Bemerkungen* to present a new picture of things. (That is why *Remarks on the Foundations of Mathematics* after Part I really are what a reader would understand by 'only remarks'; for after Part I they are a mere selection, preserving chronological order, from Wittgenstein's first-draft notebooks.)

So we have a very large number of worked and polished building blocks put together to make a whole. And it is here that the contrast with the *Tractatus* comes out most strongly. It is not a question of order; there is in fact little deficiency of order. But from the *Tractatus* as it were a face looks out very clearly. With *Philosophical Investigations* I at least have the impression of a veiled face, or one which does not appear strongly.

Strange contrast! In the *Tractatus* it is said that what is shown cannot be said — there is something that our sentences try to speak out but gulp on. Yet the *Tractatus* seems to succeed in saying what, according to it, 'can't be said'. The *Investigations* insists that it is an error to think that there *is* something that can't be said, and yet it seems often to be nearly revealing something which yet does not come into view: a picture, not supposed to be constructed out of its elements, the *Bemerkungen* in assemblage, but in a substance from which they cleanse the encrustations and engrained deposits.

17

A Theory of
Language?

> But such a sound is an expression only in a particular language-game, which now has to be described. (*Philosophical Investigations* [*PI*], §261.)

I take this sentence out of context and I will leave out the first two and last six words. I derive a possible basic statement of a theory of language:

> A sound is an expression only in a particular language-game.

This will be a basic statement of a theory of language only if we regard the task of 'describing the language-game' as one whose point is to show how noises are significant speech. The idea has quite a lot of attraction and it attracted me for a long time. Indeed, I once thought that that was the main thing, or the most fundamental thing, that was going on in Wittgenstein. Now I believe that the idea of such an enterprise is one which quite quickly goes up in smoke.

All the same it is worth showing this, because it will give us some clues to better understanding.

If one pursues that conception, one at once feels constrained to distinguish between 'primitive' and 'non-primitive' language-games, because one can't describe many without presupposing others. And so one starts something like this:

> A primitive language-game is an action or procedure into which words, or perhaps we should rather say, sounds (e.g.) are interwoven. Just their role in the procedure makes them to be words or signs.

* Reprinted from Irving Block (ed) *Perspectives on the Philosophy of Wittgenstein* (Oxford: Basil Blackwell, 1981), pp. 148–158, with the permission of the publishers, Wiley-Blackwell.

In describing this role one makes no assumption about the occurrence of the same sounds in other procedures. Naturally, one thinks there are very few primitive language-games that determine sounds to be the signs they become. Greeting would be an example.

'A great deal of stage-setting in the language is presupposed to any act of naming.' (*PI*, §257) If that is so, then 'naming' couldn't be the name of a primitive language-game. Or better: naming couldn't be accomplished in a primitive language-game. 'Naming' there of course meant *conferring* a name. But we could say the same of using a word to name something, i.e. as a name of something.

A *non-primitive* language-game will be a procedure using what are already words. And here there will be two cases. In one, nothing but what are already words will be used in the new procedure. In the other — and this one is nearer to the 'primitive games' — there will be some old words and some new sounds together woven into, i.e. given a role in, the new procedure. An obvious example is given by Wittgenstein's builders, who are first described as using just four words, 'Slab', 'Block', etc (which was to be conceived as 'a complete primitive language') and then as having the extra words 'a', 'b', 'c', etc., together with 'this' and 'over there'. These appear in utterances like 'd-slab-over there' by A, accompanied by a pointing gesture, in response to which B carries four slabs to the place indicated.

If it is the use of a word that constitutes it as a name, but the use of a word as a name cannot be said to occur in any primitive language-game, then in what sort of non-primitive language-games do we get it? For the word doesn't occur as a new sign (it isn't a new sound) like 'd' and 'there'.

Is it like this: there are *several* primitive *and* near-primitive language-games played with the four original sounds 'Slab' etc., and it takes occurrences in several language-games to constitute 'Slab' as a name? That 'Slab' is a *name* of a certain shape of building stone isn't established just because language-game (2) is played. Consider Wittgenstein's discussion of whether 'Slab' in (2) means 'Bring me a slab' or just means 'slab'; and of whether it is a sentence or a word. 'In fact it is our "elliptical" sentence.' This he says in spite of obvious objections (which he considers). The point is: 'When I call "Slab!" what I want is *that he should bring me a slab!*' — and that was what 'Slab!' amounted to in (2). Wanting that doesn't consist in thinking (in some form or other) a *different* sentence from the one you utter. This raises the question whether 'Bring me a slab' might be meant as one long word corresponding to 'Slab!'.

We should not be put off by the extreme simplicity of the example. Language and human capacity are so complex that e.g. different words can come to be counted as in some way the same word. Cf. different *inflections*, as we call them. Or it might be that one used a different sound the next time: 'Slab', 'Tink', 'Noffle' might all be the 'same word' — you say 'Tink' if *last* time you said 'Slab' etc. but otherwise the role is the same. I don't know of any language in which that happens, but it *might*. That people master different inflections is impressive. 'Romam' is after all quite as different from 'Roma' as 'broken' is from 'broker'. But let us forget the possible complications in order to see the difficulty even in very simple cases. The 'theory' before us is that a sufficient number of different language-games with the same word can make that word into a name. It will occur in combination with other words. First we have a mere sound, say 'Slab', whose use has a certain point in an activity; no more reason to call it a name than the shout 'Bingo!' *in* the game of that name. Then we have it fitted together with other sounds, e.g. 'Slab there', 'Four slabs' — but *what is the identity*? We have the same sound, equally fitted together with others, in 'This lab work'. And, of course the sound 'Slab' itself was already a conjunction of sounds.

Our attention is now called to the question: What is the difference between a 'mere' phonemic combination and a morphemic or verbal one? Many philosophers of otherwise diverse tendency (e.g. Aristotle, Russell) have explained a simple sign as one which has no parts which are signs; or, more strictly, no parts which function as signs within the sign in which they occur. Only for a crossword-puzzle man does 'Churchill' contain 'Church' and 'hill' and 'ill'.

But how can we pretend to that account from the position that we have taken up? We are trying to say *what* about the occurrence of a sound constitutes it as a sign, and in particular as a name. So the idea of a part's not being a sign can't be used to discriminate between what occurs as a sign and what occurs as a 'mere' phoneme or 'mere' syllable.

'The sound which is a sign has a certain role as part of a procedure' — but isn't that *also* true of the mere phoneme? We are accustomed to think that Plato in the *Cratylus* was extraordinarily blind in assuming that phonemes have meaning-roles. But this, as often, may be a failure on our part to see a problem.

We may be inclined to say: the most elementary sounds usually form clusters, and it is certain clusters that can be recognised as having what we've called 'a role' in an activity and so as being signs.

In the limiting case, as with 'I', 'a', etc. the elementary sound *itself* has a 'role' and is a sign. In all other cases the most elementary sounds themselves have what we are calling a 'role' merely *as* parts of a cluster which has one.

The latter expression demands explanation. Shall we say: by itself the phoneme S does not have the kind of role we mean, the role of the sound in the language-game, but only when combined with other phonemes to make the sound 'slab'? Only the sequence has that role, and the single phoneme's contribution is that it is part of that sequence. To be sure the individual phoneme matters, witness the difference between 'slab' and 'slat'; we can't deny that it 'matters for the meaning'; Plato was wrong only in thinking it mattered by making a *meaning-contribution*.

We are talking ourselves into greater difficulty, not reducing it. *What* is the difference between 'mattering for the meaning' and 'making a meaning-contribution'?

We may say: Very well, the mere phoneme does make a meaning-contribution, but not in the way Plato thought. A cluster of phonemes plays a role in a language-game and its elements play the role collectively. There is a difference between phonemic and morphemic concatenation. It is when you have morphemic concatenations that you have the same sign, the same *word*, occurring in a new combination with other signs. Whatever 'language-game' you may introduce 'This lab work' into, if this is the familiar phrase, the concatenation of the S phoneme with the cluster l-a-b isn't morphemic. — But now, of course, we want to know the criterion for morphemic as opposed to phonemic concatenation. — Someone may wish to introduce pronunciation, thus retreating to the acoustic qualities of what is said; but the suggestion that the actual stretch of sounds s-l-a is regularly different according to whether a word beginning 'sla' is occurring or not, is not one I'm willing to buy.

If Zellig Harris is right (and I am willing to believe that it is often so), there is a way of generally ascertaining the morphemes of a language without making any more appeal to meaning than is made in an assumed preliminary process of ascertaining its phonemes. Starting with any old phoneme of the language, you put another possible one after it (i.e. one that does occur after it) and ask how wide open the possibilities are now, for the next place. The morphemic divisions of sample sequences of phonemes generated in this way will be at the peaks of possibility for the next phoneme. (If in doubt, try it backwards!) Of course in giving examples one relies on grasp of the possibilities for the language, but if the 'possibilities' were established just as a matter of frequencies for a language that was not understood, the method would work — if Harris is right — as long as the acoustic identifications of the phonemes was reasonably reliable. Now in telling us this method for determining what are the morphemes of language, Harris does not suggest that it is a criterion: the method can be investigated for its success in identifying morphemes or in morphemic segmentation. So it doesn't tell us what we are to *call* correct morphemic division but assumes we already have a fair idea of that. Now Harris's actual explanation of morphemic segmentation seems not to be successful.[1] One cannot help suspecting a covert reliance on etymological knowledge, which nevertheless is also scouted; cf. his observation that 'ice' is no morpheme in 'notice': but, after all, the 'ice' in 'notice' also occurs in 'service', if etymology is relevant; and if it is not, one feels grave doubts whether the concept of a morpheme has any validity. (Cf. Chomsky's bogus treatment of 'eous' in 'righteous'. The matter is of some importance vis-à-vis post-Harris linguistics, especially when there are claims to base something about *the mind* on the 'transformations'.) I have turned to Harris because he is noticeably conscious of the question I have raised, and also because he attempted a theory which is 'micro-reductionist' in spirit; such a theory is also what I tried to read into Wittgenstein. Harris is of course correct in observing that 'the morphemic boundaries in an utterance are determined, not on the basis of considerations interior to the utterance, but on the basis of comparison with other utterances'. Now this is equally true of the break-up of utterances into 'words'. Cf. Wittgenstein's observation:

> But now it looks as if when someone says 'Bring me a slab' he could mean this as one long word corresponding to the single word 'Slab!' ... We mean the sentence as four words when we use it in contrast with other sentences such as '*Hand* me a slab', 'Bring *him* a slab', 'Bring two slabs', etc; ... that is, in contrast with other sentences containing the words of our order in other combinations. — But what does using one sentence in contrast with others consist in? ... We say we use the order in contrast with other sentences because *our language* contains the possibility of those other sentences ... a foreigner might believe the whole series of sounds was one word.†

---

† *Philosophical Investigations,* §20.

[1] See Zellig Harris, *Methods in Structural Linguistics* (Chicago: University of Chicago Press, 1951), pp. 160–2, including the footnote.

In fact the concept of 'an individual word' is so familiar to us largely because of the division into 'separate words' by printers. Printers' divisions, and lack of them, are in part purely conventional. Without the familiarity engendered by the printed word, the concept of an individual word is a product of rather sophisticated reflection. The more primitive idea is that still retained in such a phrase as 'a word in your ear', or 'word came to me that …'.

I once had the following dialogue with a four-year-old who had a piece of paper in her hand:

I: Give me that.

C: Whose is it? (Hands it over)

I: How many words did I say?

C: When?

I: When I asked you to give it to me.

C: One.

I: What was that one word?

C: 'Can I have the paper, please.'

The last utterance of the child is in quotation marks because it was quite clearly an answer — which came quite pat — to my last question; she did not want the paper back. This story is no very weighty support for, but is an excellent illustration of, my contention: the division of utterances into distinct words is a sophisticated proceeding. Not just the historically but the psychologically and epistemologically primitive sense of the 'word' is 'thing said'. If this is right, then either Wittgenstein is wrong to say 'We mean the sentence as four words … because *our language* contains the possibility of those other sentences', or 'meaning the sentence as four words' does not involve having the idea of four distinct words. The latter is the correct interpretation.

Harris's effort was an unsuccessful enterprise of micro-reduction, and if we conceive Wittgenstein as also engaged in such an enterprise we must equally say that he fails. Indeed the pretended attempt would be positively fraudulent. He deliberately constructs a very small number of proceedings with a very small number of noises, each of which is a cluster of phonemes, and invites us to consider the very first type of proceeding as a 'complete primitive language'. When the additions are given, we are presumably to consider the whole set of procedures of the builders as now constituting their 'complete language'. Certainly, as it happens, the problem of re-identification does not arise, that is to say, as the thing was set up, there was no possibility of the occurrence within a 'game' of any of the sound-clusters that are designated as words, without their being *those* words. Thus no problem is presented such as appears when we say we are quite sure that the word 'red' doesn't occur in 'Get ready', 'He's read it', 'Don't tread there', 'Better edit it', 'Have you any bread?', 'It's ready to shred', 'It's predatory', etc., etc. If what we have at the beginning of *Philosophical Investigation* is an embryonic micro-reductionist theory of language such as we envisaged, and we are given those 'objects of comparison' the 'clear and simple language games', to illustrate the theory by presenting it in a simple model — then the presentation is fraudulent. The difficulties of identification would be supposed to be overcome by a wave of the hand and muttering about 'complexity'.

When Wittgenstein adds the new words and introduces 'd-slab-there', the question 'What determines that "slab" is the same word as in the first language-game?' has the same answer as the question: 'What determines that "Horatio" is the name of Hamlet's friend?' The author determines it: explicitly or implicitly, he tells us it is so.

We could formulate an exercise: Assume that the builders proceed as described, except that the vocal part of their activity is only described as their making those noises at these points. Now construct further developments such that when we consider the whole, the sound-cluster 's-l-a-b' occurring in 'deeslabthere' was not after all a word, or not the same word as at its first appearance. Or again, the sound-clusters 'Slab' etc,. though identifiable as repetition of the same morphemes, turn out not to be names of shapes of building stone.

The main purpose of the opening of the *Investigations* is to persuade us not to look at the connection between a word and its meaning either as set up or as explained (a) by ostensive definition, or (b) by association, or (c) by mental pictures, or (d) by experiences characteristic of meaning one thing rather than another, or (e) by a general relation of reference or naming or designation or signifying which has (logically) different kinds of objects as its terms in different cases. The 'clear and simple language-games' are offered as objects of comparison, not models — to give us the idea of the possible functioning of a word in use, without even invoking that of meaning. For 'it surrounds our consideration with a fog'.

This was an enormously difficult trick to pull off, because there is an internal relation between a word and its meaning such that under some circumstances we would so use the expression 'that word' that 'it' wouldn't 'be the same word' if it hadn't the same meaning.

The question then arises: was Wittgenstein trying to break the 'internal relation' — to set up external relations instead? To speak of words without faces, offering them to us without their peculiar physiognomy? That would be a misunderstanding, as comes out if we reflect (a) on his free assumption of authority to identify words and (b) on his claims about grammar. (a) alone might betoken blindness, but (b) rules out that possibility. We must therefore turn our attention to (b).

Surgeons may order the manufacture of instruments adapted to catch hold of different items. Catching-hold-of is in every case the same kind of thing, but the objects caught hold of vary in shape and so they may need instruments the business parts of which are differently shaped. Consider now the difference between naming a number, naming a particular man, and naming a kind of fruit. We might conceive it on the analogy of the surgeon's instruments, and, while this would suggest that naming, or 'using a word for a —' was always the same kind of thing, still it would also give us the idea of the analogue of a 'difference of shape' in the catching-hold part of the instrument. But what is in question is a difference of *logical* shape. I speak in metaphors: what I thereby seek to express is what according to Wittgenstein belongs to the grammatical characterization of words. If I am right, it would for example be perfectly correct according to his thinking to call 'numeral' the name of a grammatical part of speech. I know of no place where he did say this, but unless I misunderstand the matter, he must have assented to it. No doubt it makes too little contribution to solving the problems about the foundations of mathematics that interested him, for him ever to have said it.

His use of the word 'grammatical' has of course been noticed, and it has been widely supposed that he had an odd taste for using 'grammatical' where others would use 'logical'. He himself claimed that when he said 'grammar' he meant grammar — more of the sort of stuff one learns at school when one learns grammar. People have found it very hard to believe this. But we ought to remember that there can be a difference of opinion *about* grammar, even though 'grammar' is the word for what the disagreement is about — just as there can be different beliefs about God, though the word is not the wrong one to use for the topic of disagreement.

Strange to say, Wittgenstein's conception of the grammatical is far closer to the Platonic-Aristotelian tradition than that of the linguistics which seem to hold the field at the present day. It is strange, because Wittgenstein is always inveighing against the influence of 'Aristotelian' logic in causing people to force uses of language all into one mould; and here 'Aristotelian' logic is to be understood so broadly that Frege and Russell are examples of it too. In this tradition Plato initiated the distinction between name and verb, or subject and predicate. This division is so generic that it covers an immense variety of diverse structures. But a man who complains of the forcing of diverse things into one generic mould may be doing so because he wants many more specific patterns described: not because he wants to change the direction of interest of the enquiry. Plato saw the *grammatical* difference between 'Theaetetus' and 'walks', Wittgenstein, the *grammatical* difference between 'Theaetetus' and 'two'. If 'proper name' is a grammatical category, then so in his conception is 'numeral' and so is 'colour-name' and so is 'psychological verb'. But by Wittgensteinian considerations even all of these turn out to be somewhat generic: that is, there are 'categorial' differences within each kind.

Now 'numerals' would often be a special chapter in the grammar of a particular language. This is, however, largely because numerals affect cases and constructions of sentences in peculiar ways. Colourwords do not in the languages I know. If there are languages in which they do, then the treatment of those languages by grammarians will equally include separate chapters for them.

The difference of opinion about what belongs to grammar arises from belief in and practice of a 'formal' science of grammar on the one hand, and a study of what a given use of words amounts to or achieves or tells us on the other. The former belief leads to an examination of the ways that words occur together and an attempt to formulate rules and explanations of this, always in terms of purely linguistic structures. The latter leads to consideration of contrasts between say 'For how long did you forget that?' and 'For how long did you reflect on that?' or between intermission of intention and intermission of attention. There is nothing obscure about calling 'grammatical' the observation of the different temporalities involved in these cases. But it is not a kind of observation that we expect from the formal grammarians. Plato's distinction at the beginning of our tradition might seem to belong to either conception of the grammatical; but his interest in making it (the problem of falsehood and negation) put it in the philosophical class of grammatical investigations: the 'formal' grammarian is interested in the structures of language for their own sake.

See how close Wittgenstein is to Plato here. Wittgenstein:

> The agreement, the harmony, between language and reality consists in this: if I say falsely that something is red, then, after all, it isn't *red*. And if I want to explain 'red' to someone in the statement that it is not red I do it by pointing to something red. (*PI*, §420)

The harmony between language and reality is found in the false statement no less than the true. This false statement says (of what is) something that (it) is not — but *something* nevertheless, which is. Here we can point to that which the thing is not.

Plato:

> A statement does not consist of names spoken in succession or verbs apart from names … it does not merely name something, but gets you somewhere by weaving together verbs with names … those that fit together make a statement … stating something *of* something (of you, say) … the false statement stating of you, as being, things which are different from the things that *are* of you, and so things that are not, but all the same things which do exist. (*Sophist*, 262-3b)

(Suppose the question arises: would the two part company about empty predicates? — Well, whatever way there is of explaining a predicate when used positively, just that way explains it too when it is used negatively.)

'If I say falsely that something is red, then all the same it isn't *red*' — the mere truism suddenly looks astonishing. If I can change a false statement to a true by negating it or cancelling a negation this is possible because of the distinction of the different kinds of words which fit together to make descriptions. The grammar of 'red' is not determined by mere experience of colours.

> If you trained someone to emit a particular sound at the sight of something red, another at the sight of something yellow, and so on for other colours, still he would not yet be describing objects by their colours. Though he might be a help to us in giving a description. A description is a representation of a distribution in a space (in that of time, for instance).

> If I let my gaze wander round a room and suddenly it lights on an object of a striking red colour, and I say 'Red!' — that is not a description. (*PI*, II, ix)

Whereas, had I said *of* the object that *it* was red, or had I said that my visual field was not suffused with (or that it did not contain) red, here there would be a 'representation of a distribution in a space'.

It is thus not the case at all that Wittgenstein means anything but 'grammatical' when he says 'grammatical'. What is contentious is his claim that a vast number of philosophical and metaphysical statements are disguised statements of grammar — and *that*, of course, is his interest in grammar. So far as I can see each such claim has to be examined separately, and when he says that something, 'like everything metaphysical', is rooted in the grammar of our language, it is difficult to form a judgment on the general claim.

I conclude, then, that there is after all no theory of language in Wittgenstein. It may be worthwhile to end with a warning. What he calls 'a grammatical proposition' is of course a proposition *of* grammar. But his references to 'grammar' and his occasional statements of the form 'That is not how the language-game is played' may have played some part in leading 'formal' grammarians to try to characterize as 'ungrammatical' various forms of statement, such as 'I mean to punish the mountain', or 'The mountain devoured the boy' where there is for example an inappropriate object for a verb or the like. In view of the pictoriality of our use of language, the endless possibilities of a metaphor and picturesque new applications of words, such attempts on the part of formal grammarians are bound to fail. If they have been at all influenced by Wittgenstein in taking this direction that can only have been through a misunderstanding.

18

Wittgenstein: Whose Philosopher?

One of the ways of dividing all philosophers into two kinds is by saying of each whether he is an ordinary man's philosopher or a philosopher's philosopher. Thus Plato is a philosopher's philosopher and Aristotle an ordinary man's philosopher. This does not depend on being easy to understand: a lot of Aristotle's *Metaphysics* is immensely difficult. Nor does being a philosopher's philosopher imply that an ordinary man cannot enjoy the writings, or many of them. Plato invented and exhausted a form: no one else has written *such* dialogues. So someone with no philosophical bent, or who has left his philosophical curiosity far behind may still enjoy reading some of them.

What I call a philosopher's philosopher is one who sees problems, interest in which is the mark of a philosopher, and whose principal thoughts can be derived from his discussion of those problems. When Socrates in the *Phaedo* says he cannot understand how both adding one to one and dividing one can yield two; when in the *Republic* he says that the domain of knowledge is being, of non-knowledge non-being; when he ties Euthyphro into knots because he thinks that the pious pleases the gods *because* it is pious and that the pious is pious *because* it pleases the gods—at least, Euthyphro seems to begin with thinking both and Socrates proceeds to derive a contradiction and to leave the question what piety is in a state of *aporia*; when Plato reproduces arguments of the Sophists to prove that there cannot be such a thing as false belief, because what

* Reprinted from A P Griffiths (ed) *Wittgenstein: Centenary Essays*. Royal Institute of Philosophy *Philosophy Supplement* 28 (Cambridge: Cambridge University Press, 1991), pp. 1–10, with the permission of the publishers.

is false *is not*, and so he who thinks what is false thinks nothing, i.e. does not think anything; when he argues that there must be more than One, Parmenides' *being*, because it has a name and if the name of the one were the same as the one you could just as well call it the one of the name as the name of the one, so the name must be something different; when Socrates argues that if anyone can speak he can be found to know the whole of mathematics, though he has forgotten it and has to be reminded of what in fact he knew before he was born — I will stop because I have given enough examples. When this quite characteristic sort of thing is found argued for in the dialogues, the arguments will say little to interest non-philosophers, but almost always are likely to excite people of philosophical bent.

There is also the fact that where Plato does — or does make Socrates — draw conclusions from discussion of his problems, they do not seem credible. That the Forms are the only really real things; reincarnation and the eternal pre-existence of the souls of men; that it is impossible to want what is bad and all evil-doing is a matter of ignorance that it *is* evil; that there is something called the 'dyad' which makes whatever is two to be two: these and many other Platonic doctrines seldom exercise much appeal to philosophers, though some may appeal to non-philosophers for non-philosophical reasons.

By contrast, Aristotle is not often so much concerned with what are apt to strike non-philosophers as weird or boring problems, and his conclusions very often seem to be down-to-earth and about pretty familiar things. Sometimes this is because he made them familiar: consider the concept of *relation*. Plato had distinguished between what was *per se* (*kath auto*) and what was *to something else*; Aristotle replaced 'to something else' by the simple 'to something', for, as we would now say, a thing may stand in a relation to itself. Again, the concept of *matter* is one we owe to Aristotle: such a concept as is implicit in the reasonings of Lavoisier when he re-obtained mercury by heating mercury calx (as it was then called) in a closed vessel. The same matter but a change of chemical substance and an increase in how much of the matter in the vessel was air.

I will say no more in explanation of my distinction, but will proceed to argue for my main thesis: Wittgenstein is, like Plato, a philosopher's philosopher.

First, however, I will note with sorrow the sad fate that seems to be befalling him. For reasons which I do not understand, there are some philosophers who become cult figures. Plotinus is one, Spinoza another. I know hardly anything about Plotinus; of Spinoza, I know a certain amount—enough to find this vulgar elevation of him incomprehensible. He is a very tough thinker and it is hard work to study him. I doubt very much that *this* fact gives him his superior aura. Nor would the same facts about Wittgenstein account for the same phenomenon in his case. Having regretfully noticed it, I wave it away from my considerations.

These concern the phenomena of mental life called 'understanding' and 'thinking'. I will begin with *understanding*. Now we (usually) understand the meaning of a word when we hear or say it. Not always: we may think we understand it and not do so. (Think of how some people are fond of using the word 'parameters' in philosophical discussion.) However, we mostly understand words that we hear or say. *When* do we understand them? Well, when we hear them or say them. So is understanding, in that context, an event of a moment? Still more, when we *suddenly* understand a word whose meaning we did not know before. Now Wittgenstein's observation at Part I, section 43 of the *Untersuchungen* (*PI*) is surely quite correct: 'For a *large* class of cases of employment of the word "meaning" — even though not for all, it can be explained thus: The meaning of a word is its use in the language.' But if the meaning is the use we make of the word, how can I grasp it in a flash? For use is sometimes extended in time. So what I grasp in a flash must, must it not, be something different from use: the whole *use* of a word cannot come before my mind in a flash. And the verb 'to mean' has the same feature. 'When you said "funny" did you mean queer, or funny like a joke?' And there is such a thing as 'experiencing the meaning of a word'. Suppose I utter the sound *bord* to you. You may be able to answer the question 'what did you hear that as: the word "board" or "bored" — the noun or the past participle of 'to bore'?' and if you say 'the first' did you hear it as meaning something like a plank or something like a group of people with some official purpose? And if you say 'the past participle' was it connected with boredom or with boring holes? Of course, you may say you didn't hear it as anything, you just heard me make that noise and wondered why I did so. But if you do have one of those answers, which you very well may, then haven't you experienced a meaning? However, we cannot say that understanding in a flash is experiencing a meaning.

Suppose you envisaged a plank, the polished leaf of a table round which a board sits—would that prove that you heard the word 'board' as meaning 'plank'? No, the same thing may come before your mind on different occasions when you hear that word and the application still be different. But, once again, application is complicated and extended in time and applications of a word 'in the same meaning' may be various: e.g. in the sentence 'The board was liquidated'. Certainly, then, there is such a thing as experience of meaning and also an experience of understanding a word, but these just by themselves do not, or need not, tell the whole use. (I say need not, because in the case of very idiomatic connectives like the German 'wohl aber' there can be an experience which gives you its whole meaning: or so it has seemed to me. To anticipate, however, this may depend on antecedent circumstances.)

Suppose you are being taught something and are given examples of the kind of thing in question — as it might be a series of numbers, and you have a sudden reaction: 'Now I know what this one is, now I can go on'. 'Various things may have happened here', Wittgenstein says. You may have thought of a formula that fits the bit of the series you have been given; you may have asked yourself 'What is the series of differences between one number and the next?' and got a familiar series; or it may strike you that the series itself is a familiar one which you know how to continue; or you may recognise the series as something and have a mnemonic for going on, like the mnemonic for π: 'How I want a drink, alcoholic of course, after all those lectures confuting Fregean doctrines one by one', or you may simply go on with the series without any device.

But 'understanding the principle of the series' cannot be any of these happenings: it must be more, or it must be something *behind* them.

Here Wittgenstein says:

> If there has to be anything 'behind the utterance of the formula', it is *certain circumstances*, which justify me in saying I can go on — when the formula occurs to me. [And further:] In the sense in which there are processes (including mental processes) which are characteristic of understanding, understanding is not a mental process.[1]

> Thus [he continues] ... when [the man] suddenly knew how to go on, ... then possibly he had a special experience ... but for us it is the *circumstances* under which he had such an experience that

---

[1]   *Philosophical Investigations* I, § 154.

justify him in saying in such a case that he understands, that he knows how to go on.[2]

I will here note that in modern philosophy since Descartes there has been a strong tendency to amplify Descartes' list of *cogitationes* to include memory, even knowledge, probably understanding. I will not pause to consider the inwardness of the limitation of Descartes' list—though I suggest it might be a fruitful enquiry.

However that may be, Wittgenstein now proceeds to a very detailed consideration of *reading*: his purpose, he says, is to make clearer the fact he has just alleged: 'it is the *circumstances* under which he had such an experience that justify him to us in saying in such a case that he understands, that he knows how to go on'.

The choice of *reading* proves to lead us on a very complicated enquiry. It is here that I can most easily justify my thesis that Wittgenstein is a philosopher's philosopher. Non-philosophers are apt to think that there are no philosophical problems about reading: reading is just a special inner experience which you may or may not accompany by utterance out loud of the words you read. And perhaps under the post-Cartesian influence some philosophers too would say this, if they thought about it at all. That understanding and thinking are topics for philosophy none would doubt; that reading might be, it takes a philosophic bent to conceive. The enquiry on reading occupies nine pages of the English edition of the *Untersuchungen*; twelve if we include the corollary enquiry into *being guided*. Not long after Wittgenstein's death I was asked to produce something about him as a BBC programme; I innocently thought: 'This examination of *reading* is a whole and not too long passage and extremely interesting, so I'll read it.' I did, but I heard only rumours of how boring people found it, going on about something not in the least problematic.

Wittgenstein explains that he will give a special restricted—but also partially widened—sense to 'reading'. He will not count understanding what is read as part of reading for purposes of his investigation: it is there the activity of writing from dictation as well as those of rendering out loud what is written or printed and playing from a score.

A reader reads a newspaper: his eye passed along the words; perhaps he says the words; some he takes in as wholes, others he reads syllable by syllable, occasionally letter by letter. Even if he says

---

[2] *Op.cit.* § 155.

nothing while reading we would count him as having read a sentence if he could afterwards reproduce it, or nearly so.

A beginner in reading, by contrast, reads the words by laboriously spelling them out. He may guess some, or know some by heart. If he does that the teacher will say he is not really *reading* those words, and perhaps that he is pretending to.

But — Wittgenstein tells us he wants to say as far as concerns uttering any *one* of the printed words, the same thing may take place in the consciousness of the pupil who is 'pretending' to read, as in that of the practised reader who *is* reading it. The word 'read' is applied differently in the two cases.

The first word that someone *reads* — it makes no sense to ask what word that is, unless you stipulate that you are, for example, going to call 'the first word' the first in a series of 50 words that he reads right or something of that sort. But if 'reading' is to stand for a certain experience of transition from marks to spoken sounds, then it does make sense to speak of the first word he really read.

Wittgenstein imagines that someone argues that if only we knew more about the brain and the nervous system, we could look into the pupil's brain and say 'Now the reading connection has been set up.' But why does it have to be like that? If we feel it *must* be, that means that we find that form of explanation very convincing. But we really do not know if it is even probable that there *is* such a mechanism with a 'reading connection'.

If on the other hand we think that the only real criterion is that the 'reader' has a conscious experience of reading, we may be thinking of the contrast with someone who is a conscious fraud, pretending he can read Cyrillic script. He of course knows he is not reading — he knows he is not having the characteristic sensations that accompany peering, guessing with some confidence, misreading, and so on. The 'and so on' includes the contrast with repeating what you have learned by heart. But now, suppose a practised reader is reading a text fluently — but has the *sensations* of repeating something learned by heart — though he never saw the text before. Or suppose that someone is presented with what look like written characters, but which belong to no known alphabet, and he comes out with words, showing all the outward signs and having the characteristic sensations that go with reading. If he is systematic and consistent in what he does with uttering sounds in connection with the text, there might be disagreement about whether he was reading or not — or, indeed, whether he was making up an alphabet and reading accordingly.

Repeating something you know by heart—is that incompatible with reading? Look at your watch after saying the numbers 1 to 12 and now *read* the numbers. What did you do to make it *reading*?

We might want to say: reading is deriving the spoken sounds from the written characters. And we can describe clear-cut cases of such derivation in which a taught rule is used, or a rule for passing from print to handwriting. Such a 'rule' might be a pair of columns with printed letters on the left and written ones on the right; the pupil is to look at a text, check what written letter is immediately to the right of a printed letter, a sample of which occurs in his text, and copy the written letter. Of course he has to have been trained in the practice of using the adjacent columns as a rule, and as *that* rule. If less simple correlations are used, we can describe a series devolving into randomness. This, however, does not mean that there is really no such thing as a clear case of derivation. There is a variety of cases—and this fits in with the fact that a variety of circumstances provide us with cases of reading; from the first, we had to admit that for a beginner and for a practised reader we would apply quite different criteria. A child once said proudly when visiting his grandmother 'I can read!' 'Good', she said, and put a book before him. 'Oh no', he said, 'that's not the right book.'

A 'special experience' or 'words coming in a special way' do not function as explanations of what reading is. A word might come to you in the 'special way', and *any* special way you care to describe otherwise than as 'the way the sounds come to you when you are reading the words' might be found in cases which are *not* cases of reading. As for *that* description, it is useless: one wants to know 'what way *is* that?'

Some generalisations we can make—but they are of a restricted sort. There is a uniformity about reading printed pages when one is familiar with the printed words—for one thing, there is a uniformity in the appearance of many such pages. But reading is not restricted to this class of 'texts'. Wittgenstein remarks on how different the text would look where a sentence was written in Morse code. And if one tries to read out printed lines from right to left, i.e. reading the *letters* from right to left, there is a struggle quite unlike what we experience reading from left to right.

'But when we read do we not feel the word-shapes somehow causing our utterance?' —One would do better to say they grounded it— we would point to the text as a justification for the way we read it out loud. —Wittgenstein says 'I would like to say I feel an *influence* of the letters on me' — but he does not want to say that about a solitary letter. The contrast is between a row of printed words and a row of arbitrary printed marks like §, ?, %, *.

We repeatedly have as an argument against explaining *reading*, or *deriving*, or *influence*, or *being guided* in some way that is supposed to apply quite generally, that our cases are particular and that cases vary according to circumstances, and our 'explanation' is not borne out in a different sort of case. In the last example the marks are perfectly familiar, and we would have no difficulty about saying we read them when they occur functionally in appropriate positions. And we might *copy* such an arbitrary row of them — which conforms to Wittgenstein's specifications of what he is counting as 'reading' for his current investigation. One of the other explanations — the use (implicit) of a rule which could be constructed in the form of two columns, one of the printed signs, the other of the written ones — would be more like a justification than an account in terms of 'feeling an influence'.

In short, the whole enquiry in these pages consists largely in rather convincing arguments against generalising particular expressions that we are inclined to use in highly particular situations and cases.

We must remember the purpose which Wittgenstein claimed for putting his investigation of *reading* at this place in the *Untersuchungen* (*PI*). It was to help his contentions about *understanding* to become clearer to us. Of these, the principal one was: 'If there has to be anything "behind the utterance of the formula" [a formula you may use to continue a series] it is *certain circumstances* which justify me in saying I can go on — when the formula occurs to me.'[3]

'Now I understand the principle' does not mean the same as 'The formula … occurs to me.' The argument that it does not is an argument for a quite clear variety of cases in which one might say 'Now I understand the principle'; the formula … occurring to me was just one of the possible cases, and a case in which no such thing happens is not thereby shown *not* to be a case in which I could justifiably say 'Now I understand the principle'. But note this: the formula occurring to me *is* a particular experienced event, and with that we have explained how there can be 'experiences of understanding'. For *that* experience in *that* case is an experience of understanding — though this is true only because of the circumstances, which include much that went before the moment of the formula's occurring to me. That is why 'Now I understand the principle' does not mean the same,

[3]   *Op.cit.*, §154.

even just in this case, as 'The formula occurs to me'. This is illuminated by the discussion of reading: there are experiences connected with reading, but 'reading' is not the same as any of them. Similarly there is a variety of experiences connected with an occasion of understanding, but 'understanding' is not the same as any of them.

Now I do not believe that the investigation into reading which Wittgenstein conducted and compressed into these tight pages is of the sort to appeal to a reader without a philosophical bent. As a contribution to a certain clarifying of the concept of understanding, it plays a part in some major themes of his work — it is not just an eccentric preoccupation with a concept of very marginal importance.

This is my case for saying that Wittgenstein is 'a philosophers' philosopher'.

Understanding was not an abnormal topic for a philosopher: it is the questions, like 'when did understanding take place?' and 'if you understand the integral calculus, when do you do so? all the time, or every now and then?' that surprise. The latter not so much, as it may excite the ready answer: 'Here we are speaking of understanding as something dispositional'. So one also speaks of belief — and of knowledge. Wittgenstein's relevant contribution here was to reject the 'scholastic' suggestion that where there is a 'dispositional' sense of a word like 'belief', there is also and primarily an 'actual' sense of it. I mean as if one could answer a question: 'What are you doing?' by saying, for example, 'Believing that smelling is having molecules hit your smelling apparatus.' 'Believing', Wittgenstein said, has no such 'actual' sense. Clearly *coming to a conclusion*, if it is not just seeing that *q* follows from *p*, is arriving at a belief; but belief is not an activity which you can, for example, practise before breakfast every morning. Yet someone can say 'Believe me, it is better to steal than to beg' or recommend you to believe what someone else has said — using an imperative again. Coming to a conclusion, I said, may be arriving at a belief, and certainly is that if it is not finding the implications of a possibly rejected proposition. That means that, here at least, thinking, unlike believing, is an activity. (I am not speaking of the usage in which 'I think' *means* 'I believe'.) Anyone might say 'So far so good: obviously thinking is an activity, which may or may not accompany your utterances and your other actions, but we want to know what this activity, thinking, *is*.' Here Wittgenstein begins to jib — thinking may *be* talking — one does not usually have to think a sentence before saying it — though there may be talking 'without thinking'. So too with other activities: in some cases 'I did it without thinking' explains what sort of mistake in action, psychologically speaking, I committed: I did not deliberately take the wrong turning. So does doing something deliberately involve doing it *with thought*? No, not necessarily, as doing something with practised competence may show us.

We have only scratched the surface, but it is already clear that Wittgenstein was right in saying that the grammar of 'to think' is extremely complicated. To think is an activity, yes, but the activity may be one of, say, sharpening a pencil with a pencil sharpener that requires the pencil to be held in a particular way if the lead is to be given a point. Familiarity means that one can do it 'without having to think about it' — but if asked: 'Why are you pressing the pencil side-ways like that?' one can immediately give the reason. The activity is one *of* thought (as speech can be) if there is no distinct *accompaniment* of thought.

Our few examples might lead into thinking that 'thinking' is like 'paying'. If someone claims to have paid some money, the question may arise 'In what way did he pay it?' For example, was it by cheque, or with money; by post or messenger, or did you in person hand something over, or cancel an equivalent debt? But no: all I have indi-cated is that certain activities may *eo ipso* be thinking; they may con-tain moves that have an aim and are decisions, as playing chess or darts do. Here, though, as with *understanding*, a background of some custom is needed to constitute the practices as what they are. Suppose — to take an example from the discussion of *being guided* — I am copying a line that describes a complicated course. Is what I do, in that I draw a line that corresponds to — is in detail *like* — the other, *copying*? That is, is it *eo ipso* copying? We say children copy their par-ents. Do sheep copy one another? But the case of copying the line is more specialised than these. What do I mean by saying that? I mean that you could *imagine* circumstances, a background in my society, even in the development of people of my ancestry, which would mean that I was not engaged in the activity of copying. This would be decidedly odd — the conception *here* is of a natural regularity like that men grow beards. The construction of such 'philosophy fiction' does not have the purpose of recommending scepticism about whether you can know that I am copying that line; but only of show-ing what, other than what can be seen to be happening here and now, is involved in the fact that I am doing so.

A lot of things that are not necessarily 'overt actions' are thinkings: deciding, forming an intention, some exercises of imagination, calculation 'in the head', interpretation. 'Interpreting is thinking, is an action; seeing is a state', Wittgenstein remarks in Part II, section xi of the *Untersuchungen*. If I say: 'First I thought I would tell him and then I thought I would not', is there a difficulty about understanding such a report? Some have thought that such a 'thought' must *be* sub-vocal movements of the larynx. But how can one know one had such thoughts without knowing anything about such movements? Besides, it seems to hint that that thinking must have been a 'saying within oneself' as one may recite a whole poem 'in one's head'. What, then, did having those two thoughts *consist in*? We have no idea — or no reasonable idea — and we ought to call the question into question. For how does one learn to say such things? Perhaps I can show you how to saw a plank; I cannot show you the way to have a thought like that — so how do you learn? And what is the relation to its expression in words? Do these constitute a sort of translation as if from one language into another? How could that be, and how could the translation be checked?

One useful method of enquiry would be to construct misuses of these terms, 'thought', 'translation', 'meaning', etc., which show hopeless error about their grammar. 'I know Russian.' 'Right, translate "I'm going out" into Russian.' Silence ensues. 'Well, do it.' 'I did do it, but I can only do it in my head.' I cannot sing in tune — suppose I said that I can think a song in tune, only not out loud.

I will end with a story. I went with my little girl, then four-years-old, to look in on Kanti Shah in Trinity.[†] He was not in his rooms, but there was an offprint on a table. I sat down and picked it up. 'Shall we go now?' asked the child. 'Yes, but first I'll read this a bit.' She waited expectantly and then said 'Read it'. 'I am reading it.' A bewildered silence followed, then she angrily shook my arm, exclaiming '*Read it, read it!*' I could not explain.

---

† The location and date: Trinity College, Cambridge, 1947.

19

Was Wittgenstein a conventionalist?

The conventionality and subjectivity of truth (but this latter not at all in Kierkegaard's sense) is one of the characteristically apathetic thoughts of our time. Nothing is, not only good or bad, fair or foul, but also true or false but thinking makes it so. The thinking may be a consensus within a society: that is where the conventionality comes in.

To this popular attitude the philosophy of Wittgenstein seems to make its contribution. That is, Wittgenstein of the *Philosophical Investigations*, not Wittgenstein of the *Tractatus*. *That* work played a part in the promotion of another attitude: truth is to be found in natural science alone. Not a new attitude, indeed, but one which in the *Tractatus* was backed up by sophisticated thinking about logic, language, mathematics, and which had the added cachet of a deeply serious tone about the ethical, the mystical, the higher.

If those propositions which seem to express insights into the essential natures of things—propositions whose contents are supposed to be the *musts* in reality—if these are to be explained as disguised propositions of grammar, or sometimes are revealed to be pure nonsense; and if their correlative contradictories in turn are not the expression of what is *necessarily* excluded from reality, but are merely forms of combination of words at present not admitted by the grammar of that part of language to which they essentially belong: if all this is so, doesn't it seem that truth itself is a matter of

---

* From a typescript without title or date with some written corrections to its first few pages by the author. Insertions in square brackets in quotations from Wittgenstein are by the author. Insertions in square brackets in the author's text are by the editor; a number were required in what was a largely unrevised typescript. Title supplied.

convention? Philosophy has no deep truths to teach; its goal is not the achievement of knowledge of what must be truth; its problems are deep *only* because the forms of language are deeply rooted in us; and even the 'truths' of everyday communication are true only within the framework of a system of conventions.

'Essence', Wittgenstein says, 'is expressed by grammar'. It isn't difficult to grasp that. Think of the association of a proper name with the name of a kind of thing, such as 'dog', such that the *proper* name is used with the same reference as it was before, if and only if it is used of the same member of that kind, the same dog, say. That gives us part of the grammar of proper names. And does not this grammar express the essence of the individual named by a proper name, if anything does? Or at any rate, part of its essence.

But grammar could be different. And that suggests, not just that essence is expressed by grammar, but that essence is the creation of grammar. Couldn't a proper name be associated with a different kind of identity? Suppose, for example, that what comes out of the mouth of one human body as personal expression (expression of personal states) were always referred to another human body so far as any body must e.g. suffer the consequences (as princes had whipping boys) — might not one personal identity be vested not in one human body but in two, be as it were distributed among two? (Or more, as we distribute the several roles of a 'person'.) — One society, it seems, cannot criticise the beliefs and practices of another if their forms of life are different from one another. *You* are talking *your* language, and anything you say is a move in a language-game which is played in *your* society: the Aztec or the consultor of poison-oracles in mid-Africa is making moves in the language-games they play there.

Or again, one can describe the grammar of verbs of perception and sensation, observing that some of them take objects while others do not. E.g. 'I see' and 'I itch'. One will describe the intentionality of such verbs and their double use: with an intentional or a material object, according to whether 'I see such-and-such' is refuted by there being no such-and-such there. One may give an account of the 'asymmetry' of such verbs in respect of the first person present indicative used assertorically — the senselessness of the question 'How do you know?' in response to such utterances (e.g. 'I am hearing a sound') except with reference to the material diagnosis of the object

('I see the sky').[1] — And now let us suppose the grammar changed. We describe a use of words which is akin to the use of the verbs of sensation and perception, but which lacks some of these features. Each person, for example, makes reports in the form 'my retina is affected thus-and-so' (etc.), and others may look and see whether this is so. If it is not, he is simply mistaken. So, though he says such things not by examining the way his organs are affected, but they come to him 'immediately' — and so there is still a certain asymmetry, for the question can be 'Did you really mean it, did you consider carefully enough?' but not 'Did you *look* carefully enough?' — still there is no 'privacy' and instead of intentionality there is incompleteness in what he is able to report. (But such incompleteness is usual in *any* report.) The question arises: should we thereby miss out things essential to perception (as it is still taking place)? Or suppose that the language we manage to describe were universal, the language of perception as we at present have it being non-existent: would that be the supposition that there was *no such thing* as perception — as it is at present?

At §497 Wittgenstein remarks: 'If someone says "If our language had not this grammar, it could not express these facts" — it should be asked what "*could*" means here.' He doesn't answer the question. Let's try: 'If our language (of perception) had not its present grammar but was replaced by a language of the sort we have imagined, then it would not include sentences about (e.g.) the visual *experiences* of people with *delirium tremens*.' — Well, doubtless it would not. The concept of 'experience', as it is used there, would make no appearance in the language we are supposing. But wouldn't the facts appear in the alcoholic's greater tendency to report wrongly what was on his retina? We might say: *Experience*, in this special sense of the word, *is* an 'essence' not just expressed but created by grammar. Now that would involve us in no general commitment.

Plato's suggestion in the *Cratylus*: words for the same thing in different languages (as 'horse', 'cheval') are like tools made of different metals but all shaped to catch hold of the same object. What these words catch hold of is the same essence. This presupposes that the essence is there to catch hold of, and that the words have in some sense the same shape. Wittgenstein might concur in the last bit: the

---

[1] This does not mean that no case is imaginable where the question is given a sense. It would be given a sense, for example, if a use of the verb of sensation in the first person present is described, where the seeing referred to is itself an hypothesis or diagnosis on the part of the user.

'shape' is *logical* shape, and this is none other than that use whose similarity justifies translation of a word in one language by a *sensibly* very different word in another.

'You learned the *concept* pain by learning language.' I.e. *not* by experiencing pain. If people have a different concept do they miss something? I mean, if they have a concept which is sufficiently like ours to be called a concept of pain, but which does not apply where there is no obvious damage or physical disorder (dislocation, for example) or incapacitation — do they misrepresent, or at least miss something out? If there are people for whom red is a degenerate form of green, do they miss anything, or make a mistake? — To render this natural we need to suppose a different world: red, say, occurring only on the edges of some leaves.

On the first example, Wittgenstein imagines the objection: don't they notice the similarity? — *sc.* of pain without damage to pain with damage. And he asks if *we* want a concept wherever we may notice a similarity.

Differences in facts of nature and differences in human practices: imagining these can render intelligible to us the formation of concepts different from ours, yet related to them. This shows us that we haven't the right to say that certain concepts are absolutely *the* correct ones.[2] But Wittgenstein also seems to speak against the idea that 'having different ones would mean not realising something that we realise'. But *wouldn't* it? E.g. wouldn't the people for whom red is a degenerate case of green fail to realise that red is a different colour? — Yet again, *would* they? They see a difference — and don't treat it the same way as we do. We *call* the difference one of colour, they do not. That doesn't make them wrong.

There is another question. May we not say: we don't claim that our concepts are absolutely *the* right ones, but are they not nevertheless *right* ones? We understand indeed how other people might form different concepts. The intelligibility of this may depend on a description of some difference in very general facts of nature — for example, colour and shape vary independently in our world; in a world in which they did not, people might have only 'simple' concepts which correspond to our 'round and blue', 'red and square', etc. But of course we have said in our description that there are not in their world the facts for which distinct words for colour and shape give us the means of description. — However, we might suppose that there were *some* such facts; these *might* then be overlooked, or might

[2]   See *Philosophical Investigations* II, xii.

be regarded as very unimportant. The possession of such a language as we have would presumably make it easier to notice such facts than it might otherwise be. But we haven't reason to say that people possessed only of the colour-shape concepts would not be able to notice these facts. They can grant similarities without having terms for the respect of similarity. Here there seems no reason to say that essences are created by grammar. But: though we do thus make no claim for our concepts to be 'absolutely' *the* right ones, still we can claim that our concepts *are* right ones. Or at least: can't we *enquire* whether our concepts are right ones, and conclude that they are, at least in some cases? And can't we *criticise* others' concepts as wrong ones, i.e. as not corresponding to anything?

We can surely prove this. We have a concept of superstition. Is there not such a thing? If not, then the concept is a wrong concept.[3] If so, then some concepts are wrong. So in any case some concepts are wrong. And you, Wittgenstein, yourself called some things superstitious. To be sure, what you called 'superstitious' were not concepts but beliefs. But if someone says 'It is superstitious to believe that there is such a thing as magic. Certainly there are people who practise magic, but their belief about what they do is superstitious' — is that not equivalent to saying that 'magic' (as believed in) is a superstitious concept, and *therefore* a wrong one. I am not at all supposing here what Wittgenstein found so stupid, namely that belief in magic is a sort of mistaken natural science. But I take it that superstition is wrong, false. Wittgenstein too presumably means that it is false, when he diagnoses something as superstition, as for example at §110: ' 'Language (or thought) is something unique' — this proves to be a superstition (*not* a mistake!) itself produced by grammatical illusions.'

However, he says 'not a mistake'. We need to ask why. We shall find that Wittgenstein would say 'It's not a mistake' in a number of cases. Suppose someone were to say, apparently seriously and not speaking in metaphor or by anticipation, 'I am dead', or to ask 'Surely I am dead, aren't I?' He can't be said straightforwardly to be making a mistake. What would it be like for him to be right *in saying this*? And if there is no answer to that, then what is he supposing himself to be saying? He is using language in such a strange way that

---

[3] I don't mean to raise any objection to empty concepts as such; but *this* one has its native place in an application to certain things. If it doesn't apply to them, or at least if it can't be called 'superstitious' to do or think *any* of the things that *have* been called 'superstitious', then surely it is a wrong concept.

we ought to hesitate to think we understand him. Of course, if he has just emerged from an accident, we may understand him in a way, as suffering from confusion of mind, and we may firmly reassure him by *telling* him that he is alive. This may get him out of it — but it would be comical to think of the situation as one in which we inform and he learns from us. Again, if someone is brought up, trained, to think he is a god and that the world began with and depends on him, his belief is a wrong, an appalling belief for him to have, and we might want to get him out of it, but it would be absurd to treat it as something the truth of which would be established by *these* observations, and refuted or rendered doubtful by *those*, and to think he is under the impression that these rather than those observations can be made.

The conception of 'mistake' which Wittgenstein has is obviously something like this: in order to say that someone thinks that *p*, and it is a mistake on his part, it has to be clear what it is for *p* to be true (or correct); he must be acquainted with this. E.g. the situation must be such that *if* he had noticed the relevant features, he would have agreed that *p* was false. Or, if it should be a calculation, he must be ready to take back a slip or false step.

Thus not every case of saying *p* when, by all familiar criteria, it is true that ~*p* is a case of making a mistake. The situation may be all wrong for this utterance of '*p*' to be straightforwardly the assertion which is the contradictory of that apparent truth that ~*p*.

It may be that the assertion '*p*' is something which we cannot understand. An example is the assertion of the deaf-mute, Mr Ballard about his childhood that

> ... even before he could speak he had had thoughts about God and the world. — What can he have meant? — Ballard writes: 'It was during those delightful rides, some two or three years before my initiation into the rudiments of written language, that I began to ask myself the question: how came the world into being?' — Are you sure — one would like to ask — that this is the correct translation of your wordless thought into words? And why does this question — which elsewhere seems not to exist at all — raise its head here? Do I want to say that the writer's memory deceives him? I don't even know if I would say that [presumably, if confronted with the man and able to converse with him]. These recollections are a queer memory phenomenon, — and I do not know

what conclusions one can draw from them about the past of the man who recounts them.[4]

That is, accepting the man's sincerity, we don't know what it means for the report to be true.

On the other hand, consider the Catholic doctrine of transubstantiation and the irrelevance of referring to chemical analysis or what everyone can see if he looks at the consecrated host. — What is said may be an assertion in a different line of country, where once again there is a definite way *for* the thing to be true. If it were a convention — say a legal convention — that someone was dead in certain circumstances, the assertion 'He is dead' would be an assertion in a different line of country from the usual one, and the method for showing it to be false is known; it can once more be a mistake.

About the Law of Excluded Middle, where p is e.g. 'There are 3 consecutive sevens in the decimal development of π', Wittgenstein's objection to $p \lor \sim p$ is that it can have as shaky or as solid a meaning only as its elements, p and $\sim p$, have themselves.

The key thought on all this comes at §241: ' "So you are saying that human agreement decides what is correct and what is wrong?" — It is what human beings *say* that is correct and wrong; and they agree in *language*. That isn't any agreement in opinions, but in form of life.'

It is what human beings *say* that is true or false, and they agree in the language that they use. You have to know or find out what that language is, before you can draw conclusions about what they say, or call it false. When the sun appears at the horizon at the beginning of the day, that is *called* 'sunrise'. That does not mean that the question 'Had the sun risen yet?' is not objective, i.e. that it is subjective in the sense that the correctness of the answer depends on, consists in, the agreement of those who said it had or had not.

You have to find out what language *we* are using, when we purport to be making assertions. What is it for that to be so, or not to be so? We often assume we know this when we don't. E.g. an anthropologist tells us that in a certain tribe they have such and such a belief about the soul. It is to the point to ask him what he *calls* people having such a belief about the soul. It is of course no use his saying 'That's what they say' because we shall need to know why he translates a word they use as 'soul'.

The idea that e.g. personal identity is a matter of convention is strongly resisted. That there might be a convention by which this

[4] *Philosophical Investigations* §342.

future object (indicated by some description) is *called* the same person as I am — that does not either comfort me or make me fear. The question is, will that be I? Conventions can be changed. How absurd a proposal, to relieve my apprehensions by proposing a new convention. (Chisholm)

But *is* there not a convention by which some future object may be identified with me? It is this: if any human body living with a human life is the same human body as *this* one (at which I lay my hand on my breast) then that will be me, E.A. The application of the convention is clear so long as we know what we mean by re-identifying a human being. Now *isn't* this a convention? I mean: if you asked why that would be E.A., there is no answer except that that's what is meant by being the same person as E.A. 'E.A.' is the name of a human being and of a person because a human being is a person; i.e. to use Boethius' definition of a person: *an individual substance of a rational nature*. We could no doubt imagine a failure, an inapplicability of this convention; e.g. if it happened for one human being to split directly into two the same size: two as it were walk simultaneously out, one to the right, the other to the left, from where there *was* a single one. Or again we could imagine the identity of the organism preserved but this lacking some of the interest it at present has, so that it was reckoned that one organism was successively two different human beings. E.g. suppose the race worked like this: everyone is born female and continues so to the age of twenty or thirty, and then undergoes a metamorphosis so as to become male. Much, both in the facts of nature connected with this development, and in the treatment that Laura and Laurence (say) universally receive in society: the emotional relation between them, what sort of vanity is exercisable by Laurence for being the same human organism as Laura was, what sort of responsibility either has in connection with the other — all this, we will suppose, surrounds and in a way supports the reckoning of these as two human beings. No doubt it will have *some* role in this if Laurence quite lacks agent-memory in respect of Laura's deeds. But the importance of this ought not to be exaggerated. The presence of such agent-memory would not *prove* anything, for 'I' is not a name. And the rule we at present have: If *N* directly says 'I …' then that is true if and only if '*N* …' is true might not hold. Any more than it would hold if there were a peculiar relation between a human being and one of his grandfathers, such that he had agent-memory in respect of his grandfather's actions. This, oddly enough, was recently made clear by Locke, who, however, took as a criterion for a new kind of identity one of the several reasons (memory) why we are (at present) *interested* in the identity of a human being (and not usually in the identity of a pin or a grain of sand). Locke saw that agent-memory could be conceived to pass from one substance to another, that is, that the spontaneous memory 'I did such-and-such' had by one substance might have a relation to the consciousness 'I am doing such-and-such' previously had by *another* substance, which constituted the former as the direct memory of the very deed referred to in the latter. *He* thought that such an occurrence would prove identity of a new sort of object, which he called a 'person'. But a person, as he defines it is not a suitable term for identity at all. For he defines a person as 'a thinking intelligent being that has reason and reflection, and can consider itself as itself, the same thinking thing, in different times and places.' That is, he defines a person as a being with certain capacities. 'Same person' by this definition is not different from 'same genius'. (This admirable insight is owing to my student Harold Noonan.) Find a being with this capacity and you find a being that is a person by Locke's definition. But the *identity* of the being will be the identity of whatever kind of being it is, a human being for example. Locke had the profundity to see that his idea led to the question whether one thinking substance might have true agent-memory which was of deeds belonging to another, and invoked the goodness of God to avoid this. Jonathan Edwards on the other hand embraced the idea and used it to explain our guilt for Adam's sin: we shall remember doing it when we are judged.

Thus in my fantasy neither the absence nor the presence of agent-memory in Laurence in respect of Laura's deeds has to determine anything. Laura and Laurence (who are but examples, these names are dummy constants and what is said using them shows what is said in *all* cases) can be supposed to be counted distinct human beings. — But, it may be asked, would they be distinct human beings? What can that mean? The case is after all imaginary: the facts of nature are different from ours. Among us, the single human organism is not distinguished from the single human being except in the twinning embryo and in very closely united Siamese twins. Nothing is determined by our present application of the concept 'human being' about what would be *the* continuation of that concept in circumstances so different from ours. But if anyone objects that, since various continuations are imaginable, any one would be merely conventional, we reply that our present use too [is] a convention, by which the aged man (or other animal) is the same X ('X' being the name of the animal kind) as the new born or new hatched. But it is an illusion to think that, because something is a convention and because we could imagine a different one, it must therefore be in human power to alter it, as it is presumably in human power to adopt a fixed date for Easter or a phonetic system of spelling for English. Altering a convention may be beyond our power.

'If it is at present a convention that the aged man is the same human being as the baby from which he developed.' It may be protested: but that, e.g. is what a single human being is! And that is quite true. But does it mean anything other than: that's what is *called* a human being — is an example of what is *called* being the same human being? If[5] an Oriental sect calls some abbot the same human being as an abbot who existed before this one was born — which we do not call being the same human being — that is a convention that parts company with ours [and] this suggests that we cannot call it a *mistake*, as Wittgenstein understands 'mistake'. It certainly is not like the mistake of thinking that this man I see here is the same as such-and-such a baby, when not that baby but some other grew up into him. It appears, then, that we, who are speaking within *our* convention, cannot contradict the belief of the sectary. But to say that is to assume that contradiction is just one thing. Negation is rejection: but there are different kinds of rejection. If any superstition is to be rejected as fake, but can be contrasted with [a] simple 'mistake', then so may be the convention and associated belief of our Oriental sectary. The interesting question is whether this is a matter of mere denunciation of one another by people of opposing parties — people whose several beliefs and practices excite powerful *feelings* of mutual opposition — but in which there can be no *showing* of anything as false or wrong. My supposed Oriental no doubt grasps, say *has*, the concept of the identity from conception or post-conceptional splitting to death, which is the only thing that we in the West are agreed on calling the identity of an individual animal, but he regards that as only one stretch of a continued identity over many such stretches which (I am supposing) he *calls* the identity of a human being. Now to say this is to assume that we shouldn't after all use some other word to translate his word, rather than 'man' or 'human'. That can surely be a justified assumption.

It may be quite clear that this is the word in that language for 'human being' but that they make these identifications, different

---

[5]   I only say 'if', as I don't know that any such do say so.

from all otherwise normal identifying practice. *This* indeed we know that the Tibetan Buddhists do, identifying the present so-and-so with all former ones; but I do not know whether they regard them all as different human beings, in whom the same individual something else (spirit, say) is successively embodied, or as all the same human being who again and again becomes an embryo, is born, grows to maturity and dies. It is this latter idea that I am ascribing to my hypothetical sectary. Now how could this be shown to be wrong? We may say we don't know what the identification means, and that no one could know: it is in fact meaningless because unintelligible. But 'it means something to them': it has consequences including logical consequences.[6] And we may very naturally suppose that it has a point in their lives: e.g. quasi-divine worship is paid to these identified Enlightened Men. If we say we cannot understand the identification, it may be retorted upon us: (a) what would you say to someone (of another utterly different society) who 'could not understand' *your* identification of the baby as the same human being with the grown man or woman? You may say: look, *this* is an identification we just do make, and it shows what our concept of a human being is. But then the objector might find that senseless, he might not be able to enter into it. — And that other one is an identification those people make, and it shows something of what *their* concept of a human being is. (For there is enough overlap for us to call it that.)

There is a place in Africa where, if a head of an immediate family dies, someone belonging to that village but not to that family is identified as that man by a visiting witch-doctor, who is summoned for the purpose from a distance (so that he shall [not] have a personal stake in the decision). The person so designated has a certain position of authority in the family; he can settle quarrels, tell them to stop misbehaving, and so on. He does not acquire any material interests in connection with it. This role can be socially useful.[7] Now this is not a mysterious story. We can take it that the identification does not in the least show a different concept of human identity — any more than Christ's saying 'Behold your mother, behold your son' to John and Mary. There is, so to speak, no meta-physics in it. It is the meta-

---

[6]   It is reported of the present Dalai Lama that when he was a small boy he was rebuked by those who were bringing him up; reference was made to the Great Fifth Dalai Lama — whereupon he rebuked his rebukers with the question 'Who *is* the Great Fifth Dalai Lama?' which quite confounded them.

[7]   I had the matter described to me by a man from that society, who seemed to me to be truthful and very sensible.

physics in the idea of the Tibetans, or of the Oriental sect that I have supposed, which puzzles us. This man 'really is', not in a manner of speaking or for particular social purposes, that man and that one and that one, all long dead.

Of course (for I am modelling my own supposition on something we know of) the belief is connected with a role: the role of the enlightened, the carrier of the solutions [to] the problems of life, who only continue with their successions of lives to confer blessing and enlightenment on men who are still struggling with desire and sorrow. In order to reject the identification one brought up to such a role would have to deny the role itself—deny its validity, or perhaps think some mistake had been made in assigning *him* to it. No information on scientific facts about life and birth, or his own origin and history, could supply a refutation.

That is why it is so futile to oppose such a belief with the characteristic beliefs going with what is called the 'scientific outlook'. To the extent that one of this outlook points to facts ascertainable by making repeatable observations, and 'mundane' facts ascertainable by historical enquiry, and to canons of evidence and checkability said to be connected with the adoption and maintenance of scientific theories—to *that* extent he cannot touch the belief that he is opposing. To the extent that he has a philosophy of the sort we may call 'scientific', he will want to oppose the whole conception of enlightenment which is the real key to the belief. But here what he says is likely to be weak. There is no incompatibility, even, between the pursuit of knowledge of physics and cosmology and biology according to scientific canons, and the practice of the grossest superstitions. Natural science cannot refute superstition. Take the superstition that it is unlucky to upset salt, but that the bad luck may be averted by throwing a pinch of it over your shoulder; or again to have a rowan tree growing in your garden. How could this possibly be refuted by any scientific considerations? People will speak of such a belief not measuring up to the proper canons of evidence but I don't suppose anyone knows, and it hardly even seems relevant, whether the general run of people who have upset salt or had such trees in their gardens have led as fortunate lives as others. (For of course there will be other causes of bad luck as well.) And a believer in these superstitions may have some tales to tell in illustration, or believe that his ancestors did. It is very difficult to say what superstition is, though it is rather easy to recognise in some of its forms. Wittgenstein said in the *Tractatus*: Superstition is belief in the causal nexus. I am not quite sure what he meant, but I believe it was this: superstition is belief that 'causality' names a tie between things, that there is such a thing as causality itself which connects up a cause with its effect, so that the cause drags the effect after it by means of the tie. The cause would drag the effect into existence. The idea of the pure causal tie is obviously involved in some kinds of superstition: there is no need felt that there be a 'how' in this causality, different in different cases according to the natural properties of things.

The thesis that the type now called 'scientific' knowledge is all that enlightenment can be is not itself a truth of any of the sciences, say of physics, cosmology, or biology; nor yet of such a claimant to the name of 'science' as sociology. It is rather an−absurd−philosophical thesis. It is absurd because it would itself have to be enlightenment but is not part of the sciences in which it says enlightenment consists.

The only way of partially avoiding this point was offered by the *Tractatus*. According to it, knowledge−what can be expressed−is only knowledge of the sciences. But what can't properly be expressed, and is far more important−is, indeed alone important, is the right way of seeing the world. For the mere facts of the world are indifferent. Enlightenment will then by no means consist in scientific knowledge, but it will not consist in anything else that can be said either. The 'clarifications' of philosophy turn out, paradoxically, to be improper expressions, strictly speaking nonsense, not framed according to the only *strictly* correct way of doing philosophy. This would consist in saying *nothing* except 'what can be said', i.e. the propositions of natural science, and, if anyone tried to say something metaphysical, in showing him that he had failed to give meaning to some part of his would-be sentences. The 'clarifications' were a sort of apparatus to help human weakness: Wittgenstein calls them a ladder, but that seems the wrong metaphor. A sort of apparatus for cripples, rather, by which we−being so far incapable of standing upright and walking and looking around−may *somehow* crawl to where we can do so.

The thing that is most striking here is the extraordinary restriction laid on language and truth: restriction to the expression of the different facts about how things are in the world−which way things are that may be one way or another, and where which way they are is indifferent: 'how the world is, is indifferent for what is higher'. In the same vein Wittgenstein also wrote 'God does not manifest himself *in* the world'. At first sight this looks like something we can set in clean

† *Epistle to the Romans*, 1:20.

opposition to that of Paul (of Tarsus): 'The invisible things of his — his eternal power and divinity — are manifest to sight since the creation of the world, being understood by the things that are made.'† But, on further reflection, this is not so. What Paul says is paradoxical: 'invisible' things are 'seen'. The invisibility is that of which Wittgenstein spoke: 'God does not manifest himself *in* the world', that is, not in the facts of the world's being this way rather than that. This is 'indifferent for what is higher', i.e. it doesn't make any difference as far as concerns the existence of 'what is higher' which way the world is. But [it is] the existence of the world itself — the 'that, not the how', as Wittgenstein called it — that makes God manifest. Only, according to the restriction which by his theory must be laid on language, this cannot be said. It is one example of 'What can be shown cannot be said'.

The *Tractatus* theory of language, however, is incredible for many reasons. E.g. it requires that all of logic be a decidable calculus; it requires the existence of atomic propositions and simple objects which, however, can never be found; there are a host of propositions which it is impossible to suppose to be truth-functions of elementary propositions, and which yet are statements of mundane fact. The restriction on language is incredible. In one way there was something greatly attractive about the silence prescribed by the *Tractatus*: an area to cut off not only much nonsense in philosophy but also much disgusting religious drivel. But that work must be left to criticism. We must be at liberty to discuss, to reason about, all these things: to discuss whether indeed natural science *is* the only kind of knowledge and enlightenment that there is. And, that being so, our former argument holds. For the decision on that question is [not] in itself a scientific one.

In the *Investigations* Wittgenstein seems to imagine a purely negative role for philosophy. Its achievement is to clear the ground of the '*Luftgebaüde*' which we are hoodwinked into constructing, hoodwinked by the suggestions made by the forms of language. There is no suggestion that the ground is cleared for the construction of a better edifice. The positive value of philosophy is the clarity for living in — if one could attain it.

20

Wittgenstein on Rules and Private Language

At article 6 of the *Discours de métaphysique*, Leibniz says that God does nothing disorderly. In the same breath he makes clear that he means an impossibility of even imagining any 'absolutely irregular happening'. To illustrate or persuade us of this he says:

> For let us suppose for example that someone were to make a lot of points on a piece of paper quite randomly, as is done by people practising the ridiculous art of geomancy. I say that a geometric line can be found, the notion of which is constant and uniform following a certain rule, such that this line passes through all those points, in the same order as that in which the hand marked them. And if someone were quite quickly tracing a line, now straight, now circular, now of some other kind, it is possible to find a notion or rule or equation common to all the points on that line, in virtue of which those very alterations would have to occur. And there isn't, for example, a single face whose contour would not make part of a geometric line and could not be traced at one go by a particular movement governed by a rule.

I believe this to be a first in philosophy and would be much obliged if anyone who knows better could point to any earlier author who had this thought. (We find echoes of it later in Russell's *Principles of Mathematics* and Wittgenstein's *Tractatus*.)

* A review of Saul A Kripke, *Wittgenstein: On Rules and Private Language* (Cambridge, Mass: Harvard University Press, 1982) published in *Ethics* 95 (January 1985): 342–352, and reprinted by permission of the publishers, Chicago University Press. This is one of two quite distinct reviews of the Kripke volume by Anscombe published in 1985. The other appeared in the *Canadian Journal of Philosophy* 15 (1985): 103–109.

What Leibniz says has a particular consequence: I don't know whether he drew it or would have liked it. If what he says is true, an indefinite number of rules should be discoverable for a line passing through all these points in that order; and, given one particular line that so passes through them all, an indefinite number of rules producing it and continuing it in different ways. This sort of fact is of course familiar to Saul Kripke:

> Given my past intentions regarding the symbol '+', one and only one answer is dictated as the one appropriate to '68 + 57'. On the other hand, although an intelligence tester may suppose that there is only one possible continuation to the sequence 2, 4, 6, 8, ..., mathematical and philosophical sophisticates know that an indefinite number of rules (even rules stated in terms of mathematical functions as conventional as ordinary polynomials) are compatible with any such finite initial segment. So if the tester urges me to respond, after 2, 4, 6, 8, ..., with *the* unique appropriate next number, the proper response is that no such unique number exists, nor is there any unique (rule determined) infinite sequence that continues the given one. (pp. 17–18)

The intelligence tester has arbitrarily fixed on *one* answer as *the* correct one.

Kripke goes on to ask: since the process of explaining which function we mean must eventually stop, with 'ultimate' functions and rules stipulated 'only by a *finite* number of examples', isn't our procedure arbitrary after all? 'In what sense is my actual computation procedure, following an algorithm that yields "125", more justified by my past instructions than an alternative procedure that would have resulted in "5"?' (p.18) At this point he has a footnote which opens with: 'Few readers ... will by this time be tempted to appeal a determination to "go on in the same way" as before.' (p. 18, n. 13) I think it a pity that he did not actually discuss this. His footnote was concerned principally to say that questions of 'relative' or 'absolute' identity have nothing to do with the matter. But the question: 'What *is* going on in the same way?' has everything to do with it.

At the faint risk of being unfair to Leibniz I will attach his name to the point that an infinite number of rules are compatible with, say, an initial segment of a series, for example, 1, 5, 11, 19, 29; or with such as he himself sketches. I don't call it a Wittgenstein point because I don't know if he ever so much as referred to it. (Perhaps §213 – 'this segment of a series obviously admitted of various interpretations' –

is a partial reference to it.)[1] But since it is true, there is no use in giving a stretch of a series and suggesting that that gives you with mathematical certainty or logical necessity *the* function to use in developing *that* series further. I take it that it is this fact that leads Kripke to his account of 'Wittgenstein's sceptical question' as a question whether there is any such fact as 'my having an intention to mean one function rather than another by "+".' (p. 28) Or again, he speaks of himself as asserting that he definitely means addition by 'plus' and insists that in asserting this 'I assert that the present meaning I give to "+" determines values for arbitrarily large amounts'. (p. 29, n. 21) He invents a name, 'quus', for a function whose values coincide with those of plus up to a point and thereafter are always 5. Given that the previous examples in which I have computed $n + m$ are within the range of coincidence, 'The sceptic argues that there is no fact as to what I meant, whether plus or quus'. (p. 39) 'There can be no fact as to what I meant by "plus", or any other word at any time.' (p. 21)

This last sentence ends a paragraph. The next begins:

> This, then, is the sceptical paradox. When I respond in one way rather than another to such a problem as '68 + 57', I can have no justification for one response rather than another. Since the sceptic who supposes that I meant quus cannot be answered, there is no fact about me that distinguishes between my meaning plus and my meaning quus. (p. 21)

I am not sure whether the 'This' at the beginning of this quotation looks backward to the previous sentence or forward to the next one. Perhaps it does not matter, for Kripke has previously said that the questions whether there is 'such a fact' and whether I am justified in giving 125 as the answer are related.

> Neither the accuracy of my computation nor of my memory is under dispute. So it ought to be agreed that *if* I meant plus, then unless I wish to change my usage, I am justified in answering (indeed compelled to answer) '125' not '5'. An answer to the sceptic must satisfy two conditions. First, it must give an account of what fact it is (about my mental state) that constitutes my meaning plus, not quus. But further, there is a condition that any putative candidate for such a fact must satisfy. It must, in some sense, show how I am justified in giving the answer '125' to '68 + 57'. (p. 11)

---

[1] Ludwig Wittgenstein, *Philosophische Untersuchungen* (Frankfurt am Main: Suhrkamp Verlag, 1977).

He has previously said:

> … I do not simply make an unjustified leap in the dark. I follow
> directions I previously gave myself that uniquely determine that
> in this new instance I should say '125'. What are these directions?
> By hypothesis, I never explicitly told myself I should say '125' in
> this very instance. Nor can I say that I should simply 'do the same
> thing I always did', if this means 'compute according to the rule
> exhibited by my previous examples'. That rule could just as well
> have been the rule for quaddition … The idea that quaddition *is*
> what I meant, that in a sudden frenzy I have changed my previ-
> ous usage, dramatizes the problem. (pp. 10–11)

Now I will justify my regret that Kripke did not discuss 'going on in
the same way'. It is a matter that the Leibniz point makes problematic in an elementary way. What is necessarily the next term in the
series, or point which the traced line has to reach, beyond the points
already on the paper? It seems that there is no such thing without the
formula, rule, or equation. For this reason the aforementioned footnote of Kripke's (pp. 18–19, n. 13) sins against what I have quoted
from his page 18. For in the footnote he says:

> If someone who computed '+' as we do for small arguments gave
> bizarre responses, in the style of 'quus' for larger arguments, and
> insisted that he was 'going on in the same way as before' *we would
> not acknowledge his claim that he was 'going on in the same way'* as for
> the small arguments. What we call the 'right' response deter-
> mines what we call 'going on in the same way'. (my italics)

It is possible — even probable — that Kripke wrote these lines as it
were adopting the mask of Wittgenstein, speaking with the intention of expressing a view of Wittgenstein's. In that case he is not
himself sinning against what he said on page 18, but making as if
Wittgenstein does so. Now I think he could not quote anything from
Wittgenstein to justify the last sentence (in spite of its sounding more
'Wittgensteiny' than 'Kripkeish'). And as for the previous, long sentence, the only evidence we have about what Wittgenstein would
say is adverse or neutral. The sentence itself is (strictly) true: we
would probably think such a person dotty or shake our heads
and say we couldn't make him out. But so might we too for
Wittgenstein's example: the man who first learns the decimal system
of numerals (*Investigations*, §143) and then does exercises in writing
down series at an order of the form +*n* (*Investigations*, §185). His exercises have been in the domain of numbers up to 1000. Now, asked to
go on from 1000 with +2, he writes 1004, 1008, 1012. When we

exclaim to him, shout: 'You were meant to add *two*: look how you began the series!' he says 'But surely I'm doing it right? I thought that *was* what I was to do!' and 'But I went on in the same way, didn't I?' Wittgenstein sketches the case and says: 'It will now be useless to say "'But can't you see … ?" and repeat the old examples and explanations'.

The passage is famous; I quote it for the sake of the way it ends: 'In such a case we might say, perhaps: It comes natural to this human being to understand that order, given our explanations, as *we* would understand the order "Add 2 up to 1000, 4 up to 2000, 6 up to 3000, etc." '

That is, there is here a different understanding — and a weird one. For Wittgenstein straightway compares it to a human being's *naturally* reacting to a pointing gesture of the hand by looking in the direction from fingertips to wrist.

In this there is no suggestion that we would say: 'He is *not* going on as he began!' Of course the example is so strange — and not meant not to be — that one doesn't exactly think of practicalities: of how 'we' would *actually* react. Probably we'd never carry it far enough to make the suggested remark, but just say he was hopeless, seemed all right at first, but for some reason it was no good teaching him beyond 1000. There are people who can't learn to tell the time, we may reflect. We don't take trouble to find out what they are doing when they 'try'. And remember how late (apparently) colour blindness was noted, how late brought to the attention of the learned world. Before then, it seems likely that, say, red-green colour-blind people just seemed stupid on various occasions.

As Wittgenstein imagines the case, however, we do go on with it long enough to find out that there is something like rule-governed reaction; the pupil understood the rule, together with the instructions, differently. If we go this far, could we say he *wasn't* going on in the same way as he began? It is a different same way from our 'same way'. That doesn't mean that 'same' means something different, except in the sense that if I had a beer and you had a whisky and we both said 'same again' my 'same' would mean beer and yours whisky. (Kripke has a pleasing footnote on objects of the verb 'to mean' on p. 9.)

The relevance of the Leibniz point is obvious. Is the imagined pupil applying the same rule? As we? No, not as we understand it; the rule is reinterpreted or changed by us in order to describe his way of going on. So he is applying the same rule — as *he* began with? Or is he applying *the* +2 rule — but wrong? Here Wittgenstein imag-

ines the comment: 'What you are saying comes to this: a new insight
—an intuition—is needed at each step to carry out the order +*n right*.'
He explodes:

> To carry it out right! How does it get decided what the right step
> is at a particular point? 'The right step is the one that agrees with
> the order—as it was meant.' So, when you gave the order, you
> meant him to write 1002 after 1000—and did you also mean him
> to write 1868 after 1866, and 100036 after 100034 and so on—an
> infinite number of such propositions?—'No, I meant him to write
> the next but one number after each number that he wrote; and
> from that all those propositions follow in their place.'—But
> [Wittgenstein replies] that is just the question: what, at any par-
> ticular place, *does* follow from that proposition. Or again—what
> are we to call agreement with that proposition (and also with the
> *mind* [intention] you were putting into it then—whatever that
> may have consisted in). (*Investigations*, §186)

(I have here made a new effort to translate *Meinung*, which in this
sentence is appallingly difficult to render in English. N.B. this use of
'mind' is a bit old-fashioned. We might say 'That was not his mind'
in discussing how something in someone's 'last will and testament'
was actually carried out.)

What is 'just the question' is evidently: 'What is the next-but-one
number here?' The pupil has only done exercises and tests up to
1000. So he has learned to write the four digit number 1000 after
999. —If he didn't know what to write next after 999, there'd be nothing surprising about that. I have sometimes given a series (see Fig. 1)

	?	§
?!	??	?§
§!	§?	§§
?!!	?!?	?!§
??!	???	??§
?§!	?§?	?§§
§!!	§!?	§!§
§?!	§??	§?§
§§!	§§?	§§§

Fig. 1

and asked a class to suggest 'the' next row; thus no doubt behaving like the intelligence tester. I suppose if I gave them ?!!! to start the new row it would help. I personally find it difficult to go on as I mean to except by actually recalling the development of numerals in the decimal notation—my intention being to produce something on those lines. Children have no such model. Yet they learn!—and eventually can go on beyond anything they've been given! Wittgenstein doesn't tell us anything about his pupil of §143 and §185, which definitely implies that he has developed the basic cardinal numbers beyond 1000, so we don't know whether he would go on with *that series*: 1002, 1004, 1006, etc., or whether we are to assume he has done it in the ordinary way. Probably the latter; but note that if the former were the case, his way of taking 'the next but one' would be perfectly intelligible. If the latter, it is his way of going on with +2 that is strange (just as we would find his development of the cardinal numbers strange in the former case). Why do the numbers 1001 and 1003 not count as determining what is the next but one? Well, the fact that something is a two-digit numeral in the decimal system 'doesn't matter' if we are speaking of the 'next but one' there. If *that* were an insurmountable obstacle to someone, we'd think him incompetent to learn, perhaps mentally defective.

Kripke quotes from *Remarks on the Foundations of Mathematics* (pt.1, §3): '*How do I know* that in working out the series +2 I must write "20,004, 20,006" and not "20,004, 20,008"? (The question "How do I know that this colour is red?" is similar.)' In *Philosophical Investigations*, §381, we find: 'How do I tell that this colour is red?—It would be an answer to say "I have learnt English".' Can we not infer that that would also answer the other question? A completer answer to the colour question might be: 'I am not blind and not colour-blind and have learnt English'. So too with the former question: 'I have learned that much English'.—But it doesn't seem important *which* language one has learnt. I have that much mastery of a language which includes this sort of thing.

It seems more obvious that one is 'doing something new' in answering a simple new arithmetical question or developing a new bit of a series—say of the cardinal numbers—than when one calls a new object 'red'. What about this?

Wittgenstein seems to set no value on it. For he says: 'If an intuition is necessary to develop the series 1 2 3 4 ..., then so it is to develop the series 2 2 2 2 ... (*Investigations*, §214). Here one wants to say: 'But merely *repeating* is different!' This will be why he goes on at once to ask: 'But isn't the *same* at least the same?' (*Investigations*, §215), which leads on to some considerations about identity, rules, and agreement. These, however, don't concern us for the moment. §214 might not definitely show that Wittgenstein regards 2 2 2 2 in the same light as 1 2 3 4, for in no case has he any respect for the idea of intuition which is suggested. 'Intuition an unnecessary dodge.' (*Investigations*, §213). So §214 may just be a coup de grace for intuition. This, however, can only work if those who want to invoke an intuition are struck by the idea that you are doing something new, something else or *different*, all the time in developing (say) the cardinal number series but would feel that you were not in just going on with 2s – as we may feel you are not in calling something of *this* colour 'red' again.

But now: Wittgenstein speaks not just of going on writing down 2 but of developing the series 2 2 2 2 .... Suppose I were a child developing the decimal series $^{10}/_3$, no one could say this wasn't finding out what it was at each step I took. To be sure, Wittgenstein is not giving us a formula for 2 2 2 2 ..., but then neither do we use a formula for 1 2 3 4 .... If writing 2 2 2 2 ... *is* developing a series, the invoker of intuition should accept §214 and say an intuition is just as necessary for 2 2 2 2 .... And so this example does show that Wittgenstein sees what we might call 'mere repetition – nothing *new*' in just the same light as the case of development of a series where we feel it *is* always 'something new' that one is doing. To repeat from §186, 'The question is, what, at any particular place, does follow from that proposition. Or what we are to call agreement with it (and with the *mind* you are uttering it with).' The 'new' thing is that this is the answer at *this* place. The place is new. And that can be seen for each place in 2 2 2 2 ... if it is the development of a series. But we are also to see it, it seems, if 'red', 'red', 'red', 'red' is a string of applications of the word 'red'. To different objects? – Not necessarily if these are utterances, for example; they are temporally distinct. (This brings out a way in which an ostensive definition of the word 'red' doesn't 'have everything in it'. Think of a German wondering what type of word is being explained. '*This* is red' I say, holding up a little red book. 'And is it *still* red?' he asks as I lay it down. 'Yes'. He is content: for he had been hesitating between 'rot' and 'aufrecht'.) And the question 'what to do at *this* place' arises even for the order 'Keep on writing 2'.

A new place in the series, a new occasion, another time – all these, it seems, are assimilated under one heading. The questions 'How do I know that 1197 is the next odd number after 1195?' 'How do I know that this taste is sweet?' and 'How do I know that this note is high?' can all be answered by 'I have learned English – that part of English'. Compare and contrast 'How do I know that this is a cockroach? a premise? a novel? oak? satire? a rainbow? a hole? laughter?'

The comparison between red and working out the series of +2 at the number 20,004 is extremely interesting. Kripke's explanation is 'a central thesis of this essay' (p. 20): namely that Wittgenstein has propounded an irrefutable sceptical paradox and come up with a 'sceptical solution' – a 'sceptical conclusion about rules and the attendant rejection of private rules'. This 'is hard enough to swallow in general, but it seems especially unnatural in two areas. The first is mathematics … another is that of a sensation or mental image … Because these two cases, mathematics and inner experience, seem so obviously to be counter-examples to Wittgenstein's view of rules, Wittgenstein treats each in detail.' (pp. 79–80)

The exegesis is wrong. Wittgenstein was not putting forward sceptical arguments: the 'new sceptical problem' about which Kripke expresses such great admiration on page 60 – is Kripke's.

Superficially it is easy to prove that Wittgenstein had no such sceptical problem as Kripke credits him with. At §§84–86, where he considers how the application of a rule, and a doubt about it, may be taken care of by another, and it in turn by another, and so on, he says, 'That is not to say that we doubt because we can *imagine* a doubt'. Also, he asks whether a table one consults by looking across from a word to a picture is incomplete without a schema to tell one this; the answer is evidently no. We have already examined §185 and §186, where indeed the idea of *the right* way of going on with a series under an order '+2' is questioned because (a) the explanations and examples are useless for demonstrating the rightness of our way *to someone who has an abnormal response to them*, even though the response is the expression of *some systematic understanding* and (b) what one is to do at each place of the series, in order to obey the rule, is exactly what is in question when we are considering someone who does something different from us and is not in any ordinary sense making a mistake.

This is, I think, the best passage for Kripke to call 'sceptical'. But what *is* the doubt? Kripke thinks – apparently – that an argument that a stretch of a series can't tell you the continuation of it is correct enough; and he seems to accept the argument that, since a rule can be reinterpreted ad lib., you cannot simply point like Leibniz to the rule or formula or equation. But he is sure that there is *the* right answer to a sum, though this now can't depend either on previous examples or on the formula $n + m$ with an interpretation. Hence he is driven, as far as I can make out, to think that the required guarantee resides in what he meant or had the 'intention to mean' by the plus symbol — that being the example which he chooses for discussion. He might seize joyfully on Leibniz's word 'notion'.

Wittgenstein's discussions several times emphasize something which Kripke does not mention: the teacher cannot succeed in teaching unless the pupil has certain reactions which he is not obliged to have and which the teacher can't teach him; is responsive in certain ways in which he does not have to be. And this does not mean that the teacher can't teach, for example, an inattentive pupil. Rather, he won't be able to teach him unless, for example, he does get the basic cardinal numbers by heart and in order and *does go on in a new stretch*, after the examples and the practice, like *this* and not in some other way. This is something that cannot be taught; it is a prerequisite of teaching. The ancients and medievals had a problem whether and how teaching is possible; the point I have been making — which is in Wittgenstein — is a contribution to that discussion; the matter, I believe, is not discussed nowadays. I have never heard of its being a question discussed in philosophy departments: Is it possible for one human being to teach another? You can tell him histories; can you teach him to calculate? You can do something which is called teaching; but he only ends up knowing, if he has had *these* reactions, not *those*, in the course of the teaching.

However, what is called teaching does end up, if successful, with the pupil able to do what in a certain sense he cannot be taught. And then, the pupil — take him to be Kripke — means addition by '+', and what he means is a function 'that determines values for arbitrarily large amounts', that is, arbitrarily large finite cardinals. Whether for anything else, we do not know, for Kripke does tell us. But he insists that 'the sceptic' argues that there can be no such fact as that he meant addition in the past by '+' and that the sceptic's argument is not only invented but accepted by Wittgenstein. Kripke could not, however, quote anything to the effect that 'there can be no such fact, etc'. It is *his* deduction from the past procedures' having been 'only finite in number' and variously continuable and from rules' being indefinitely reinterpretable.

Wittgenstein, however, does not say or imply that there can be no such fact.

Is it correct for someone to say 'When I gave you this rule, I meant you to … in this case'? Even if he did not think of this case at all as he gave the rule? Of course it is correct. For 'meaning it' did *not* mean: thinking of it. But now the question is: how are we to judge whether someone meant this? — That he mastered a particular technique of arithmetic and algebra and gave the other the usual instruction in the development of series, is such a criterion. (*Investigations*, §692)

Nor do we have to look away from our passages §§185 and following to get this information; it is not an afterthought, nor does it belong to a movement of thought in Wittgenstein: 'How can I cope with this ghastly sceptical problem?' I have discussed §185 and §186; §187 begins:

'But I already knew, at the time when I gave the order, that he ought to write 1002 after 1000.' — Certainly; and you can also say you *meant* it then; only you should not let yourself be misled by the grammar of the words 'know' and 'mean'. For you don't think that you thought of the step from 1000 to 1002 then — and even if you did, you didn't think of others. Your 'I already knew then …' means something like: 'If anyone had asked me then what number he ought to write after 1000, I'd have answered '1002'.' And that I don't doubt. This is an assumption of the same kind as, say, the following: 'If he had fallen into the water then, I'd have jumped in after him.' — Now, where was the mistake in your idea?

On pages 69–70 Kripke indicates that Wittgenstein does not state broad philosophical theses: it is easier so to avoid the danger of denial of any ordinary belief.

Whenever our opponent insists on the perfect propriety of an ordinary form of expression (e.g. that 'the steps are determined by the formula', 'the future application is already present' [!]) we can insist that if these expressions are properly understood, we agree. The danger comes when we try to give a precise formulation of what we *are* denying — *what* 'erroneous interpretation' our opponent is placing on ordinary means of expression.

What Kripke doesn't seem to recognise here is that correctly attacking a philosophical idea — at any rate of the kind which gets a grip on us as nonsensical is likely to involve difficulties about characterising it. 'The steps are determined by the formula' — one may be contrasting formulas in saying this; and that is harmless. But — there is something else one may be saying, something difficult to distinguish; and which may have a sense which is not what one supposes.

All the same, we should note that Wittgenstein does not fail to give expression to what he is attacking. He says that the first thing he would like to say (having asked 'Where did your idea go wrong?') is: 'Your idea was that meaning the order had already, in its own way, taken all those steps: that your mind, in meaning the order, as it were flew ahead and made all the transitions before you physically reached this or that one.' (*Investigations*, §188) He adds: 'So you were inclined to use expressions like "The steps are *really* already taken, even before I take them in writing, or orally, or in thought". And it seemed as if they were in a *peculiar way* determined beforehand, anticipated—as only meaning can anticipate reality.' Kripke does not mention some of these formulations by Wittgenstein of what he is attacking. It is possible that this is because he himself would want to embrace them but would not—could not—deny their absurdity.

At §190 Wittgenstein imagines someone using an unfamiliar sign in a formula, and our saying, 'If with "$x!2$" your intention is x^2, you get *this* value for y, but if you mean $2x$, you get *that* one.' He then invites us to ask ourselves 'How does one have the one or the other intention in using "$x!2$'?" He declares that *that* will be how one's meaning can determine the steps in advance. This is an interesting example because it involves the use of a sign not in common use. How could one train someone who knew neither 'x^2' nor '$2x$', in the use of '$x!2$' with the meaning of one of them? How (assuming one's own innocence of both 'x^2' and '$2x$') would one explain '$x!2$', when it does have one of these meanings for oneself?

The passage implies that, whatever intending such a meaning as x^2 for an unfamiliar sign would be, that will be how one's intention for a sign can determine steps in advance. This seems to be a somewhat roundabout way of saying that the criteria for N.N.'s having meant the pupil to do this in this place of this series include N.N.'s possession of a certain technique of arithmetic. I only say 'include' because I am obviously not sketching the rest of the situation of N.N. and the pupil. But this part of the total set of criteria is the business part for Kripke's problem.

At this point we should stress that Wittgenstein does not think, as Kripke does, that a stretch of a series can't rightly be taken as to be continued *so*. It can: either from familiarity with it or by guessing at a formula or principle of development and having one's guess confirmed by the next number one is given. (See *Investigations*, §151) To the objection: 'You must have chosen *one* out of the various possible interpretations', he replies: 'Not a bit of it! In some circumstances a doubt was possible. But that is not to say that I did have, or even could have had, any doubt.' (*Investigations*, §213) Neither the Leibniz point nor the reinterpretability of a formula or rule makes Wittgenstein fault the exclamation 'Now I can go on!'

They make Kripke fall back on a mental state of meaning and want an account of 'the fact about his mental state' which constitutes his meaning whatever he does mean. It has got to be an account which will justify, for example, his computations of *n* + *m*. What he will allow as justification has got to be formally (not merely in practice) immune to objections based on the Leibniz point or the reinterpretability of rules.

Wittgenstein's accounts, which I have quoted, of the sort of thing it is for you to have meant me to give 1868 as successor of 1866 in the +2 series, Kripke would no doubt count as a bit of 'the sceptical solution' (though I fear he doesn't actually attend to it).

Kripke can't prove the existence of the fact that 'the sceptic' denies. Now scepticism cannot endure the imaginability of doubt. You ought to doubt if you can think of a doubt. So Kripke is faced with a dreadful threat if he can't answer the sceptic. How can he say he knows? — Knows what? — That he has 'reason to be so confident that he should answer "125" and not "5".' (See p. 11) Clearly he does not feel justified in replying like Wittgenstein, 'I do not doubt'. And 'My eyes are shut'. I do not know if he has gravely considered this possibility as anything but a sort of bluff.

And yet he said that the problem 'is not [A] "How do I know that 68 plus 57 is 125?", which should be answered by giving an arithmetical computation, but rather [C] "How do I know that 68 plus 57 as I *meant* 'plus' in the *past* should denote 125?" ' (p. 12) But: only if A cannot be settled as it is and as he says it is, does C relevantly arise. The demand that whatever mental state was meaning plus should in some sense show how Kripke is justified in giving the answer '125' means that he wants some account of his past mental state to justify saying that 68 plus 57 is 125 — contrary to what he says on p. 12. Why not simply give the computation as the justification and leave it at that? The answer must be: because after all Kripke thinks that you can raise a doubt about the computation itself if the sceptical question about past meaning cannot be answered.

Let us accept it that the sceptical doubt turns into a doubt about present as well as past meaning, and about meaning any word; and that this *is* necessarily a doubt about whether '125' is the right answer to the sum.

Then we can scrutinise Kripke's 'condition that any putative candidate for such a fact must satisfy', that is, such a fact about one's mental state as constitutes one's meaning plus. This was that it must in some sense show how one is justified in giving the answer '125' to '68 + 57'. This demand seems to be an impossible one for any 'fact about a mental state' to satisfy unless one is to be extremely generous about what is to count as a 'fact about a mental state'. For example, Wittgenstein, replying to the question 'How are we to judge whether someone meant such and such?' says: 'The fact that he has, for example, mastered a particular technique in arithmetic and algebra, and that he taught someone else the expansion of a series in the usual way, is such a criterion.' (*Investigations*, §692) Now can we say: There you are, there's the fact about the mental state he *was in* or *was having* or *which was his mental state* — when he told that pupil to go on adding 2? All of those italicised phrases sound queer; they seem to express something different from what we want. But never mind that: my present point is that calling that 'a fact about a mental state' is like calling 'somebody had been playing chess in the next room five minutes before' a description of a 'fact about my physical state' at a certain time. What one would naturally mean by 'a fact about one's mental state' (taking this in the way philosophers in the empiricist tradition have taken it) would be some current feature of one's (possibly momentary) mental posture. Of course if one says that some mental state terms are 'dispositional', one may not mean just that. Kripke devotes a lot of space to dealing with this suggestion, made to him as a solution to his sceptical problem; he deals with what I gather was meant by his interlocutors in making it, very efficiently. They do on the whole seem to have meant something like the set of an alarm clock; something which theoretically could be directly inspected by someone looking directly inside the mechanism. Such is not the sense in which knowledge, for example, is a dispositional concept. In neither sense is having meant plus by '+' dispositional. So I will say no more on this part of the book. It is worth noting, with some curiosity, that Kripke speaks of a mental state rather than of a mental act; possibly he would accept Wittgenstein's remark that it is thoroughly wrongheaded to think of the verb 'to mean' (with personal subject) as the name of an intellectual (or mental) activity. (*Investigations*, §693)

This leads me to Kripke's good observations on the difficulty of arguing 'that meaning addition by "plus" denotes an irreducible experience, with its own special *quale*, known directly to each of us by introspection. (Headaches, tickles, nausea are examples of inner states with such *qualia*)'. (p. 41) If one did argue thus, one would say that 'the fact that I mean addition by "plus" is to be identified with my possession of experience of this quality'.

He criticises this idea as being 'Off target as an answer to the original challenge of the sceptic'. For the sceptic wanted to know why he was so sure that he ought to say '125' when asked about 68 + 57. But, he asks, how could experience with a very special quality help him figure out whether he ought to answer '125' or '5'. (p. 42)

Quite so. Such is *the* difficulty. What sort of mental somewhat meets it?

Kripke's problem: how do I know I meant plus? is indeed interesting, if sceptical problems ever are.

More interesting is the problem with which he is implicitly confronting himself: what *is* the fact that he knows, namely that he meant, and means, plus? His account of Wittgenstein as giving a 'sceptical solution' to the first problem is far less interesting and is I fear affected by his not letting himself be *épris* by *this* problem.

The sceptical question about past meaning is not supposed to be part of a general sceptical question about memory of mental events, states and processes. One might wonder why it matters for the justification of Kripke's answer to the sum. If he meant plus and has not changed his usage, he says, he *is* justified. But 'if' is not 'only if'. For this reason, one might well think that the sceptic's challenge: 'You are making a mistake about the meaning of "+"; going by what you have meant before, your answer should be "5",' was merely a device for arousing us to the essential problem: 'What is the mental fact of meaning?' with the attendant considerations about rules and the Leibniz point.

But the sceptical question about past meaning has a peculiar interest: one says 'I meant such and such' as a direct memory of a fact. One is not recalling one's possession of such-and-such techniques, previous training of the pupil, et cetera, though one might refer to these if one were arguing with the sceptic. At the same time 'I meant ...' is not, surely, the expression of a Cartesian *cogitatio*. This problem, about the first person past indicative of psychological verbs, was barely scratched by Wittgenstein.

My friend Yorick Smythies once said to me that what was needed was an attack on Wittgenstein. Such as there have been are no use at all, as far as I have seen them. Kripke's express intention was not to attack but to expound the argument which he, Kripke, got out of Wittgenstein. In my opinion it ought to be useful in the way Smythies thought a serious attack would be. The great chapter for this purpose is the one called 'The Wittgensteinian Paradox'. For this reason I have simply tackled its main line. I hope it may lead readers (partly in perceiving what is wrong with it) to a stronger perception of and further enquiry into the questions involved. And I say to Kripke, Much thanks.

Index